THE ROAD TO SUCCESS

VOL.2

Published by CelebrityPress®, Orlando, FL.

CelebrityPress® is a registered trademark.

Printed in the United States of America.

ISBN: 978-0-9975366-3-8
LCCN: 2016942368

For more information, please write:
CelebrityPress®
520 N. Orlando Ave, #2
Winter Park, FL 32789
or call 1.877.261.4930

Visit us online at: www.CelebrityPressPublishing.com

THE ROAD TO SUCCESS

VOL.2

CelebrityPress®
Winter Park, Florida

CONTENTS

CHAPTER 1

YOUR ROADMAP TO SUCCESS

BY JACK CANFIELD

All you need is the plan, the road map,
and the courage to press on to your destination.
~ Earl Nightingale

Success is possible in every area of your life—job and career, financial, health and fitness, relationships, fun and recreation, sports, politics and service. From my work with millions of people in more than 50 countries I have discovered that there actually is a "science of success." There is a set of universal principles and techniques that all but guarantee that anyone who knows and applies them can achieve anything they want. Obviously, there is only going to be one Super Bowl champion each year, and only one gold medalist in each of the Olympic sporting events. But what is also true is that you don't get into the top tier of any field or profession if you don't apply these principles and strategies.

My intention here is to outline the core principles that, if applied in the right way at the right time in the right sequence, will take you from where you currently are to where you want to go in life—a roadmap to success. Like all roadmaps, GPS systems, and digital navigation systems, all you have to do is follow the directions. And one of those principles is to respond to feedback. I recently downloaded an app called WAZE, and what I love about it is that I continually get feedback from those people who are ahead of me on the road I am travelling—not only telling me where there are traffic jams and accidents, but it also reroutes me to avoid those obstacles. My intention is that this chapter will help you avoid some of the traffic jams and potholes along your journey to success and get to where you want to go faster and with less effort. So let's get started.

1. DECIDE WHAT YOU WANT

In order to get what you want, you must first decide what you want. Most people foul up at this crucial first step because they simply can't see how it's possible to get what they want — so they don't even let themselves want it. Don't sabotage yourself that way! What scientists now know about how the brain works, is that you must first decide WHAT you want, before your brain can figure out HOW to get it.

Be Willing to Dream Big Dreams

It doesn't take any more effort to dream a big dream
than it takes to dream a small dream.
~ General Wesley C. Clark
Former U.S. Supreme Allied Commander of European Forces

As soon as you commit to a big dream and really go after it, your creative mind will come up with the big ideas needed to make it happen. You'll start attracting the ideas, people, opportunities, and resources (including money) that you need into your life to make your dream come true. Big dreams not only inspire you, they also inspire others to want to play big, and to help you succeed as well.

Set Goals That Will Stretch You

Another value in giving yourself permission to go after the big dreams is that big dreams require you to grow in order to achieve them. In fact, in the long run, that is the greatest benefit you will receive from pursuing your dreams — not so much the outer trappings of fulfilling the dream (an expensive car, impressive house, lots of money and philanthropic opportunities), but who you become in the process. As we all have seen many times over, the outer symbols of success, can all be easily lost. Houses burn down, companies go bankrupt, relationships end in divorce, cars get old, bodies age and fame wanes, but who you are, what you have learned and the new skills you have developed, never go away. These are the true prizes of success. My mentor, self-made multimillionaire W. Clement Stone, advised, "You should set a goal big enough that in the process of achieving it, you become someone worth becoming."

Service to Others

Something else you'll discover is that when your dreams include service to others — accomplishing something that contributes to the well-being of others — it also accelerates the accomplishment of that goal. People want to be part of something that contributes and makes a difference.

Turn Your Dreams into Goals and Objectives

Once you are clear about what you want, you must turn each item into a measurable objective. By measurable, I mean measurable in space and time — how much and by when. For instance, if you were to tell me that you wanted more money, I might pull out a dollar and give it to you, but you would probably protest, saying, "No, I meant a lot more money — like $20,000!" Well, how am I supposed to know unless you tell me? Similarly, your boss, your friends, your spouse, your brain — God, the Universe — can't figure out what you want unless you tell them specifically what it is. What exactly do you want, and by what specific date and time do you want it?

2. BELIEVE IN YOURSELF: USE POSITIVE SELF TALK

The second strategy that you must employ in order to achieve all of your dreams is to develop an unshakeable belief in your worthiness to have what you desire — and in your ability to achieve what you set out to accomplish — from financial abundance and a fulfilling career to dynamic health and nurturing relationships.

Ultimately, you must learn to control your self-talk, eliminate any negative and limiting beliefs, and maintain a constant state of positive expectations.

Control Your Self-Talk

Researchers have found that the average person thinks as many as 50,000 thoughts a day. Sadly, many of those thoughts are negative — "I'm not management material." ... "I'll never lose weight." ... "It doesn't matter what I do, nothing ever works out for me." This is what psychologists call victim language. Victim language actually keeps you in a victim state of mind. It is a form of self-hypnosis that lulls you into a belief that you are unlovable and incompetent.

In order to live your dreams, you need to give up this victim language and start talking to yourself like a winner — "I can do it!" ... "I know there is a solution." ... "I am smart enough and strong enough to achieve anything I want." ... "Everything I eat helps me maintain my perfect body weight."

You Are Always Programming Your Subconscious Mind

Your subconscious mind is like the crew of a ship. You are its captain. It is your job to give the crew orders. When you do this, the crew takes everything you say literally. The crew (your subconscious) has no sense of humor. It just blindly follows orders. When you say, "Everything I eat goes straight to my hips," the crew hears that as an order: "Take everything she eats, turn it into fat and put it on her hips." On the other hand, if you say, "Everything I eat helps me maintain my perfect body weight," the crew will begin to make that into reality by helping you make better food choices, exercise more often and maintain the right metabolism rate for your body.

This power of your subconscious mind is the reason you must become very vigilant and pay careful attention to your spoken and internal statements. Unfortunately, most people don't realize they are committing negative self-talk, which is why it is best to enlist another person — your accountability partner — in monitoring each other's speaking. You can have a signal for interrupting each other when you use victim language.

Use Affirmations to Build Self-Confidence

One of the most powerful tools for building worthiness and self-confidence is the repetition of positive statements until they become a natural part of the way you think. These "affirmations" act to crowd out and replace the negative orders you have been sending your crew (your subconscious mind) all these past years. I suggest that you create a list of 10 to 20 statements that affirm your belief in your worthiness and your ability to create the life of your dreams. Here are some examples of affirmations that have worked for my students in the past:

I am worthy of love, joy and success.
I am smart.
I am loveable and capable.
I can create anything I want.

I am able to solve any problem that comes my way.
I can handle anything that life hands me.
I have all the energy I need to do everything I want to do.
I am attracting all the right people into my life.

3. BUILD ON YOUR STRENGTHS AND YOUR UNIQUE ABILITIES

Everyone is born with a unique set of talents and abilities — what I refer to as your areas of brilliance or your genius. There are certain things you do that are easy for you, that you love to do, and from which you get feedback that people receive value from them. In fact, you probably do these things you do so easily and so well that you feel almost embarrassed or guilty about taking money for them.

For me, my core genius lies in the area of teaching, inspiring, motivating and empowering people in workshops, trainings, teleseminars, and coaching. I love to do it, I do it well, and people report that they get great value from it. Another core genius is compiling and writing books. Along with my *Chicken Soup for the Soul*® co-author Mark Victor Hansen, Janet Switzer and others, I have written, co-authored, compiled and edited more than 175 books—46 of which have become *New York Times* bestsellers.

Take time to determine what your core genius is and begin to focus more of your time on it. Begin to delegate the tasks that are not your core genius to other people who love to do those tasks. I believe that you can trade, barter, pay for and find volunteer help to do almost everything you don't want to do, leaving you to do what you are best at — and which will ultimately make you the most money and bring you the most happiness.

4. BUILD AN AWESOME DREAM TEAM

One of the most critical elements of living your dreams is having your own "Dream Team." It is a powerful way to support your dreams and bring unlimited resources to your professional and personal life.

Sometimes called a mastermind group, your dream team is two or more individuals that voluntarily come together to creatively put their energy behind a definite purpose — increasing each other's income, building a business, raising their kids better, or solving a social problem. Within your mastermind group, you benefit from the other members who empower you and draw out your full talents, resources and abilities. They trigger you, stimulate you and motivate you to become all you are capable of being. As part of a dream team, you use blended mind-power in action to obtain your desired result.

Creating Your Dream Team

In forming your Dream Team, start by carefully enrolling another friendly, on-purpose, like-minded individual. Start by meeting together and then adding other selected, unanimously agreed-upon individuals who will work in total harmony for the good of each other and for the good of the group.

1. Your Dream Team should consist of 4-8 people (most people find that 6 is the ideal number).
2. Meet weekly or twice a month (in person, by conference call, Skype, or Google Hangouts) for an hour to an hour and a half. This meeting must be held sacred as a life-enhancing priority. The meetings should be upbeat, enriching, encouraging and beneficial to each individual and the group's purposes. We always start our meetings with a prayer or an invocation. You could also start with an inspiring story.
3. Each member must agree to play full out — to openly share ideas, support, contacts, information, feedback, and anything else that will help advance the individual and group goals.
4. Start by having each member share something positive and good that happened since the last meeting.
5. Next, have each member share an opportunity or problem they have experienced since the last meeting, and then ask for whatever support they would like on it. This can include brainstorming ideas, addressing limiting beliefs, and suggesting people to contact. Appoint a timekeeper to make sure that everyone gets the same amount of time. This is important if you want your Dream Team to last. Everyone must get value at every meeting or people will begin to drop out. Also make sure to end on time.
6. Have everyone commit to one or more action steps they will take before the next meeting.
7. End by sharing appreciations and acknowledgements with each other.

5. VISUALIZE AND AFFIRM YOUR DESIRED OUTCOMES

You have within you an awesome power that most of us have never been taught to use. Elite athletes use it. The super rich use it. And peak performers in all fields are now starting to use it. That power is called visualization. The daily practice of visualizing your dreams as already complete can rapidly accelerate your achievement of those dreams. Visualization of your goals and desires accomplishes four very important things.

1. It activates your creative subconscious mind, which will then start generating creative ideas to achieve your goal.
2. It programs your brain to more readily perceive and recognize the resources you will need to achieve your dreams.
3. It activates the law of attraction, thereby drawing into your life the people, resources, and circumstances you will need to achieve your goals.
4. It builds your internal motivation to take the necessary actions to achieve your dreams.

Visualization is really quite simple. You sit in a comfortable position, close your eyes and imagine — in as vivid detail as you can — a movie of what you would be looking at out through your own eyes if the dream you have were already realized. Imagine being inside of yourself, looking out through your eyes at the ideal result. See it in as much detail as you can create. Add in any sounds you would be hearing — traffic, music, other people talking, cheering. And finally, once you have created the image, do your best to generate in your body the feelings—gratitude, happiness, joy, excitement, abundance, peace—that you think you will feel when you actually achieve your end results.

When you have finished this process — it should take less than five minutes — you can open your eyes and go about your business. If you make this part of your daily routine, you will be amazed at how much improvement you will see in your life.

Create Goal Pictures

Another powerful technique is to create a photograph or picture of yourself with your goal, as if it were already completed. If one of your goals is to own a new car, take your camera down to your local auto dealer and have a picture taken of yourself sitting behind the wheel of your dream car. If your goal is to visit Paris, find a picture or poster of the Eiffel Tower and cut out a picture of yourself and place it into the picture. You can make an even more convincing image using Photoshop® on your computer.

Create a Visual Picture and an Affirmation for Each Goal

I recommend that you find or create a picture of every aspect of your ideal dream life. Create a picture or a visual representation for every goal you have — financial, job and career, relationships, recreation, new skills and abilities, things you want to own, and so on.

When we were writing the very first Chicken Soup for the Soul® book, we took a copy of the New York Times best seller list, scanned it into our computer, and using the same font as the newspaper, typed Chicken Soup for the Soul into the number one position in the "Paperback Advice, How-To and Miscellaneous" category. We printed several copies and hung them up around the office. Less than two years later, our book was the number one book in that category and stayed there for over a year!

Index Cards

I practice a similar discipline every day. I have a list of about 20 goals I am currently working on. I write each goal on a 3x5 index card and keep those cards near my bed and take them with me when I travel. Each morning and each night I go through the stack of cards, one at a time, read the card, close my eyes, see the completion of that goal in its perfect desired state for about 15 seconds, open my eyes and repeat the process with the next card.

Use Affirmations to Support Your Visualization

An affirmation is a statement that evokes not only a picture, but the experience of already having what you want. Here's an example of an affirmation:

I am happily enjoying my two-week vacation in Maui watching the sunset over Ka'anapali Bay.

Repeating an affirmation several times a day keeps you focused on your goal, strengthens your motivation, and programs your subconscious by sending an order to your crew to do whatever it takes to make that goal happen.

Expect Results
Through writing down your goals, repeating your affirmations and using the power of visualization, you can achieve amazing results. Visualization and affirmations allow you to change your beliefs, assumptions, and opinions about the most important person in your life — YOU! They allow you to harness the 18 billion brain cells in your brain and get them all working in a singular and purposeful direction.

Your subconscious will become engaged in a process that transforms you forever. The process is invisible and doesn't take a long time. It just happens over time, as long as you put in the time to visualize and affirm, surround yourself with positive people, read uplifting books and listen to audio programs that flood your mind with positive, life-affirming messages.

Repeat your affirmations every morning and night for one month without missing a day, and they will become an automatic part of your thinking. They will become woven into the very fabric of your being.

6. ACT TO CREATE IT

The thing that most separates winners from losers in life is that winners take action. If you want to live your dreams, not only must you decide what you want, turn your dream into measurable goals, break those goals down into a plan of specific action steps, and visualize and affirm your desired outcomes — you must start taking action. I recommend making the commitment to do something every day in at least three different areas of your life that move you in the direction of your dreams. If one of your goals is physical fitness, make a commitment to do some sort of exercise — aerobics, weight training, stretching — four to five times a week for a minimum of twenty minutes. I read recently that if you simply go for a 30-minute walk four times a week, that would put you in the top 1% of those people getting physical exercise in America! If your goal is financial independence, start saving and investing a portion of your income every month with no exceptions. If your goal is to write a book, write for a minimum of one hour every day.

Don't Let FEAR Stop You
Most people never get what they want because they let their fears stop them. They are afraid of making a mistake, looking foolish, getting

ripped off, being rejected, being hurt, wasting their time, and feeling uncomfortable. Remember this—all fear is self-created by imagining catastrophic consequences that have not yet happened. It is all in your mind. One solution is to replace any fearful thought or image with a positive thought or image. Another powerful new technology to release any fear that you might have is tapping. Developed by Gary Craig, tapping consists of tapping on 9 acupressure points on your head and upper body while focusing on your fear. It is amazing how powerful this simple technique is in disappearing fear (even phobias you've had for years) in often as little as 5 to 10 minutes, you can learn how to use tapping from the book I coauthored with Pamela Bruner—Tapping into Ultimate Success. It also contains a 90-minute DVD illustrating Pamela and I guiding several students through the technique. You can get the book at Amazon.com

Rejection Is a Myth

One of the biggest fears that stops people from asking for support, guidance, advice, money, a date, a job, the sale, or anything else is the fear of rejection. In fact, it's been known to literally paralyze people. They become tongue-tied and refuse to reach for the phone or get up and walk across the room. They break out in a sweat at the mere thought of asking for what they want.

I have come to realize that the whole concept of rejection is false — that rejection doesn't really exist. Think about it for a moment. If you asked someone to join you for dinner, and they said no, you could tell yourself that you had been rejected, but it is all in your mind. But think about it. Did you have anyone to eat dinner with before you asked them? No! Did you have anyone to eat dinner with after you asked them? No! Did your life really get worse? No. It stayed the same!

Act As If

One of the secrets of success is to start acting like a success before you are one. Act as if. If you had already achieved your dream, what kinds of clothes would you be wearing? How would you act? How would you treat others? Would you tithe a portion of your income to your church or favorite charities? Would you have more self-confidence? Would you take more time to spend with your loved ones?

I suggest that you begin to do those things now. When I decided that

I wanted to be an "international" consultant, I immediately went and applied for a passport, bought an international clock that told me what time it was anywhere in the world, printed business cards with the words "International Peak Performance Consultant," and decided I would like to first go to Australia. I bought a poster of the Sydney Opera House and placed it on my refrigerator. Within one month, I received an invitation to speak in Sydney and Brisbane. Since then, I have spoken and conducted trainings in over 40 countries.

You may not be able to fill your closets with expensive Italian suits and designer clothing, but why not invest in one or two really great outfits, so that when you do need them, they are there. When you dress like you've already made it, you will look the part, and successful people will naturally be attracted to you and invite you to participate with them.

Start acting as if you already have everything you want. Most people think that if they have a lot of money, they could do the things they want to do, and they would be much happier. In fact, the reverse is true. If you start by creating a state of happiness, abundance and gratitude, then do the things you are inspired to do from that state of being, you will end up having all the things you ultimately desire. The Law of Attraction states that you will attract to you those things that match your state of being. If you focus on having gratitude for what you do have, you will feel rich, and you will attract more abundance into your life. If you focus on what you don't have, you will send out a message of lack and you will attract more lack into your life.

7. RESPOND TO FEEDBACK

As you begin to take action toward the fulfillment of your dreams, you must realize that not every action you take will produce your desired result. Not every action will work. Making mistakes, getting it almost right, and constantly experimenting with new approaches to see what happens are all part of the process of eventually getting something right.

Thomas Edison is reported to have tried over 2,000 different experiments that failed before he finally got the light bulb to work. He once told a reporter that, from his perspective, he had never failed at all. Inventing the light bulb was just a 2,000-step process! If you can adopt that attitude, then you can be free to take an action, notice what result you get, then adjust your next actions based on the feedback you have received. The faster you can make mistakes, learn from them and take action again, the faster you will become successful.

Ready, Fire, Aim!

Don't be afraid to just jump in and get started moving toward your goals. As long as you pay attention to the feedback you receive and make corrections based on that, you will definitely make progress. Just getting into the game and firing allows you to correct and refine your aim.

Ask Others for Feedback

One of the most valuable questions I have ever learned for soliciting valuable feedback is this:

On a scale of 1 to 10, how would you rate the quality of our relationship during the last week?

Here are a number of variations on the same question that have served me well in both my business and my personal life.

On a scale of 1 to 10, how would you rate...

- our service?
- our product?
- this meeting?
- our performance?
- my coaching/managing?
- my parenting/babysitting?
- my teaching?
- this class/seminar/workshop/training?
- our date/vacation?
- this meal?
- this book/recording/show?

Any answer less than a 10 always gets this follow-up question:

What would it take to make it a 10?

This is where the valuable information comes from. Knowing that a person is dissatisfied is not enough. Knowing in detail what will satisfy them gives you the information you need to do whatever it takes to create a winning product, service or relationship.

Ask Yourself for Feedback

In addition to asking others for feedback, you need to ask yourself for feedback, too. More than any other source of feedback, your body will tell you whether or not you are living your dream or not. When you feel relaxed, happy and alive, your body is telling you that you are on track. When you are constantly exhausted, tense, in pain, unhappy and angry, then you are definitely off track.

Take time to listen to what your body is saying to you. Take time to listen to your physical sensations and your feelings. They are sending you important messages. Are you listening?

If you are not feeling joyful and alive, start doing those things that make you come alive and feel joy.

8. NEVER GIVE UP: THE POWER OF PERSEVERANCE

After taking action, the most important quality you will need to develop in order to live your dreams is persistence. You must be persistent in your disciplines and habits; perseverant in the face of adversity, hardship and challenge; and determined to achieve your dreams, no matter what.

There will be many times when you will want to quit, give up, and go back to doing something else, but the one quality that will guarantee you success is the willingness to stick with it, to see it through to the end — to refuse to settle for anything less than your dream.

Adversity and Discouragement Is Inevitable

No matter how well you plan and how well you execute your plan, you are bound to meet with disappointments, adversity and failure along the way to your ultimate triumph. Adversity is what gives you the opportunity to develop your inner resources of character and courage. Adversity is a great teacher. It will test you and make you stronger. But you have to hang in there and not give up.

More than 4000 years ago in China, Confucius wrote, "Our greatest glory is not in never falling, but in rising every time we fall." As long as you know there will be times when you will fail, then you will know that failing is simply part of the process. Just take it in stride and press on — no matter what. And just when you think things are never going to change, press on a bit further, and that is when the tide will turn.

On my journey to living my dreams, I found the following facts very encouraging: The average millionaire in America has gone bankrupt or out of business 3.5 times on his or her way to becoming a millionaire, and there are now over 10.1 million millionaires in America. The Deloitte Center for Financial Services estimates that nearly one out of every 11 American workers is a millionaire. If financial independence is part of your dream, you too can fail your way to success if you simply stay the course.

9. CELEBRATE YOUR VICTORIES AND GIVE THANKS

If you do stay the course, you will eventually begin to realize all your goals. Once that happens, you need to do two things:

(1) celebrate your successes, and

(2) express your gratitude to everyone — including God — who helped you along the way. Let's take a look at some ways to do that.

Celebrate Your Victories

In order to justify all of the sacrifice and persistence that is required to create the life of your dreams, you have to enroll your family, your friends, your colleagues and co-workers, your employees, your clients and, most importantly, yourself to pay the price. In order for them to do that, there need to be payoffs along the way. Every time you reach a milestone on the path to ultimate success, and every time you achieve a major goal, you need to celebrate by doing something fun and nurturing.

Your Inner Child

It is important to reward your inner child, as well. Every time you work hard to meet a goal, the part of you that just wants to have fun has to sit still and be good. However, just like any kid, if it knows it will be rewarded later with a treat, it will hang in there with you.

How can you reward your inner child?

- Take a 20-minute walk after an hour or two of concentrated work
- Go for walks in the morning with your spouse
- Take 20 minutes to listen to music and daydream
- Take most weekends totally off
- Take several weeklong vacations throughout the year
- Get regular massages

- Engage in daily meditation, exercise and yoga
- Take music lessons
- Go to movies, concerts and plays
- Listen to comedy on CDs, SiriusXM Radio and the Comedy Channel
- Listen to motivational audio programs when driving

Have an Attitude of Gratitude

Take the time to thank every one that helped you achieve your goal. Write them a letter, call them, send them a card or an email, or send them a gift. It can be as simple as a hug and a thank you — to something as elaborate as letting someone use your summer vacation home for a week.

The Power of Acknowledgment

When you take the time to thank someone, they feel acknowledged for their contribution and will be more likely to want to help again.

Thank Your Higher Power

Finally, it is important to thank God, or however you perceive the Higher Power, for all of the abundance that comes into your life. Start with the little stuff — another day of life, healthy children, a sunny day, people who love you, family and friends. Be thankful for the birds, your pets, the clothes you have and the food you eat.

And be especially thankful for any additional blessings that come into your life. Take time each day to say a prayer of thanks when you first arise, before meals, and again at night before bed. Having an attitude of gratitude opens up the channels for even more abundance to flow into your life. The more grateful you are, the more you will attract to be grateful for.

10. GIVE SOMETHING BACK

A great philosopher once said, "Whatever you want more of, first give it away." If you want more love, first give away more love to others. The same is true for money. The best way to ensure an ongoing flow of abundance into your life is to share with others the wealth you have already received. I am a big believer in tithing — giving away 10% of your income to your church and/or favorite charities and causes. I believe that it does indeed come back multiplied. This has been demonstrated in my life and the lives of *Chicken Soup for the Soul*® readers over and over again.

My *Chicken Soup* co-author Mark Victor Hansen and I have been tithing for years and believe it is one of the major factors of our phenomenal success. Along with Peter Vegso, our original publisher at Health Communications, Mark and I have given away millions of dollars to more than 70 charities and non-profit organizations. We also distributed nearly 150,000 copies of *Chicken Soup for the Soul®* and *Chicken Soup for the Prisoner's Soul* to inmates in all of America's prisons.

If you have never tried tithing, give it a three-month trial and see what happens. Remember that, when you are giving, like attracts like. The more you give, the more will come back to you. If need be, start with one percent of your income, time, energy or effort, and then slowly build up to ten percent.

Tithe Your Time, as Well as Your Money

You can tithe your time, as well as your money. If you are uncomfortable tithing ten percent of your income, try tithing ten percent of your time. You can make a huge difference in so many areas of your community by giving of your time. There are numerous schools, churches, and other non-profits that are all clamoring for help.

****

The roadmap I have covered here is the essence of what I know works and what I have seen proven to work time and time again for individuals from all walks of life. You have the opportunity to create the life of your dreams, and you now have a proven road map for success — but it takes determination, planning resolve and effort on your part to actually travel that road. Remember, the only two things that will create the future of your dreams are the decisions you make and the actions you take— today! Don't wait. Get started today.

About Jack

Known as America's #1 Success Coach, Jack Canfield is the CEO of the Canfield Training Group in Santa Barbara, CA, which trains and coaches entrepreneurs, corporate leaders, managers, sales professionals and the general public in how to accelerate the achievement of their personal, professional and financial goals.

Jack Canfield is best known as the coauthor of the #1 New York Times bestselling *Chicken Soup for the Soul®* book series, which has sold more than 500 million books in 47 languages, including 11 New York Times #1 bestsellers. As the former CEO of Chicken Soup for the Soul Enterprises he helped grow the Chicken Soup for the Soul® brand into a virtual empire of books, children's books, audios, videos, CDs, classroom materials, a syndicated column and a television show, as well as a vigorous program of licensed products that includes everything from clothing and board games to nutraceuticals and a successful line of Chicken Soup for the Pet Lover's Soul® cat and dog foods.

His other books include *The Success Principles™: How to Get from Where You Are to Where You Want to Be* (recently revised as the 10th Anniversary Edition,) *The Success Principles for Teens, The Aladdin Factor, Dare to Win, Heart at Work, The Power of Focus: How to Hit Your Personal, Financial and Business Goals with Absolute Certainty, You've Got to Read This Book, Tapping into Ultimate Success, Jack Canfield's Key to Living the Law of Attraction*, and his recent novel—*The Golden Motorcycle Gang: A Story of Transformation.*

Jack is a dynamic speaker and was recently inducted into the National Speakers Association's Speakers Hall of Fame. He has appeared on more than 1000 radio and television shows including Oprah, Montel, Larry King Live, the Today Show, Fox and Friends, and 2 hour-long PBS Specials devoted exclusively to his work. Jack is also a featured teacher in 12 movies including *The Secret, The Meta-Secret, The Truth, The Keeper of the Keys, Tapping into the Source*, and *The Tapping Solution.*

Jack has personally helped hundreds of thousands of people on six different continents become multi-millionaires, business leaders, best-selling authors, leading sales professionals, successful entrepreneurs, and world-class athletes while at the same time creating balanced, fulfilling and healthy lives.

His corporate clients have included Virgin Records, SONY Pictures, Daimler-Chrysler, Federal Express, GE, Johnson & Johnson, Merrill Lynch, Campbell's Soup, Re/Max, The Million Dollar Forum, The Million Dollar Roundtable, The Entrepreneur Organization, The Young Presidents Organization, the Executive Committee, and the World Business Council.

He is the founder of the Transformational Leadership Council and a member of Evolutionary Leaders, two groups devoted to helping create a world that works for everyone.

Jack is a graduate of Harvard, earned his M.Ed. from the University of Massachusetts and has received three honorary doctorates in psychology and public service. He is married, has three children, two step-children and a grandson.

For more information, visit: www.JackCanfield.com

CHAPTER 2

LEARN HOW TO AVOID ENTREPRENEURIAL A.D.D.

BY DAVID GOODMAN

Don't suffer from "Entrepreneurial Attention Deficit Disorder." Choose a passion and stay laser focused on it.

My experience, throughout my business career, has been that virtually everyone possesses some form of the entrepreneurial spirit. It's there, living inside us, waiting to emerge. Only, with many of us, it stays hidden because, well, life gets in the way. We fear taking chances. Or don't believe strongly enough in our idea. Or lack the confidence to determine our destiny. Too many of us remain miserable or unsatisfied in our jobs, and like the characters in the Billy Joel song "Piano Man," believe we could achieve our dream if only we "could get out of this place."

And, should you choose to go out on your own, you'll certainly fail if you don't have the necessary passion and the ability to stay focused.

Being successful in life has nothing to do with "school smarts." George W. Bush once said in a college commencement address at Southern Methodist University in Dallas, "As I like to tell the C students – you too can be president." This certainly speaks to me. Throughout my school years, I too was an undistinguished student. Yet, from a very early age, I knew I was a born entrepreneur. At the age of five, I made candles and sold them door to door (of course, in those days it was safe to do this). After graduating college, rather than look for a job, I chose to start my own business. More than 30 years later, I've never had a boss – and have never looked back.

I had two objectives in choosing a business: I wanted to do something that would allow me to live the lifestyle I wanted and, as importantly, would make me feel good about what I did. Unless you can say this, it can be hard waking up every morning. After several months of contemplation, I chose an industry that, for all practical matters, didn't exist at the time. Unlike the Eskimos who send their elderly loved ones downriver on ice floes, when mom or dad in the 1980s grew elderly and infirm their children typically had two options: they would take their parents into their own home or ship them out to a nursing home. Having someone come into the home to provide private duty "home care" – a term that didn't exist at the time – was unnatural. After all, the thought of leaving the responsibility of caring for a loved one in the hands of a total stranger was as foreign as, well, carrying a phone in your pocket or having your car give you directions.

At the time, however, I sensed that both the country's financial and social mores were changing. Many households depended on two paychecks, resulting in more and more women entering the workforce. Additionally, families were becoming increasingly reluctant to remove aging parents from the familiarity and comfort of their homes and place them in impersonal facilities where, at an advanced age, they would be expected to adjust to a new way of life. Combine this with the reality that people were living longer, though not necessarily healthier lives, and the opportunities in this burgeoning industry spoke clearly to me.

I believed back then that the concept of live-in home care – bringing trusted, highly-trained people into one's parents' homes to provide the service the children themselves were no longer able or willing to perform – was the best of all solutions. Time would prove me right – today, surveys show that nine out of ten people prefer home care.

Even more so, I felt very good about the service my agency performed. I was making a difference in the lives of these families, providing them with an answer to the dilemma of who will care for mom and dad when the family cannot. As a result, over time my agency prospered and grew into the largest of its kind in New Jersey.

After spending years building my own brand, I came across another idea. What if I took these 25 years of knowledge and packaged it for people who, for a modest cost and an ongoing monthly fee (and without paying royalties or being required to report to the "mother ship" as franchises do), could own their own home care business? The graying of America, after all, was only causing even greater need for such services. In 2004, I launched this concept, naming the business, Companion Connection Senior Care. "Members" would purchase my knowledge – I would help them license their business, recruit caregivers, market their services to referral sources and families, etc. – and give them unlimited and immediate access to my support. The idea took off. Today, there are well over 100 Companion Connection Senior Care members – all independent home care agencies – throughout North America.

Many of my member organizations have prospered as well. These people come from all walks of life: healthcare, education, social services, sales, corporate, marketing, technology. Some have turned their businesses into multi-million dollar enterprises (in some cases later selling what they developed for tidy profits), while others have chosen to run them as part-time ventures.

Stacy Benjamin, our very first member, is the President of At-Home Companions in Hackensack, New Jersey. Today, Stacy runs a business with 70 caregivers and gross annual income of more than $1.6 million. Below, in her own words, Stacy offers her thoughts on her reasons for choosing this industry, the responsibility she feels in running such a business, her relationship with clients' families, and her take on being a member of the Companion Connection Senior Care network.

I had been working as a social worker for many years, at that time running two small non-profit organizations where I worked with children. I had also run non-profits for seniors. These were run like businesses, but with a social service piece. I was 40 at the time and feeling I had to do something with my life. I was bored and restless, and very intrigued with the idea of combining business and social service.

Home care is a very intimate business, one that's all about relationships. It's about going into people's homes, bathing, toileting them, seeing people at their worst, at a time when they're most vulnerable. It's also about working with people from different cultures and being open to their lifestyle.

The most satisfying part of this job is working with the families. I often identify with the adult daughters. The responsibility is huge, one that can keep you up at night. I often take families through to the end of the process, where there are crises and their parents are dying. I don't often meet them personally (the family members); the contact is usually by phone. But recently I went to the wake of a patient and I saw the daughter who I had been talking to daily for some time. Neither one of us recognized the other by sight, but when I went up to her and said 'I'm Stacy,' we both started crying. Chances are we'll never meet again, but for a time we shared a vital connection. For me, these are really warm memories.

It's the family connections that have always come more naturally for me than the business part. As compassionate as you have to be, you have to remember that it's also a business. You don't always look at the bottom line, but you have to. I train our caregivers to be consistent, to watch the details and keep boundaries, and I remind them that we're getting paid to be there.

Companion Connection Senior Care provided me with the start-up kit I needed back then. They gave me the training I needed to learn how to run the business and the backup and support I've required moving forward. I've spent a lot of time getting to know David and I trust him implicitly. There is a level of integrity here that might not exist with other opportunities. They have been invaluable to my success in both building meaningful relationships with families and doing extremely well financially.

So, what advice can I impart to those individuals looking to unleash the entrepreneurial side of their being? Here are my 16 takeaways to success:

Words of Advice

1.) Choose a business that serves others. Yes, it is possible to build a successful business platform while helping others. Make a difference in this world and the rewards will follow.

2.) Do as much due diligence as possible on the opportunity being considered. Talk to experts, go to conferences, trust your instincts, and leverage the expertise of others.

3.) Make sure you have the proper capital for a start-up. You should have enough capital to last you at least 12 months – not just for your living expenses but for the development and marketing of your startup. Undercapitalization is a common cause of failure, regardless of how great the idea may be.

4.) The path to financial reward lies in a residual income business. Look to build a business with a recurring revenue model, as opposed to a widget business where you only get paid for every widget you sell.

5.) Diversify your payment sources. Remember the old adage, "don't put all your eggs in one basket." Nothing could be truer when it comes to a customer base or payment sources for services. Diversification is the key to success.

6.) Don't be afraid to pay for leveraged expertise. This will greatly increase your chances of success. The learning curve can be steep, and having a mentor committed to your success will mean less lost opportunity and income while you learn about the industry.

7.) Own every part of a startup business. This entails doing every job possible. The best delegators are those who have walked a mile in the shoes of others.

8.) You are the only one who will be responsible for your success. You can't point fingers at others. Work hard, burn the midnight oil, and reach outside your comfort level. You will be surprised how much talent and confidence you have living inside of you.

9.) Entrepreneurs are artists. Only, our canvas is a whiteboard and our success, at least partially, is in the profits. Yet, a great entrepreneur is no different than Picasso or Monet. You, too, have created something from nothing, relying only on your imagination and commitment.

10.) Negative thoughts and input is fear by others disguised as well-meaning (or not so well-meaning) advice. You need to search for your own answers!

11.) Being your own boss in a startup can be as lonely as sitting in a room by yourself writing a novel (especially if, like in many cases, you start out working at home). Make sure you have a great support network committed to your success.

12.) Smile – don't shirk – at every challenge. Life is for living. Go for it!

13.) Don't limit yourself. Almost everything is scalable. Prove it in a local market and then leave your mark on the world with your brand. Believe unconditionally in yourself and your product or service. View success as not only possible, but as a foregone conclusion.

14.) Look at your business like you were raising a child. It too needs a steady hand, consistency and nurturing for success.

15.) Regardless of what you do, realize there will always be competition. Just like a football coach going over film of the opposition, you need to know every weakness of your competitor so you can make it your strength. Just like the big boys – the Apples, Nikes, Microsofts and Pfizers of the world – do a detailed SWOT analysis (Strength, Opportunity, Weaknesses and Threats) of the competition so you know where you stand and can plot your strategy accordingly.

16.) Don't suffer from Entrepreneurial A.D.D., where you're held captive by too many ideas. Stay on one path and take it to the end of the road before you move on to another. Concentrate on doing one thing exceptionally well before you focus on something else.

About Dave

David M. Goodman is a successful entrepreneur and true visionary. Over the years, he has had the knack for growing businesses in areas where such opportunities did not previously exist.

This began in the 1980s, when at the age of 23 he opened a home care agency. It was at a time when the concept of private duty home care barely existed in America. Over the next three decades, he built Expert Home Care into one of New Jersey's largest and most successful home care agencies. During this time, David has become a leading voice on improving the quality of care for seniors and disabled people. He has served on legislative bodies, hosted a national radio show, and written for and been featured in countless publications. This has included trade and industry journals as well as such major media outlets as *The Wall Street Journal, Entrepreneur Magazine* and ABC Television.

After 20 years of dedicating his life to the well-being of New Jersey seniors, David utilized this wealth of experience and knowledge to found the Companion Connection Senior Care National Membership Organization. This membership organization is dedicated to teaching others how to start their own non-medical home care business. Today, there are more than 100 members in North America, many of whom have credited David with not only helping them start their business, but changing their lives.

David is now introducing a new chapter in home care with a brand that he plans on scaling nationally and ultimately worldwide. There is a great deal of anticipation around the launch of Careshyft, which offers an innovative online care seeker solution in the home healthcare marketplace.

You can connect with David at:

- david@companionconnectionseniorcare.com
- www.companionconnectionseniorcare.com
- 800-270-6949 Ext 101

CHAPTER 3

THE ROAD TO SUCCESS WITH MUSIC LESSONS

BY STEPHEN RICHES

INTRODUCTION

When I published my first book two years ago, *Talent CAN Be Taught: The Book on Creating Music Ability*, it was a response to my realization that most students give up on private music training within three years. I was writing primarily to document the problems with conventional methods, as well as the highly successful solutions that I had implemented. Further, it is a fact that today more than ever, music lessons need to be recognized as an essential part of education and training. Steps need to be taken by parents and educators alike to ensure that all students have every opportunity to develop music skills as well as to enjoy the many added benefits that come from developing music skills. As a lifelong music educator, it's my mission to provide a better legacy for music students everywhere.

WHY EVERYONE SHOULD TAKE MUSIC LESSONS: INSIGHTS FROM NEUROSCIENCE

Recent studies have revealed an important connection between the development of music skills and an increase in both brain structure and function. In short, if you value higher intelligence, you should place a strong emphasis on music education and training. According to neuroscientists, developing music skills leads to the creation of more grey matter in the brain and increased IQ, along with improvement in memory, better reading comprehension and mental arithmetic skills, greater interconnectivity between right and left areas of the brain that improves creative thinking and problem solving skills, and even up to 20% higher scores on standardized tests. Even studies many decades earlier in Europe revealed that students who divided time between math and music studies did better even on the math than those who spent double the time on math alone. Yet many education administrators still look upon music as a frill, rather than as the single most important and primary focus or foundation for all learning as it rightly deserves to be.

WHERE HAVE ALL THE STUDENTS GONE: A SYSTEMIC FAILURE

The problem is not only that not enough parents or even educators value music education, but that even those who do and who enroll their children in private music lessons don't achieve the results that should be expected. About half of all beginners give up during their first year of lessons, and almost all quit within three years. So the additional benefits that could and should come from exposure to music training isn't occurring because the music experience is too limited. A distinct pattern has been emerging for decades. Students struggle with practice issues, begin to lose interest, perhaps even develop a negative attitude which leads to further frustration and decline in progress and enjoyment until eventually everyone involved gives up. In some cases, those who survive are even worse off because without the critical skills, the workload becomes ever more tedious at each advancing level. While some survive and may even manage to achieve certificates predominantly through rote learning, they soon forget how to perform everything they ever learned, and are unable to either re-learn or learn anything new without the basic music skills. Of course, all of the added benefits to brain structure and function are also undeveloped.

NOW SUCCESS CAN BE GUARANTEED: BUILDING CRITICAL SKILLS

The heart of the matter is that the words "Talent" and "Skills" are synonyms. And skills in anything can be taught and learned. The unique Talent CAN Be Taught™ system, about which I write in my first book, actually ensures that these critical skills are developed first. When it comes down to it, there are only two ways that anyone can learn music. You either learn how to read music notation so that you can translate the music symbols into your fingers, or you train your ear so that you can learn to perform the music that you hear. These are the two critical skills that must be taught and learned. With a high degree of competency in at least one of them, there is great potential for success. There are many wonderful stories of blind musicians who accomplished great things exclusively from listening and exploring their instrument. With both skills, of course, potential is unlimited. But if neither are developed to any significant level, success will be extremely limited. Sadly, less than 1% of all beginning music students ever develop a high degree of proficiency in either of these skills. As a result, they are never able to build a collection of music selections that they can perform for any occasion.

SO WHY DOESN'T EVERYONE SUCCEED: PAYING THE PRICE

Like so many things in life, achieving success comes down to choices and priorities. Frequently, people are unwilling to pay the price for success. It's really just a decision. There are many ways that life can get in the way if there is no will to overcome the obstacles. Many people are unwilling to commit to the instructional time that is necessary. Some will claim that they can't afford more than one lesson per week. But what is the cost of months or years of less frequent lessons with disappointing or ineffective results? There is a fast-track to success, but there are no short-cuts. All students who learn and follow the Talent CAN Be Taught™ system enjoy success and enjoy it more quickly than most people believe possible.

IMPORTANT LESSONS FROM THE WORLD OF SPORTS: THE MOMENTUM FACTOR

My Powerful PRAISE Techniques represent a 12-part blueprint for successful music training. Most teachers and studios provide several of these components, although many to only a very limited extent. There is one very important aspect of the learning process, however, that is always entirely missing with conventional approaches to private music education. Interestingly, the sporting community recognizes this factor as perhaps the most influential key to success. That factor is enjoying a learning synergy. The power of momentum, accelerated learning, discernable growth of skills, inspiring moments, and both internal and external competition not only for athletes, but music students is profound. However, with the traditional approach to training this powerful synergistic experience is missing, and there are many days where learning not only is minimal for the beginning music student, but harmful bad habits creep in which then require additional time to eliminate. Progress eventually becomes so slow that the entire experience becomes very discouraging. It is well known that the energy curve comprised of inspiration, memory, confidence, etc., drops nearly to zero within 48 hours. So, with the typical single lesson per week, for five out of every seven days most students accomplish little or nothing of any value through independent practice. Even worse, independent, unguided practice often instills errors that actually have to be unlearned, wasting future lesson time. Many teachers attempt to overcome the challenge of slow progress by skipping steps in the learning process. This creates an illusion of faster progress, but leads to predictably unfortunate results due to learning gaps.

WHEN CERTIFICATES DON'T REPRESENT ACTUAL ACHIEVEMENT: THE TOM SAWYER SCHOOL

Many students achieve Conservatory of Music certificates, but have serious weaknesses in basic skill development. In extreme cases, there have been students who even manage to acquire Grade 8 music certificates by learning their exam requirements almost entirely by rote, and in some instances, despite having reading skills at or near a Pre-Grade 1 level. So when they stop playing even the very few pieces they learn, they cannot be recovered to perform for any occasion. I refer to this as the Tom Sawyer school of learning, in recognition of the penchant that Mark Twain's fictional character had for getting credit for things he hadn't actually achieved. Certificates should indicate the development of lifetime music skills such as the ability to read music notation well enough to learn and perform a new page of music in 30 minutes or less, or the ability to learn and perform music by ear. Without these core skills, however, frustration, and a loss of interest sets in, eventually leading most students to quit.

HOW CONVENTIONAL WISDOM IS FLAWED: DISPELLING THE MYTHS

Most people believe that the key to success with music lessons is to find a very experienced and highly qualified teacher. Or, that the way to Carnegie Hall is to practice, practice, practice…as the old joke says. Both of these beliefs, however, have serious flaws. A student's success depends very little upon either the qualifications or experience of the teacher, but rather on the system being used to train the student. It's because of a system that McDonald's is able to hire children to run their multi-billion-dollar empire. And practicing hard and long may only serve to entrench serious problems if the right approach is not being used. Contrary to popular opinion, practice alone never makes perfect. What the legendary football coach, Vince Lombardi actually said was that "Perfect practice makes perfect." And few, if any, music students have the maturity, knowledge, or even the basic music skills in the early levels of training to be able to practice well, never mind perfectly. And so it is that the very small minority of students who progress well with the traditional system do so in spite of that system, and not because of it. Access to outside music support and development such as significant exposure to music and singing, for example, can help them to overcome the liabilities that cause almost all others to struggle. Some teachers also have better results either because they insist on more frequent lessons in order to fully and effectively develop student capability and/or because they choose to work only with the more advanced students who have already survived the flaws of the traditional system.

WHY STRATEGIES THAT HAVE NEVER REALLY WORKED ARE STILL USED: IGNORANCE ISN'T BLISS

Most people don't know that the conventional wisdom is flawed, and many assumptions are made that are without merit. Many assume that talent is genetically endowed, when in fact, talent is a skill that is developed. Many people believe that success depends upon the effort of the student rather than the system of training and strategies being used by the teacher or studio. This is a convenient belief for those in charge of instruction, because it effectively absolves them from all responsibility for ensuring student success. Responsibility is transferred to the student, and failure is blamed on a lack of effort or pre-existing talent. Further, the usual system, which predominantly centres around a single weekly one-on-one lesson, often totalling just 30 minutes, is easier to market and cheaper for parents, and this formula has worked for many teachers and studios who have no inclination to fix what from a financial perspective isn't broken. And, a new group of six year olds emerges every year making change unnecessary. It apparently doesn't occur to most people that since one lesson a week would be a ridiculous idea for developing arithmetic skills, applying the same formula for developing music skills might also be problematic. And so, the Talent CAN Be Taught™ system has been created specifically to ensure a learning-based model for success with music training, rather than continuing the traditional business or financial model and criteria that entirely disregard the success of the student.

HOW THE SYSTEM IS THE SECRET TO SUCCESS: A BLUEPRINT FOR SUCCESS

The Powerful PRAISE Techniques™ which were the primary subject for my first book form a blueprint for success with music training. Each component of the acronym "PRAISE" addresses specific needs for all music students.

***P**erformance & Repertory: The Core Essence of Music*
Students must learn to perform and have opportunities to do so right from their first lesson. Building a collection of music that can be performed by memory is a key part of the process that requires continual daily review at home and periodic review during lessons.

***R**esults & Accreditation: The Benchmarks of Achievement*
Development of essential music skills must be given first priority rather than the more limited benefit to be derived from preparation for exams. It's a case of priorities – making sure that the metaphorical cart is not rendered ineffective by having it placed before the horse.

Acceleration & Motivation: The MAGIC of Synergy™
This aspect of student success is the one factor that is neglected almost in its entirety by all teachers and studios. And that is because the traditional formula of one weekly lesson simply cannot create a learning synergy for the student. The TCBT system ensures an ideal frequency of instruction to create the important motivational and inspirational experiences that lead to accelerated learning.

Insights & Learning Strategies: The Philosophy of Education
A plan for continual review, provision of frequent performance opportunities, and strategies to teach students how to practice before they are ever told what to practice are just a few examples of a great many tried-and-true practices and principles for success that are well-known to educators everywhere but under-utilized almost everywhere. Wherever the TCBT system is adopted, student success is guaranteed.

Supervision & Curriculum: The Tools for Training
A key component of success is found by ensuring that an outstanding progressive and sequential curriculum is used, and that it is followed uncompromisingly. No pages, books, or levels of our curriculum are ever skipped, ensuring that learning gaps that cause students to struggle are avoided. Teachers following our system benefit from the ongoing supervision and training that we provide, and students benefit from the FREE supervisory classes that allow their progress to be tracked and enable better, more strategic communication among the team comprised of parents, students, teachers, and administrators who work together to ensure ongoing successful skill development.

Ear Training & Reading Skills: The Fundamentals for Learning
These two critical skills represent the only two possible ways that any music student can succeed. And yet, they are also the two most neglected skills by all teachers often due to the desire by parents to prepare for exams and acquire higher level certificates sooner. Predictably, the failure to develop these two skills actually leads to the frustration and loss of interest that causes students either to quit altogether, or to obtain certificates that really don't reflect their actual level of skill development.

EPILOGUE: HOW TCBT IS MAKING A DIFFERENCE: CREATING A NEW AND BETTER LEGACY

TCBT is expanding its reach to locations wherever an interest has been expressed by parents, teachers, and organizations who want to make a difference by adopting the highly successful and proven strategies of our system for music training and skill development. Students of the TCBT system accelerate through as many as eight grade levels in three years, achieving up to 11% higher results on graded music exams at all levels. And because music skill development is also connected to overall brain structure and function, students are likewise achieving up to 20%

higher on academic standardized test results. As author and founder of the Talent CAN Be Taught system, I am actively engaged in providing leadership training for all who want to improve their level of success when it comes to developing the music skills of their students.

About Stephen

Stephen Riches holds Bachelor of Music and Bachelor of Education degrees from the University of Toronto, and an ARCT in Piano Performance. In 1977, he was winner of Canada's prestigious Dr. Heinz Unger Conducting Competition.

Stephen is an experienced pianist, conductor, teacher, accompanist, adjudicator, vocal coach, arranger, and composer. In addition to teaching music privately, he has directed elementary and secondary school band and orchestra programs in both public and private sectors.

Apart from his work relating to the Talent CAN Be Taught system, Stephen also provides leadership in Christian music ministries, and is active in both writing and speaking on topics relating to music and education.

CHAPTER 4

PRECISION MEDICINE: CLUES TO BETTER HEALTH EXIST WITHIN US

BY DR. TONY BOGGESS

No real sense of where I was going or how I would get there. That was me in college. Due to a difficult family life in California, and an ill father in Montana, I was essentially on my own by fifteen. To secure a summer job my final year of high school (and to upgrade my car stereo which matters at that age in small-town Montana), I impulsively signed the dotted line with the Army recruiter. After a summer of drill-sergeant style whooping, I matured a bit and earned numerous accolades in leadership, including the coveted Army Medal of Achievement for graduating first in my class. From then on, I was basically hooked on "high marks" as the primary indicator of my success.

As a result, my grades in college were too perfect! I went from struggling to finish high school to having an unhealthy perseveration for getting A's in college. Graduating with high honors from my college pre-med program, I saw medicine as the next notch in my achievement belt, so to speak. While I sincerely wanted to be a doctor, I admit it was for all the wrong reasons at first...

They often say it is the trials and tribulations in our lives that bring out our best qualities. For me, it was getting sick—really sick! It hit me like a lightning bolt out of nowhere, and it wasn't easy to appreciate or embrace in the moment.

It's not uncommon to feel like sickness and hard times come out of nowhere. **One day we're happy and healthy, and the next day we have a serious problem.** I'll never forget it. I was a thriving medical student at the peak of my youth. Then suddenly I'm dealing with psychiatric illness due to an antibiotic! I had developed what is called a metabolic encephalopathy, which in basic terms is a sudden change in the brain's electrolytes and chemicals. It was perplexing, yet there I was being contemplated over by several doctors—my future peers—sensing I was like a roulette wheel and they had to spin me to see what drug to offer next. I was told there were no other choices. But it only made things worse…

Eventually, I learned that I had a genetic weakness in certain detoxification pathways. This explained a lot! Why I had such a bizarre reaction to an antibiotic. Why my father, who owned an auto-body shop, suffered a midlife crisis that never ended. AND why, for some of my extended family, success and happiness was written in their stars, and for others, misfortune and triggered mental illness was their lot. Tracing back to our royal European roots, we Boggesses had always known we carried some type of genetic blessing or curse, but that it was a crap shoot which one you'd get.

THE JOURNEY BEGINS

My original plans for becoming a doctor were methodical, and a series of to-dos, which had been interrupted by my sudden adverse reaction. The events that derailed me took two years to recover from, and I surrendered my hard earned slot in MD school. They invited me to return, but I declined and chose a more holistic track in Osteopathic Medical School. Once there, I started right where I left off and I resumed my quest for the academic top of the class and ultimately ranked in the top 5 percent. I earned interviews at all the top institutions for residency (Harvard, Mayo, Michigan, Stanford, et cetera). Apparently, I hadn't learned enough yet. As this young, ambitious, and "sought after" doctor with "high marks," I felt like nothing would derail me again…

Then a second health crisis happened. This time it rattled me fully. It was so unexpected, and far worse than the first episode. I was brought to my knees as I anticipated the end of my education, future career, and possibly even my marriage. During this trying time, I was gifted with a number of emotional, mental, and spiritual milestones that exploded healthier motivations and a grander appreciation for life. Luckily I bounced back after taking leave for a second time from medical school—this time without medications! That is when I realized that it wasn't about strength or being smart. It was about knowing who you are. Your weaknesses, your strengths. AND specifically in my case, allowing myself to be molded into something worthwhile to others.

Today I recognize this second episode as the greatest blessing in my life because it changed my entire perspective. Emotionally. Professionally. With new inspiration I began focusing on learning all I could about the alternative approaches that had become my saving grace. I was motivated for the right reason because I realized that true professional and personal fulfillment would come through offering unique solutions to others. Competing to be the best in the class fell to the wayside as I began to develop unique skills for the purpose of helping myself and serving others. I finally knew exactly why I was studying to be a doctor!

This awareness quite honestly liberated me and punctuated my career goals. Yet it also showed me how traditional medicine viewed "docs like me." To many of my colleagues, then and now, alternative medicine isn't legitimate because it lacks double blind, placebo-controlled backing. Well the hard truth is: it never will earn such backing; at least not what I do. It is too personalized and too dynamic to fit into such a tiny box. It moves with, and is unique to, each patient and circumstance—and that is exactly why it has the potential to be so effective.

BUCKING THE SYSTEM

During my hospital training years, I was not fully understood by many of my mentors and colleagues for my out-of-the-box thinking, but I didn't let it bother me much. Ultimately, I gained the support of my program director and certain faculty members to offer alternatives like acupuncture to patients at the University of Michigan.

At the conclusion of my training, only a select few considered my aspirations viable. But those who knew me well, knew I was passionate about my goals, and supported them. My gumption did ultimately win out and when I completed my hospital training I did what only one in thousands do right out of residency. I opened up my own practice. Less than 10 years later, that practice has developed into a reputable Integrative medical clinic, attracting patients to Ann Arbor from all over the country and even outside the U.S.A.

PRECISION-BASED SOLUTIONS

As a result of working with patients who needed me to go the extra mile, I realized my clinical decisions needed to be guided by more than just the prevailing ideas of alternative medicine. With life lessons propelling me forward, I started looking wholeheartedly into how the knowledge of genetics could assist with complex patients (often at their wits end). It is as if someone had turned on the light for me to assist with increasingly challenging and refractory patients finding their way to our clinic. Soon my entire approach began to center around genetic susceptibility.

You see, we all have unique areas where our biology and chemistry may not keep up. For my family it was weak detox pathways. For others (many more than who realize) their weaknesses are also things that are easy to accommodate for, once they know. Then there are others who suffer differently, with abnormalities in their immune systems, hormones, or a predisposition to diseases such as cancer or arthritis, for example. Why the differences? Is it by chance? No, it's due in large part to individual genetic weaknesses.

Think of your body as an engine. If we push it hard we might break something. Perhaps a piston will go or maybe a gasket. Why? Over time, engines reveal their weakness. If you want to find the weakest part of your car's engine sooner, for example, put it in park, and redline the RPMs until something blows! Whatever breaks first is the weakest part.

With Precision Medicine, we begin by identifying what your genetic susceptibilities are before the imbalance or dysfunction goes from hidden to obvious. How we feel. Our energy, mood, sleep, digestion, physical pain, etc. are ALL like engine warning lights that something is breaking. Once you understand the genetic blueprint, much akin to a mechanic's manual, you can heed the warning and address the problem.

With Precision Medicine, the approach is individualized. Not one size fits all. Not one diagnosis fits all. We need to know who you are genetically, then know your "condition." When we know the cards we hold around the game table of life, we can play a better game. As doctors, we can also coach a better game. In order to succeed, we need to approach from the perspective that what breaks in us is not only determined by what is injured by our environment, exposures, and lifestyles, BUT also by what is weak in us to begin with.

INDIVIDUALIZED APPROACH TO TREATING "DIS-EASE"

We have witnessed this "Precision" approach providing real answers and solutions for desperate patients when all else had failed them. Approaching the problem first from the perspective of genetic weakness also helps people to stop spinning their wheels when trying to figure out their health dilemmas; especially ones that run in the family. Like mood problems, autoimmunity, hormonal, learning, and neurological problems often do.

Through our efforts at Natural Balance Wellness Medical Center, we are helping people who haven't been helped otherwise by being precise and careful. We identify genetic susceptibilities using cutting edge polymorphism and point mutation testing. Those results are then cross-referenced with equally cutting-edge medical testing (of the blood, urine, stool, saliva, etc.). We essentially leave no stone unturned, which makes the difference!

Ideally, what we offer is something that everyone would seek out before illness hits. However, we usually work with people who are already quite ill and exhausted. AND sadly, most people don't know what they need to know in order to fix themselves based on who THEY are.

OUR MOTIVATION

Many people seek out a doctor's advice and get the "standard-of-care." For me, the wisdom I bring comes from my own experiences, both personally and professionally. I've been where my patients are. All our stories are different, but the underlying themes are similar. We simply can't ignore the genetic cards we've been dealt.

I also remember what it was like to miss out on parts of my life, so I am highly compelled by the fact that so many people miss out because they are burdened with aches, pains, and conditions that have not YET been resolved. Getting to the root cause of that suffering drives me to continually refine this craft. I know that after years of suffering and frustration it is easy to become downhearted and give up. But I encourage you not to.

By reframing illness into something more meaningful and manageable through our team's educational efforts, we encourage patients to keep trying. By addressing the rational and motivational component, we are able to transform "hopeless" into "hopeful," because full understanding of one's suffering is, in fact, therapeutic.

OUR MISSION

Our clinic wants everyone to understand their biological weakness and strengths! Regardless of the diagnosis or stated illness (or how much you believe you already know about your condition), there is a next-level explanation we want to teach you.

In our efforts we focus on three main areas of education, which include:

1. ***Consumers*** via our public online video clinic and self-starter member's area. Through consumer awareness, we hope to change the conversation and the expectations that people have for their doctors and with respect to their overall health status.

2. ***Patients*** via our group education and our patient-only video library. By cross-referencing genetic susceptibilities with individualized medical testing and thoroughly educating our patients, we are able to restore hope and heal perplexing conditions.

3. ***Physicians*** via our VideoPrescribe consulting services. By educating and acting as consultants to physicians about patient-centered education and precision solutions we are able to influence health and healing in the broadest sense possible.

All of these things are why every day is a new day for our clinic, our patients, our website members, and our physician clients. There are literally endless opportunities to reach others and help as many people as possible become more informed, healthier, and happier.

A parting snippet for your consideration: When it comes to rehabbing your health it needs to be stepwise and precise. You have to build the dam brick by brick to hold back the water. Things that happen overnight, fall apart overnight – friendships, houses, and half-cocked health solutions included. Patients who have successfully navigated our program would attest it is worth taking your time and healing well, rather than opting for mass crowd solutions. By offering this next-level awareness, partnering with patients, and motivating them to learn who THEY are, our team has the privilege to play witness to people's greatest successes in becoming healthy again. This really speaks to what has made us unique and successful. And, yes, I still love the fact that I'm getting "high marks" (from patients that is).

About Dr. Tony

Dr. Tony Boggess is a Physical Medicine and Rehabilitation (PM&R) physician, speaker, and writer who specializes in Nutritional and Biomedical Rehab for adults and children. He and his wife, Lilian founded Natural Balance Wellness Medical Center, which has developed into a nationally-recognized center known for its individualized and multimodal approach to patients.

Dr. Boggess earned his Doctorate from Midwestern University in Chicago, completed his specialty training at the University of Michigan, and earned additional certification in Medical Acupuncture through Stanford University. He has a long list of academic accolades, including the Army Medal of Achievement and many letters, lists, and honors related to his undergraduate and graduate careers. As a physician, he has received multiple Patient Choice and Compassionate Care nominations and awards since the clinic first opened its doors in 2008.

Known for his pioneering approach to assessing genetic predisposition, Dr. Boggess is the visionary back bone to the center's "Precision Medicine & Advanced NeuroCare" programs, attracting patients to Ann Arbor from all over the US and abroad. Recognized for its reputation for addressing perplexing illness, the Natural Balance Wellness Medical Center is able to boast successes in helping patients and families with problems considered unsolvable, or otherwise not fully addressed by other doctors and clinics.

As the medical director of Natural Balance, Dr. Boggess is interested in a wide variety of clinical approaches, but he especially enjoys leading patient education sessions for his Precision Medicine clinics. He is passionate about teaching and his enthusiasm rains through in his style of facilitating both small and large group seminars. He also has a special affinity for working with families, especially those with struggling children, and he strives to help them understand their genetics as a unit. His story is a labor of love and the novel programs and medical center he has created were born from overcoming his own personal health challenges and professional frustrations.

His professional mission can be summarized as an effort to educate patients and the public about genomics and other novel approaches to health and healing through his medical center and video clinics. He also assists other healthcare professionals, doctors, and clinics to provide patient-centered education services through his third-party consulting company, VideoPrescribe.

To learn more about our clinic, doctors, or video clinic, visit: nbwellness.com
To learn more about our consulting services and VideoPrescribe visit:
videoprescribe.com

CHAPTER 5

A CREATIVE BRAIN IN A BUSINESS WORLD

– FINDING CONFIDENCE AND SUCCESS IN AN UNLIKELY CAREER

BY STEVEN DIADOO, LICENSED REALTOR®

Creativity, as has been said, consists largely of rearranging what we know in order to find out what we do not know. Hence, to think creatively, we must be able to look afresh at what we normally take for granted.
~ George Kneller

Me. Known by Spock, Elf, and sometimes worse. What a life it's been—one laden with more insecurity than I can even grasp at times. I've had a tumor removed from my jaw line, leaving me with a deformity that I'll have my entire life. Yelling "stop" didn't work, so eventually I just surrendered to my insecurity and dealt with the fact that I'd never look like everyone else, but inside I was angry and fearful of rejection. I coped by drinking too much during uncomfortable social situations and eventually I paid a price for it. I flipped my car. Well, I can assure you—a newfound faith in God comes to you quickly when you find yourself fortunate enough to walk away from a situation like that without so much as a scratch.

I've lived in the shadows of the beautiful and many of you may relate to that. It's depressing to feel that way and have people judge you outwardly, not giving a second thought to the person inside—the one who truly defines who you are. I still get the occasional reminder that I'm not "normal" from some child or adult making a comment. They don't think twice about it, but I sure do. It still hurts, and I'm a grown man. Like many who have suffered from a lack of confidence, I wonder how life would be not living in the shadows of the beautiful. Once upon a time I would have given anything to be them, and parts of me still long for that today, but I'm a smarter guy now, at least I like to think.

Today I get it…we are defined by what's inside of us, not our outward appearances. So, although I still struggle at times—like even getting my picture taken for this chapter—I go on and I know that I have every reason to be confident, because I am in this world to do good.

Confidence comes from knowing who you are.
~ Napoleon Hill

I see my skills today and I know my value. I'm a guy who learned to be a decent painter, specializing in murals and the Venetian plastering technique common in the decorative finishing industry. That's why I often hear, "How did you ever become a guy who works in real estate?" To them, there's no logical connection, but to me, that creative side that has always shown itself in me is the very reason that I've found success in an industry that many may assume a "guy like me" would have no interest in, much less success in.

Of course, my journey has involved its fair share of hard work and learning curves, but the transition has not been as unlikely as some people assume. It began with a creative spark that was similar to the one I had when I began painting for a living. The recognition that creativity—that beautiful gift from our right brain—is a tool we can use to gain confidence and success in our careers, is liberating, because it provides us with limitless options. The fusion of creativity and business leads to great things, especially in marketing. For my clients, this is what sets me apart in the highly competitive real estate market. In case you didn't realize, there are a lot of realtors, sales people, and entrepreneurs in this world. But I'm driven by this: How many of us stand apart? And my peers often ask me how I've managed to do it.

Through the application of doing everything necessary for my job, I have seen the frustrations that come with buying and selling houses; creative solutions are needed to solve and alleviate problems and frustrations to ensure we move forward with confidence. Clients who see that you are addressing their needs and striving to meet their expectations are calmer. They see your value in motion, which is very rewarding for everyone.

THE PROCESS OF CONFIDENCE THROUGH CREATIVITY

The best creative efforts have a process, just like any successful business model does.

When I began painting, I had one goal: get the job done as quickly as possible. Get in and get out. Get on to the next job. Time is money. That "me" wasn't geared up for success with the right attitude. Thankfully, I met inspiration. His name was Eli Lucero from Arizona who was a master of his trade. He taught me a great many things that have been very applicable to building a successful real estate business that has processes that benefit all my clients.

A trend in art schools today is to focus on creativity and forgo the process. I'm not referencing paint-by-number type instruction, but the specific processes that an artist can use to create works of art that are appealing and sell. It's important, just like it is for the musician to hit the right note. Creative expression for the sake of it is one thing, but if you want to use it for a career, there's more to it.

Experience has taught me to look at situations with both my creative and business mind, seeing specific takeaways that give me an edge in real estate, just as it did in painting. It's working and I'm growing. It's all in the system that gears us for success. It's called the Trivium.

Definition of the Trivium: The Latin word trivium means "the place where three roads meet." Studies consist of grammar, logic, and rhetoric.

> By understanding the deeper meaning of this procedure, we become capable of teaching ourselves any subject or topic that we choose to focus on. My real estate process and the foundation for my confidence are based on the Trivium. It's broken down into precise action that leads to predictable, desired results.

The first aspect of systematic thinking is to learn the elements of a subject in order to critically define a problem or an opportunity. This is done in the grammar and logic stages.
~ Richard Grove

Grammar: The who, what, where, and when.
More than punctuation marks in a sentence, or linguistic structural rules, it's the raw, factual data in a specific body of knowledge. In real estate, we speak about: search criteria, appraisals, market analysis, FHA financing, inspection contingencies.

Logic: The why.
Understanding the interrelationships within that body of knowledge and eliminating all stated contradictions within it. For example, a larger loan downpayment on a mortgage isn't always more advantageous when it might be better to write a larger earnest money check with your offer.

Once defined, we use our creative thought capacity to solve the problem or find ways to take advantage of the opportunity. The classical rhetorical mode accomplishes this task.
~ Richard Grove

Rhetoric: The how.
A skill involving the effective use or expression of your newfound understanding. Choosing the right method in painting or financing strategy in real estate and writing or expressing the procedures, instructions, recommendations, and so on.

By putting the Trivium to work with real estate, clients gain a better understanding of what to expect throughout their entire process. There's no need to reinvent something just to say it's unique—take what works and blend it with your strengths. The outcome is better for everyone, plus time and stress are saved. It's a win/win!

In a world where we must prove to our clients that they are a priority, we must be creative in how we find ways to best service their needs.

There is logic to this very personal, big financial decision of buying and selling real estate. Using someone who brings it all together with less stress and better results makes the experience one to embrace, not agonize over. I strive to be an expert in what I can do to deliver results.

- For a listing (selling a home) – I created a system that works for me based on proven systems from successful realtors. My concept: my clients receive a calendar showing what needs to take place up until the point of the listing going live. It includes:
  - How we service the listing
  - A step by step breakdown of the entire process

  This works incredibly well, as it is logical and easy to follow, appealing to clients of all personalities. People selling homes want to know that action is taking place and what is going on.

- For buyers, I create six pages for them on a website. These pages include information and details on:
  - Listings
  - Resources such as lenders, telephone numbers, inspectors, title companies, and other information that may benefit them

  It's also important to determine a buyer's preferred method of communication. Regardless of whether it's telephone, email, or text, they receive initial correspondence via their preferred method. From there, they can decide what's next. As a Realtor®, I find that it is essential to work with clients in the way that works best for them. It demonstrates my commitment to their results while allowing me to use a system that is efficient for me.

The process I've created is really exciting for the buy side of transactions. You see, it's rather common to show potential properties to just one spouse. Lives are busy and coordination isn't always easy. While some realtors require both spouses be present, I don't need to accept that limitation because of my process. Through the personalized client portal website my clients have, I can show one spouse properties. I also take notes on the spot for the website that shows their specific feedback. Then at their convenience they can share the information with the other spouse. It's incredible: the other spouse wasn't there, but they are up to speed. It's efficient and leads to more sales with fewer hours spent touring homes.

Real estate is highly regulated and there are many specific rules and procedures that must be followed. So, creativity in those areas –not recommended! But enticing clients through creative ways to earn their business is important. That's why the quicker that we latch on to effective and efficient ways to meet client needs, the more confident and less limited we'll be.

Here are the lessons that I've learned that help creativity pave a path to distinction…

Lesson #1
Do not try to market everything you do, but one thing you do exceptionally well.

When I first began working with Eli, I learned the grammar of Venetian plaster—what is lime plaster, what a trowel is, and how to choose the right tools. Then I learned the logic behind what trowel was best for what situation, and then the rhetoric (video training) behind applying the layers of plaster. This system allowed me the opportunity to highlight an expertise that I had. I knew how to do much more than that, of course, but it was that technique that was the draw.

In real estate, I love working with both buyers and sellers, because staying connected with all their needs helps me be more effective for them. Everyone has certain parts of any endeavor that they take on which they do exceptionally well. For some, it's speaking and presenting, for others it's communicating through writing or something visual. Then there are those who have an abundance of patience and are phenomenal at handling stress. Whatever your strength is, you focus on that as your competitive advantage and perfect it. There's no other way. Make it your personal brand—that one thing that everyone identifies with you.

Lesson #2
The righteous are bold as a lion. (The Holy Bible, Proverbs 28:1)

There is no way to reach our potential without pursuing goals that require extending ourselves to the limit. For me, some examples are: the creation of my brainchild, a thirty-two page, full color infotaining magazine; new lead follow-up in five minutes or less; custom webpages for clients, as mentioned before; webpages for agents on my team; top performing lead generation websites for my team; large-scale high-ROI postcard marketing campaigns to half our city. By embracing the Trivium process, I've learned about editing, Adobe Illustrator, psychology, photography, data analysis, and art. Every nuance—large or small—was factored in that I could think of. More than one time I thought, what did I get myself into? Just give it up while you're still ahead. But I didn't. A mix of pride and resilience demanded that I see it through. The result was actually quite incredible, a magazine with articles and features for all demographics, making it a publication that offered something for everyone. By going big I learned a lot and also saw that the magazine was something that people enjoyed—both peers and clients. And marketing efforts with a high return on investment. If I hadn't tried, I could have only speculated.

Lesson #3
Embrace technology because it is here to stay.

Tech savvy consumers used to clash with veteran sales people, and many still do. Business owners who find ways to use technology to create a stronger connection with their clients will catapult ahead at the end of the day. People love convenience, even in real estate, but in the end, they still need a human being. So draw them in with technology and your knowledge, and keep them there through the rapport you build with them. Plus, with all the technology and Social Media out there you can put one message into motion and have it go to all your platforms with no extra effort. That's a smart and efficient use of time that reaches exponentially more people than you would otherwise. Technology is our friend—unless you're scared of it, then it becomes your frenemy. Successful people embrace what their target market craves; they don't struggle against, because that's tiring and leads to giving up.

WHAT DOES THIS ALL BOIL DOWN TO?

When we are confident, we are more effective.

Throughout my life, I've found that I could use the processes available to me to help achieve life goals. Because of this, I've been able to create wonderful connections with clients that I enjoy and are formed through mutual goals. This has all happened because I found confidence in myself and the process. This success couldn't have happened without my creative mind's merger with my business mind. I'm not just talk, I'm action. And I'm sales. And I'm the one who guides them to that property. So maybe, in a world where it's often said that we cannot be all things to all people, we can see that by creating processes that use our strengths, gives us a better chance at succeeding and building unstoppable confidence.

About Steve

Steve Diadoo is known as the Realtor® who maximizes his creativity to give his clients the best real estate experience possible. Before becoming a licensed Realtor® and Team Leader for his real estate practice in Lakeville, Minnesota, he received invaluable training in the fundamentals of business from his first career of faux painting, where he specialized in Venetian plastering techniques and murals. He credits those experiences to his successes today.

With a thriving real estate career, Steve offers unique services that are not offered by many other realtors, including something that is his signature in his community—personal web pages for buyers that make their real estate process an amazing experience. With sellers, he has a process in place that lets them see what is happening and to be expected every step of the way. With all his clients, he brings assurance that their needs are being met.

Throughout his life, Steve has found that the best way to serve others is through gaining confidence in how you approach all the goals and obstacles in your life. In his personal life, he's had some challenges that caused insecurities but he recognized that those moments were opportunities and a chance to do something meaningful through recognizing that there were lessons in the experiences. By following a process of growth, he was able to take away those lessons and come out successfully, gaining confidence along the way. His clients and the causes he's vested in are grateful for his personality, determination, and ability to create something meaningful out of everything he involves himself with.

Steve is the founder of North Real Estate Team at Bridge Realty, publisher of NORTH Real Estate and Lifestyle Letter, and the author of *New American Dream, Story of a First Time Home Buyer.* In addition to that, he is now co-authoring a chapter in the Jack Canfield book, *Road to Success, Volume II.* With all the opportunities he has to reach out and connect with people he finds inspiration in being able to inspire them to greater confidence and reaching their goals. It's a joy to see his success come to fruition in this way. He has also been seen on DIY TV, Bathtastic's episode Blood Bath, which featured handmade reptile wallpaper, and has been a guest on Paint Paper Crafts show, which is seen on the Create Channel and PBS, where he showcased *trompe l'oeil* techniques.

Although born in Seychelles Island, Steven has made his home in Minnesota with his wife and two children. His family is a constant inspiration and motivation for him, as well as wonderful creative partners to help him with the causes that are dear to his heart, including the non-profit Bowling for Brains, an event that benefits the American

Brain Tumor Association (BowlingforBrainsMN.org), which he is also a Board Member for. Steve practices gratitude every day because he has so much to be thankful for.

Contact Steve at: www.StevenDiadoo.com or email him at: Steve@StevenDiadoo.com.

CHAPTER 6

THE ANSWER IS "YES" - I'LL FIGURE IT OUT

BY JENNIFER BAKER

"Please God, I was only kidding when I said I'll sleep when I'm dead. Just let me get through this and I'll figure it out." I whispered. There I was—Miss Strong and Successful—lying on the pre-op bed, being prepped for an emergency surgery. It was terrifying for many reasons, but the one that really got to me was that I hadn't seen it coming. Sure, I felt the pain and noticed changes in my body, but I was "on top of my game." It all changed that morning, because before the beginning of the business day, the only thing I was on top of was a surgical bed, as my health was at rock bottom.

How could I go from handling everything, eloquently and in control, to a state of helplessness? It scared me and was only made worse when my misplaced Italian New Yorker doctor, a guy from the "old school of medicine" said, "Jenn, do me a favor, hold your babies a little longer and give them lots of kisses. Kiss them goodbye—just in case." I sensed his fear and it made my heart sink. Choking back another bout of tears, I did my part and reassured my kids and my "soon-to-be" ex-husband that I'd be fine and back up and running in no time. But was I convincing them or me?

Thankfully, I kept my word and made it through. And over time, my fear of mortality faded away. I delved right back into that double-edged fast-pace life that I'd been living. It was the life of an Executive in the Casino Industry with the largest gaming company in the world; a life filled with plenty of fun, issues, and 24/7 action to keep me busy—that was it, my successful life.

I have always been 'busy being busy' and believed I had conquered mountains, rising up from my humble beginnings. I made what I considered to be great money, and felt I had a great career, which provided a comfortable lifestyle for everyone. I acted like a stay-at-home mom by day and an executive by night, making things happen as everyone else slept. It seemed like the best of both worlds, but that was an illusion. It had come with a cost—no sleep. I thrived on achievement and daily praise. So it was worth it, right? What woman didn't struggle a bit, time and again, to be the best mom and professional possible? Everyone was happy, so I was happy, but yikes—how far could that really take me?

The amount of pressure that we put on ourselves to find success usually blinds us to seeing what success truly is.

None of this was a part of my original plan, but I worked hard and was promoted often because others recognized my talents. I moved up the success ladder by doing right by others, working smarter and harder than those around me, and being in service to others. This approach earned me a lot of respect in the industry, and within my community. I was often approached with lucrative job offers and my superiors sought me out for advice and as a trusted source to confide in. However, change was on the horizon…

The world around me decided to show me what success looked like from a brand new perspective. It would be up to me to see the "big picture."

There I was in the middle of a busy room full of people with important things to do and I had a world-stopping moment—I was frozen in time and something forced me to stand still and be silent. I didn't know why it was happening, but I knew it demanded my attention. I was forced to witness and absorb every tiny detail around me at a very intense level.

I was fully submersed in this suffocating reality that felt like a dream where I was stuck under water. The pains in my body, head, and feet were gone. It was just me watching everything weightlessly, observing a room full of people and private conversations. I began analyzing everyone and everything around me. I was surrounded by genuinely happy, satisfied, relaxed and content people who were fully engaged in life and conversation, they appeared to have what they wanted out of life. Everyone else was in a place they wanted to be at that moment. As for me, I had no idea what any of that felt like; I couldn't remember the last time that I had a deep meaningful conversation with someone… not even my husband.

My heart was breaking because I yearned for an understanding of what it was that I was missing.

Self-evaluation can often be painful; it certainly knocked me to my knees, demanding that I face things I didn't want to know, and certainly not feel. For example, the only vacation I had ever taken was a honeymoon that took place years after I was married. There was always too much going on; so much to achieve so we could be "happy." Also, I was now a mother to two young children and wanted to be the best I could for them—always available. The problem was that there were never enough hours in a day to do it all, so everything outside of work suffered, but no one suffered more than me. I had no friendships outside of work or opportunities to recharge and relax. With only a precious four hours of sleep averaged day in and day out, I'd shut out everyone and everything outside of my world. But geez, I was on top of my game—just not anything else that lent to my health and happiness.

What was all the sacrifice for? I had no idea. This was tough to admit, tougher than I would have ever imagined. *Who does that; who lives that way; what was it that I hoped to gain?* I couldn't help but wonder. The answer—someone who does too much for everyone else, while forgetting about their own needs.

Knowing what I hadn't done meant I now had to take action. A transformational revolution took place inside of me after that; and I began to act on what I needed. I redefined success. It started with leaving my fast-paced executive position and going toward something that brought abundant rewards—public speaking, motivational and business seminars, working with entrepreneurs and being sponsored by billion-dollar companies. Through serving my purpose and helping others on my terms, I was able to take time to care for myself, and suddenly it all made sense.

Things began happening, including fulfilling dreams like zip lining with my children while on vacation in Hawaii. My children had matured and become a huge help to me. Today, they are my supporters, encouragers, business partners, and occasionally the friendly faces in a crowd during a speech or seminar I'm giving. Their presence defines a new and wonderful way for me to appreciate the success that has come my way—not forced or through me having to outwork and outsmart anyone. It's because I care and through me finding my happiness, everything else happens. Life doesn't involve what I have to say "no" to; it involves what I can say "yes" to. The days of denying myself in every area of life, "sacrificing" for others, are no longer there.

Saying "YES" invigorates the mind and creates opportunities to really appreciate authentic success.

As these changes began, it took me about a year to systematically clear up my space, mistakes, and clean out my emotional house. By eliminating "no" I overcame that automatic response that was generated out of fear and taught to me as I grew up in a "no" environment. These new habits could not be ignored. People around me took note.

Admittedly, occasionally my new desire butted heads with my structured ways, making the shift difficult at times; and yes, we struggled. However, it just took a few rewards, like waking up and knowing I was working from home and could walk across the hall and see my children, to cement that what I was doing was worth it. Far more rewarding than a paycheck, and more emotionally fulfilling than running around frantically to prove my worth. It was when this all came together that I realized something—and it is a BIG SOMETHING!

Success does not come from a paycheck. It comes from a reality check of what you truly value in your life.

Knowing what I didn't want in life—the unhealthy and unfulfilling things I used to fight hard for—I began focusing on what I actually wanted. I was the type of person who worked best with structure. I started with a list of things that I could do that would make a difference every day in my life and give me a chance to help others, while celebrating my newfound liberation—because it is liberating to finally recognize authentic success! These principles are something I place a high value on every day.

1. **Secure your own oxygen mask.**
   We hear this statement every time we board a plane. "In case of emergency, secure your own oxygen mask first before assisting others." This is good advice and it should be applied to your life. I learned the hard way and taking care of myself makes me a better friend, mother, and mentor to those I work with.

2. **Learn to say "Yes."**
   The answer is always "no" until you ask… So ask and assume the "yes". Really, it is okay to say "yes" to yourself even when it doesn't "pencil out." Don't deny yourself great opportunities because you don't feel worthy or prepared. Just enjoy the challenge of figuring it out. I love feeling the butterflies in my stomach when I say yes to something big and have no idea how to achieve it. That is what happened my first time on the Legislative floor during session, when I was introduced to the concept of running my own business, of becoming a professional speaker, and now writing this book. I firmly believe and have experienced that when we have the desire to do something, the path in which we will achieve it is already there. We just have to begin trying—live and love learning!

3. **Follow your heart and live purposefully.**
   Our hearts are full of wisdom and when we acknowledge our purpose it is nearly impossible to deny the path to achieve it. When you veer off track, there is always a strong pull that guides you back on course. There is nothing in life that is worth denying your path and living outside of your purpose.

4. **Life is about deeply feeling the peaks and valleys and appreciating the lesson.**
   We are meant to feel deep emotions. The pendulum of emotions is always swinging, giving us both happy and painful experiences. If you numb or deny feelings, you are denying the growth you need to move to the next lesson, and worst yet, you could possibly repeat the past you are denying.

5. **Live in the small moments you create as often as you can.**
   Even when you do not believe that you've arrived at success, you still have to feel it and claim it—as often as you can. We're born with freedom of choice and by choosing to celebrate all that happens to

us for the lessons it offers is a wonderful choice! Often, enjoying the journey is exciting and more rewarding than achieving the goal itself.

6. **Don't be afraid to ask for help!**
   Reach out to those people and tools that can assist in your success.
   Using mentors, safety nets, and seeking out the right information to help leverage so you can achieve your goals and dreams is important. So many inspiring people have had incredible experiences that they are willing to share and help you grow from. However, these incredible resources are people who will expect you to do more than listen. They want to see you act, and succeed!

7. **Look within and around you often to seek out what is similar to what you want.**
   Whether it's a picture, moment, person, or thing, study it and determine how it fits for you. Then write it into your life's love note. Create it into reality.

Somebody once asked me how I would define success right now. I can't adequately express how joyful it was to know that I knew the answer. I didn't even have to think twice about it. We all define success differently, but my authentic success is this:

I don't look at people and see dollar signs; I see people with specific needs, obstacles to overcome, and untapped potential with their talents. Success is when you can serve your community because it makes you feel good to give something and have no fear attached and/or be concerned if you get paid, or if the favor will ever be returned.

Holding strong to my values and guiding principles has brought me to an amazing place—a place filled with wonderful adventures and opportunities. Today, I get the privilege of helping my community and always see endless ways that my "yes" can lead to success. It's not about the money, because as strange as it may seem, the money comes when you have a good business strategy and the right attitude about how you can contribute to the world around you and to your own wellbeing. My 'me' time is the best gift that I can give those I love, care about, and help throughout my work day. And the greatest joy is how aware I am of the positive ripple impact I make and how conscientious I am of how my daily decisions can move mountains.

Today, I am a mom in the present, happy and generating good life lessons, not through my paycheck, but through my actions in the moment. I do this through my career of helping my clients burst into success. I get to see faces of people eager to learn and who want to take their lives and businesses to that next level. Nothing tops these experiences! By the end of each day, when I have time to reflect, I feel something amazing: I've done my part to guide people to recognize that success is not numbers on a white board or wall of achievements; it's about the small daily choices to enjoy the challenges and journeys that make up our lives. I know that I'm truly fortunate and that every day is another opportunity to play in the sandbox of life.

About Jenn

Jennifer Baker is a servant-driven leader, author, speaker, trainer and consultant helping her clients operate based on their values, purpose, authenticity, emotional intelligence, accountability, and balance.

Jennifer has been selected as one of America's Premier Experts™, and spends her time speaking to, training, and supporting tens of thousands of companies that range from 'Solopreneurs' and home-based businesses to Fortune 100 companies worldwide. Focusing on systems, processes, behavior measurements, and key performance indicators for success, she shares relevant insight and power-packed stories to help others realize their potential through mindset, planning, leverage and personal accountability.

An author, Talk Show creator and radio host, business and political consultant, professional speaker, trainer, certified digital marketer and expert in online marketing; Jennifer still thrives on growth and daily praise from clients and her audience. Jennifer Baker is also one of the top-ranked Master Certified Authorized Expert Solution Providers, Speakers and Trainers with Constant Contact and other online marketing tools.

These proven marketing and business development systems not only dramatically increase the key buzzwords in the industry such as SEO, ROI, open rates, and engagement, but helps actualize client success by increasing business development efforts and income through a customized holistic approach. Unlike most online marketers, Jennifer implements concepts from her extensive business experience, client engagement and constant feedback while maximizing the most advanced technology available for her clients. She then keeps it authentic by coaching her clients through the process so they understand and engage in their business growth.

Jennifer 'retired' in her 30's from her executive-level position with the largest gaming company in the world to pursue her purposeful path of helping others create a positive life of balance and impact. She thrives on daily 'pay-it-forward' moments that help others realize their greatness, how to apply it to their business, and create a ripple effect in the business and professional climate to help support our nation's economic and family stability.

CHAPTER 7

WE ARE THE MEN

BY ANTONIO GAGNON

We all create our own outcome. *I went about this mammoth task by taking in all the lessons that I had learned through conversations and lessons with my father.* He had wisdom and knew how to break it down into a kid's language. The guy was funny and I'm grateful that I inherited that from him, as well as his awareness of the importance of business and commerce.

Growing up, I watched Dad work hard. He was a millwright—a good job—but it took him away from us for six months at a time. It was all work and no play. Then it would be time for six months off. This was our "family time" and it meant vacations and adventures and for me. I remember going to auctions with my Dad to make bulk estate purchases, which he'd later resell in a small resale store he also owned with my mother. He was a tinkerer and could fix anything. Those are not my traits; I am a guy who knows how to inspire, grow and delegate; which is more in my wheelhouse. Our family also owned a small Coney Island style restaurant that was located in a not-so-great part of downtown Detroit. *I was always around business and adults. It was worth it, because I got to be around my father and mother at these times as well.* I was a spoiled kid, feeling like I had a wealth of riches from the life I got to live, and even thought you would not know it by looking at us. My Dad taught me how to save by putting half of all of my money in the bank, and using the other half to purchase materials or supplies for my business which was baseball cards. At a young age, I realized that this was far more valuable than the classroom which had me sitting still, being patient and listening to theory.

My father passed away when I was only fourteen. I was grateful for what I had learned from him and it was time to put it all into play. Those words he'd spoken for years had been pounded into my head and they were there to stay. I could hear them like they were being spoken in real time. "Tony, hard work gets you results." "Always remain positive, because our thoughts become reality." Those statements may have been canned ideas for some people, but not for my dad; he'd always been a man who didn't just like to hear his own voice—he was a man of action, a doer.

No doubts about it. Although I didn't have him for nearly as long as I should have, my Dad and Mother helped me gain the foundation to become the man I am today. The thought strikes me as strange once in a while. After all, Dad got sick when I was just twelve, a boy not old enough to date or even have a beer with his father. However, I was old enough to understand that to be a man, I had to take control of what I did in life to find success, regardless of what life delivered.

Mom and I were left to deal with Dad's death and it was not easy. Although he'd been sick for a few years it wasn't until the "moneymaker" was gone that we really felt the impact. No Dad. No Money. Life as we had known it would never be the same again. Not only because he was gone, but because Mom and I had to find a way to meet our most basic everyday needs on our own.

My life had always been fast paced, but it was about to double in speed.

Mom got a job as a housekeeper in a hotel, the best job she could find. My Grandmother moved in with us to help take care of me during those long hours that Mom worked, also becoming a leader in the household to help keep me on the straight and narrow. I had always gone to Catholic school after fifth grade and that required money, the one thing we did not have. It would have been easy and certainly less hassle to just accept the shaky Detroit public school system as my fate, but I wanted to stay with where I'd been. So, I sold my baseball card collection to pay for the tuition and started to work to cover the rest. I was always clever. I always found ways to work more to attain my goals. I was getting it done and not complaining that others had it easier.

Now, I was in high school and time was flying by. I was the protector to

Mom and Grandma, having this compelling desire to make sure that they were all right as well. My time was at a premium. School and work—day in and day out. I never got to do anything in the school that I worked so hard to attend. Well, I did play baseball and I will never forget that. My friends would have fun on the weekends, at parties and festivals and I would work. But it was worth it. My fun came from entertaining the people I was around. Making others laugh and getting a reaction from them was a gift that I had, although I didn't have any idea of how I could use that "in the real world" for "real-world results."

Then it came time to graduate and make the "big decisions" that came for most kids who were on the cusp of adulthood. Only I already felt like I was an adult. I had insights. College was not right for me at that time. I knew what I had to work with—skills, willingness to work hard, and a clear understanding of both my strengths and weaknesses. So, when a Marine Corps recruiter said, "You can learn how to lead in the Marines," I was in. I signed on the dotted line. It was something school did not teach.

My excitement about joining the Marines was not the same for my Mom. She wanted me to go to college because "that's what people did." It was not easy to show them that I was making the best choice for me. Going with the grain wasn't as important as going with my instincts. It paid off, too. What I learned in the Marine Corps delivered what that recruiter had said it would, and a whole lot more.

Money matters exist everywhere in this world, even in the service. I made about $660 a month. Dad's saving policy was still my motto so half of that money would go into the bank the other half was for fun and adventure. If I couldn't afford to do something with the money I had available, I didn't do it. This took discipline, but I was in the perfect place to show I had it. I still have it today, in fact. If it can't be done with half of the money I earn, it shouldn't be done. Then my days in the Marine Corps came to an end and it was back to civilian life; new tools for a new era.

There was a better man waiting for the world when my service was complete.

The big picture of my life was taking shape and my ability to lead within the scope of my personality and ambition took hold. I went back to what was familiar—the restaurant business—and worked...a lot! 100% of my time was invested in learning how to run a business and how to work my way up through the ranks. I used my entertainment talents to be successful. Things were shaping up. I'd even gotten the girl—or so I thought. Surprise! She wasn't a fan of me switching jobs so much in my ambitious pursuits and that was all she needed to take a pass on me. It didn't distract me from working even harder, though. I knew the industry and what I had to do. If I didn't do it, no one would. I was the driver.

Hard work paid off. I became a working partner in a restaurant and was the "face of the place." I'd found a great way to run a high-end restaurant that drew in the movers, shakers, deal makers, athletes, and everyone that others considered "someone." People loved coming to the restaurant because it was more than food, it was an experience. *This was when I recognized that the power I had to connect with people was being underutilized, and that I should be doing something that extended to a larger audience.* I knew what it was that I should do, too. I wanted to be the man who could guide people toward significant financial decisions for their life through a better conversation that connected them with their needs. I began with the basics—healthcare.

I started a health insurance company out of my home where I was a broker for large insurance carriers that offered health insurance. I had the connections and I knew how to leverage them for my very genuine purpose. And over time, my small "at home" business had grown to about a thousand clients strong and a rather nice supplemental income. Helping people structure their lives for financial stability was incredible—it's not how much money you have, but how you structure it that makes the biggest impact. *Life felt great, and before long, I decided I'd rather be talking to people about these important issues of their lives more than being at the restaurant.* The potential of it all resonated with me greatly. My thinking from the Marines: *I protected our country, now let me protect your family.*

This is where I learned the value of taking notes and listening. I had to be smart, after all, as much as I loved helping people, remembering a thousand peoples' life stories was no easy feat. I found a way to document what they shared with me and remember it so I could ask about it when I saw them next. It was highly effective!

When people know that you care about their life's events they will engage with you and allow you to help them better.

As my rapport with people continued to grow, they would begin to ask me about other types of insurance and investments and that's when my story really came full circle. Offering life insurance to families and guaranteeing lifetime income was something that I saw great value in for obvious reasons. Not having any money after Dad's passing meant huge financial struggles for my family to just maintain the status quo. I'd always been driven by the thought, *never again*. Why not help others with their "why" by supporting it. It has to be bigger than me. If I do something for money, I will burnout. This, combined with the expanding variety of ways I can strengthen people's financial picture, is now my consuming passion. I am the man who helps families be better prepared for the unexpected and the uncertainties of the future by protecting them from everyday risk and running out of money; a true why and a reason to get up every day.

My passion for what I do is now backed by a wealth of experience and expertise. Without the passion, it's tough for me to believe that anyone can do their best for others. Everyone deserves a committed person rallying around them to help them prevent distressful financial situations and create better financial outcomes for their lives and the lives of those they may leave behind. Things happen that we can't control. I say, "Listen, in order to take care of your family and leave a legacy you need to do this—it's not an option any longer. It'll be too late if you don't do this." Life could end tomorrow, so today's actions—and lack of action—do matter. Knowing this is what gets me up every morning and drives me to connect with as many people as I can. This is the man I always want to be.

It is not about getting up to make money; it's about getting up each morning to make a positive difference in a family's life.

Today, the people I meet understand my "why", which helps them relate to their "why". Leaving a family high and dry is not loving or kind. Neither is leaving them drowning in their financial picture. That's reality. But my mission is larger than just that, alone. If I had a machine to duplicate myself, I'd do it and there would be Tony Gagnon's worldwide to help people connect with their "why" that helps them focus on their financial picture. For every action I perform for myself or anyone I come in contact with, I ask myself this question, "Does this decision support my __(fill in the blank)__?" It all draws into my inability to sit by and let people be bullied. I'm a protector. What I do helps to protect. Sometimes people do not know what that means. It is my job to let them know and support them as I do it.

These great things are happening, but there is still so much work to be done. There are underdogs out there and none tug at my heartstrings more than the battered women who cannot get out of their current situation. I want to help them change that, and I will through my forthcoming non-profit, **We Are The Men**. As a man who has a high disdain for bullies I am appalled by the thought of anyone using muscle to manipulate and control another person, whether it's emotional or physical. It's something that I can't stand for. For me, showing the world that men also care about fighting for women in bad situations is important. I can think of no greater reward of my skills, time, and talent than to help women remove themselves from the threat, get on their feet, and find them a job—whatever it takes to support them. They need to know that more people do have their backs in this world than do not.

What do I really want to accomplish? I want people to look at me and the contributions I've made and have no doubts. I don't have to inspire everyone I meet, but there is a reason why I cross people's paths. I believe that if I meet you, there is a reason and I ought to try to figure out and contribute in some way to your life; even if it's just to give you a brief respite from your day so I can make you laugh or you can reconnect with your strength and dreams. Be in the "now" and pay attention because you may miss something. Once I accomplish this I can say to myself, *"I was the best man that I could be, to as many people as I could be."*

About Antonio

Antonio Gagnon helps his clients reduce everyday risk. Having been born and raised in the city of Detroit in the 70's and 80's, Antonio was taught how to be risk averse early on and he took this to heart, mastering it at a young age. Before his father passed away, when he was only 14, Antonio had learned much from him about business and used his skills to generate income. For Antonio, personally, he used to sell dandelions in the neighborhood for a $1.00 a bunch. He soon figured out that if he recruited five people to do the same thing he was doing, he could make a lot more money.

Through the big lessons learned at a young age, Antonio found a calling and discovered that he was a guy meant to get things done. He helped his friends and family accomplish tasks that no one wanted to do. He was a protector and helped fend off the bullies in the neighborhood. Through his experiences, he discovered that he had a gift and that the best way to develop it was to join the United States Marine Corps so he could learn how to lead.

After life in the service, Antonio saw that he could combine his leadership skills with his business acumen. He spent the next 26 years in the hospitality business, working in hotels and restaurants, learning how to schmooze the movers and shakers of Metro Detroit and give them the type of dining environment that they gravitated toward. During this time, Antonio also started his own health insurance broker business called, "Alliance Health Care Systems" which helped launch him into his current perfect career.

Antonio's financial career is centered on his philosophy that "people buy people." He helps his clients reduce their risk through protecting their health, income, and life, while ensuring longevity (outliving their money).

Today, Antonio wants to make a difference and leave a legacy behind. Through his new role of Best Selling Author with the book, *Road To Success, Volume II,* which he co-wrote with the legendary Jack Canfield, he is spreading the message of "why" he gets up in the morning. He's also hoping to bring light to his charity that will be launching—*We Are The Men.* The charity is dedicated to helping battered women find new hope through being removed from their situations and given the tools they need to succeed both emotionally and financially. To achieve this goal, he would like to work in conjunction with current successful foundations dedicated to this same purpose.

Antonio believes that if you're not moving forward, you're moving backwards. Ever inspired by change and helping others, he always remembers Martin Luther King Jr.'s words: "Faith is taking the first step even when you don't see the whole staircase."

CHAPTER 8

A JOURNEY OF A THOUSAND MILES

BY SHAHRAM GHANBARI

If you love what you do, you'll never work a day in your life. So, I have never worked in my life since I have always done what I loved. I started my career as a teacher and tutor when I was still a university student. This way, I became the CEO of my personal services company selling my services to institutes, schools, and those who wanted to learn. Then, I thought it was not enough and I had better start a real business and that led to my first language school in Iran in 1991.

When I was a teenager, I always had a dream. My dream was to live in an English speaking country one day. Therefore, I started my English studies when I was at high school. By the time I got admission to university, I could teach English to my classmates. Moreover, when I think of the past, I clearly see how my career as an English teacher and manager of three language schools helped me get prepared for my dream I had as a teenager. In fact, the whole universe conspired to make my dream come true. Knowing another language expanded my horizons and I could access more resources and data.

As you may have also read or heard, knowledge is power. Some say that it's not true and they correct it as: knowledge is power when applied. Anyway, I defined a mission for myself and that was to help people to go to the next level in terms of quality and quantity of life. To accomplish this mission, I set a goal for myself to study thirty books a year so that I could serve others better, and in a better way.

Later in my career, a colleague and friend asked me to help someone who had recently moved from another city, and because he didn't know anybody and he couldn't get a decent job, his family was struggling. At that time, we were about to open a new school and we needed someone to manage it. Therefore, based on his experience, I decided to appoint him as the manager of our new school. A few years later, he left us and opened his own business. A few years later, I received a telephone call from him that put us in contact with a friend of his which led to my entering a new area of business.

In three years, I opened my new company in the oil and gas services field. Although part of the work was training which was my expertise, it was a different world and it took me some time to learn and get to know this new world and its challenges. Fortunately, this business was transformed into a multimillion-dollar business within a year or so. As Winston Churchill said: "We make a living by what we get. We make a life by what we give." You can only have more for yourself by giving away to others.

The business we started in the energy sector, which turned into a success in a short time, came to an end due to economic sanctions. We couldn't work because the multinational oil companies stopped their activities and started leaving the country.

At that stage, I decided to work in other countries, but each time we encountered an obstacle because of the company's identity. Hence, we decided to dissolve the company and I decided to create another identity for myself so that I could easily work and live all over the world. After some investigations and studying different countries, I decided to immigrate to Canada. I started the procedure in 2010 and made my exploratory visit in December 2010. Afterwards, I submitted my business plan and it was approved, and later I gave them the rest of the documents needed for the immigration process. It took me five years to end up in Canada and receive my Permanent Residency Status. Meanwhile, because the procedure took so long, I started another language school and we also changed it to a multi-million-dollar business in five years before I left the country. Happy are those who dream dreams and are ready to pay the price to make them come true. I paid a lot and started to build up my life in a new environment.

To keep myself updated when I was in Iran and make myself ready for the challenges of a new and changing world, I attended a lot of seminars and workshops with some of the world's gurus and learned a lot from their expertise. I read a lot of books and listened to every audio program available, and in fact, changed my car to a university on wheels.

When I came to Canada in 2015, since I knew what I wanted, i.e., I had clear goals and plans in place, I had my office in a week and started to build up my network and business. Our goals can only be reached through the vehicle of a plan in which we must strongly believe, and upon which we must vigorously act. There is no other route to success. This isn't an end for me and I still have a long way to go and more to achieve. Michelangelo said the greater danger for most of us isn't that our aim is too high and we miss the target, but that it is too low and we reach it. Although I have taken a long journey so far, I still have a long way to go.

Success leaves tracks.
~ Anthony Robins

Success leaves tracks. Therefore, if we study the lives of successful men and women, we can come up with rules they have applied in their lives to achieve their goals.

Setting goals is the first step in turning the invisible into the visible.
~ Anthony Robbins

1. The first step to move toward success is to have goals. Besides, it's not just enough to have goals but to have clear goals. Clarity is everything. Now take time and think about your past goals and resolutions, the ones you achieved and the ones you never saw through. Reflect on them and determine why you achieved some goals but not others. The most important factor in setting a goal is clarity. It must be **S**pecific. It must be **M**easurable. You should be able to measure your progress. It must be realistic or **A**ttainable. Your goal must serve a meaning and it must be important. In other words, it must be **R**elevant. All your goals must have a deadline. Goals without deadlines are just fantasies. Your goals must be **T**ime-bound. That is to say, your goals must be **SMART**.

Plans are nothing; planning is everything.
~ Dwight Eisenhower

2. The second step is planning since a goal without a plan is just a wish. As Benjamin Franklin once said: By failing to prepare, you are preparing to fail. A plan is a list of actions arranged in whatever sequence is thought likely to achieve an objective. Now it's time to identify the obstacles, the knowledge, information and skills you will need to achieve your goals. You also need other people to help you on the way. You should identify who those people are and how you can collaborate with them.

Action is the foundational key to all success.
~ Pablo Picasso

3. So far, you have set your goals and prepared your plan or your roadmap, which shows you how to move forward and where to go so that you can achieve your goals, and now it's time to take action. Another characteristic of successful people is that they are action-oriented. They select their most important tasks for each day and then act. You must do the same. Act intelligently. Do something each day that moves you toward your goals.

Great works are performed not by strength but by perseverance.
~ Samuel Johnson

4. Perseverance is the key to success. In our life journey, we encounter a lot of setbacks and obstacles and only the most persistent succeed. Those who do not fear in the face of problems and difficulties and go beyond the common boundaries. Successful people are self-disciplined. They discipline themselves to do what they should do, when they should do it, whether they feel like it or not. That's why you should develop the habit of self-discipline. The good news is that despite what many may think, self-discipline is a learned behavior and you can improve it by practice and repetition in your daily life. Discipline is the bridge between goals and accomplishment. John Adams says patience and perseverance have a magical effect before which difficulties disappear and obstacles vanish.

Life is either a daring adventure or nothing at all.
~ Helen Keller

5. Take risks. Do not fear. Albert Einstein said, "A ship is safe at the shore, but that is not what it is built for." When I wanted to start my own business, a lot of friends and family members told me that starting a business from scratch involves a lot of risk and most of people fail. My answer to them was that even crossing the street involves some sort of risk, but you don't stay in one side only. What you do is you mitigate the risk and you cross the street. This is what we call a calculated risk. Anyway, I started my business and took a calculated risk. With a plan and perseverance, I finally succeeded. This happened again when I decided to immigrate. They told me that it's a big change and lots of risks are involved. They were right. It is a big change, but I did not believe it involved a big risk. Again, with enough planning, I succeeded and ended up in a country a thousand kilometers away with a different culture and different ways of doing things. Pearls don't lie on the beach at the seashore. If you want one, you must dive for it. The best quote I have ever read is from Mark Zuckerberg, the founder of Facebook: The biggest risk is not taking any risk… In a world that is changing really quickly, the only strategy that is guaranteed to fail is not taking risks.

I am fond of pigs. Dogs look up to us. Cats look down on us.
Pigs treat us as equals.
~ Winston Churchill

6. Treat people well. Helping people opens doors that you could never imagine. No one has ever become poor by giving. Remember that you have two hands, the first is to help yourself, and the second is to help others. Beginning today, treat everyone you meet as if they are the most important. Extend to them all the care, kindness and understanding you can bring together, and do it with no thought of any reward. Your life will be never the same again.

Surround yourself with only people who are going to lift you higher.
~ Oprah Winfrey

7. Surround yourself with successful people. To be successful, you must surround yourself with the right people. By the right people,

I mean people with a positive attitude, people who provide support and love. This way you also become a positive and supportive person. One way to surround yourself with people that can lift you higher is trying to make up a mastermind group. A mastermind group is set to sharpen your business and personal skills. The concept of "mastermind alliance" was formally introduced by Napoleon Hill in his book, "Think And Grow Rich." Napoleon Hill wrote about the mastermind group principle as: "The coordination of knowledge and effect of two or more people, who work toward a definite purpose, in the spirit of harmony."

Intellectual growth should commence at birth and cease only at death.
~ Albert Einstein

8. Try to learn something new each day. Ask others when you don't know. Anyone who stops learning is old, whether at twenty or eighty. Anyone who keeps learning stays young. Commit yourself to life-long learning. Only this way can you succeed in this knowledge-driven and changing world. As Brian Tracy says, "your lives gets better when you get better." Therefore, try to make yourself better by reading books, listening to audio programs, watching visual programs, and attending seminars and workshops. When I landed in Canada, since my native language was not English and despite the fact that in my opinion and also other people's opinion, my English was at a good level and standard, I decided to join Toastmasters so that I can improve my English, and at the same time my public speaking skills, because public speaking has always been one of my passions and Toastmasters was an opportunity for me to enhance my speaking skills and at the same time increase my network. The art and science of asking questions is the source of all knowledge. Thus, try to use other people's knowledge and expertise to understand how to proceed. We are born to do big things in this world. We should leave mediocrity and stick to excellence if we want to achieve real success in our life, and help others to achieve their goals and objectives. Thomas Edison mentioned, "If we did all the things we are capable of, we would literally astonish ourselves."

To be successful in your life's journey, you should have clear written goals, plan what you want to do in advance and then take action. The most important factors are your persistence and taking calculated risks.

On your way to success, you need the help and contribution of many people, treat them well and surround yourself with the people that add to your values and support you. And most importantly, commit yourself to life-long learning since this alone can transform your life completely.

About Shahram

Shahram Bagher Ghanbari has a **BS** in Physics and his **MBA** – Master of Business Administration. He has attended many workshops and seminars on personal and business success with the world's gurus. He's a member of **ISMM** (International Sales and Marketing Management). This combination of science and business has made him an exceptional personal and business consultant.

Shahram has been the director of three language schools. He is also the president and CEO of his own company in Canada now. His mission is to help people and businesses to get to the next level of success and achievement. He has spent all his life in education and training and that has made him an expert and master in training and education. He helps companies to achieve the standards defined in the industry.

He loves to see people succeed.

CHAPTER 9

A LAWYER'S JOURNEY TO SUCCESS

BY KEN NUNN, ESQ.

My name is Ken Nunn. I am an injury lawyer in Indiana. After 48 years and more than 28,000 clients, I am here today to tell you about my journey to success.

They taught me in law school that advertising was unethical and unprofessional. A "good lawyer" would always have lots of clients. They went on to say . . . "If you're a good lawyer, no matter where your office is, clients will seek you out." Well let me tell you, that was not exactly true!

I am the founder and sole owner of the Ken Nunn Law Office. Today, we have 92 employees, 16 attorneys and a 30,000 square foot building that was paid for in five years. We are injury lawyers. We have collected over $700 million dollars for our clients and are fast approaching the billion-dollar mark.

One of the advantages I have had throughout my career is that I have never forgotten my roots. I grew up poor. I was not a particularly good student. I had to work my way through college and law school. I got my law degree from Indiana University and I barely got through law school. I graduated near the bottom of my class. So I wasn't born rich, I wasn't a particularly good student – but I made up for all that by working very hard. During my freshman year in law school, I was at the school 14 hours a day.

When I got out of law school I had nowhere to go except UP – plus I had an enormous amount of determination. I passed the bar exam on my first try. I was sworn in as a lawyer and opened my own office.

I started as a solo practitioner. It was just me, one inexperienced secretary, a folding card table and four folding chairs. I opened my office on July 1, 1968. For the next ten years I worked very hard. I did great work. I won cases that many lawyers turned down. I spent many nights at 3:00 a.m. at my kitchen table writing my closing argument for the jury the next day. I did not take a vacation for 8 years. There were many days that I stood in my office, gazing out the window, waiting for the phone to ring and waiting for a prospective client to come and see me. It was routine for me to come home at the end of the week and say to my wife, "Honey, there's no money this week."

To make ends meet, I would search the automobile classified ads in the local newspaper looking for individuals who were selling cars. I would buy the car as cheaply as possible, clean and polish the car and put the car back in the newspaper the next day. I would make $100 or so profit. The profit came just in time to pay my rent and my inexperienced secretary. I was doing great work and I got great results for my clients, but they were all "small fee" cases. I wondered where all the big cases went.

During my first 10 years of practicing, it was popular to wear plaid suits, plaid sports jackets, plaid pants – everything was plaid. I thought I was a pretty snappy dresser. My "look" did not help my practice. All of that changed and now I have become a conservative dresser. I have 35 dark blue suits which I rotate on a daily basis. I always come to work in one of those suits with a white shirt and a tie. It also helps that I have gray hair.

My turnaround year began around 1978. The U.S. Supreme Court ruled in Bates v. State Bar of Ariz., 433 US 350, 97 S. Ct. 2691, 53 L. Ed. 2d 810 – 1977, ruling for the first time that lawyers could advertise legally. It was a major ruling for me. Many lawyers in Indiana were opposed to the Supreme Court ruling. I received a lot of criticism from my fellow lawyers.

Even today, I still get a lot of criticism and disrespect from my fellow lawyers. They still believe that I am a sub-standard lawyer. I work hard every day to prove them wrong! Their criticism actually motivates me and so I say to my critics, "THANK YOU!"

I started out very cautiously by placing a small ad in the Yellow Pages of the phone book. I was ridiculed by almost all of the other lawyers in my state. One of my town's senior lawyers (in front of a lot of other lawyers), spoke to me in a very loud voice, "Ken, you're too good a lawyer to advertise." I was very embarrassed and I simply didn't know what to say in response. That first phone book ad was small and very conservative. Then I noticed another law firm had an ad right next to mine and it was larger than my ad. I made a promise to myself that no one in my city would ever have a bigger ad in the Yellow Pages than my ad.

My biggest fear during those early years was that my Aunt Ruthie would find out that I was an advertising lawyer and she would think I was a sub-standard lawyer. That's how strong the pressure was because of the criticism of my peers. Were my critics correct? There was a certain amount of shame associated with being an advertising lawyer. Ironically, here we are in 2016, and there is still a lot of ridicule directed at me and a large amount of shame sent my way by other "so-called good lawyers" who do not advertise.

Thanks to that first ad in the phone book, my phone started to ring like it never had before. I quickly needed a second secretary. Then a third. Then a fourth. I expanded my office space within the building. I increased my Yellow Pages advertising. I was on the back cover of 42 phone books in all the surrounding counties. I had about a dozen billboards and I advertised in the newspaper every day. I soon had to move out of that building and into a larger building with more space. I kept right on increasing my advertising and eventually I had to build a larger office because my practice literally exploded. More and more staff meant I needed more and more space. Eventually I needed more space than the new building could provide. I then expanded into a second building, splitting up my office staff between the two buildings. Splitting my office between two buildings was complicated, so I decided to build yet another brand new law office and that is the building we are in right now. That building is 30,000 square feet.

Now the new building is full and I have bought additional land anticipating future needs. Our law office is next to a major highway with about 40,000 cars passing by each day. The building is well lit at night and is very visible. The building is truly a silent partner because it helps my image. It brings in a lot of clients. For example, I had a client recently tell me that he drove past my building every day and that client referred a family member to our office. That referral case settled for $16.5 million dollars. Thank you building!

Now, with the avalanche of new clients and new employees, I had a whole deluge of new problems to solve. Managing all of the employees required a lot of planning and a lot of training. Throughout my growth period, I added additional lawyers. Our lawyers are excellent! They had the same level of determination that I did. We all put our hearts and souls into each and every case. We have received many National awards. I am very proud of our attorneys and other employees.

During all this time, I gave our clients absolutely 100% great service. Our office returned phone calls the same day and our attorneys fought very hard to win the clients' cases. By the way, our attorneys have won huge jury verdicts.

More clients and more employees resulted in a major challenge. I created approximately 250 written systems to help run my law office so that I could provide great training for my staff, and also great service for my clients.

One of my most important decisions occurred 16 years ago. I decided I would get more money for my clients if we took their case to a jury. The insurance companies are inherently stingy. I believed in the jury system. That was a fantastic decision! Thousands of my clients have benefitted from that decision I made 16 years ago. We made the insurance companies pay BIG checks. Today, our law office is ranked #1 in the state of Indiana for doing the most jury trials for injured people. We have been ranked #1 for 15 years in a row. We have left a trail of multi-million dollar verdicts throughout the state. Our largest jury verdict was $157 million, which ranked #6 nationally. We love it when insurance companies make silly, disrespectful offers to our clients, and a jury awards the client a monster verdict.

I cannot begin to describe my success for the past 48 years without also including the very talented attorneys and non-attorneys who have been part of this office for many years – some as many as 40 years. It is common to walk through my office and see staff members who have been with us for 20, 25, 30 and 35 years.

Another reason for my success is that we protected and looked out for our clients, and we also protected and looked out for the employees. We have a policy in our office to give annual raises. I bring up the topic each year. I believe it is awkward for the employee and for me to require the employee to ask for a raise. We give raises annually. Our staff is among the highest paid in the state of Indiana. We have many non-lawyers who are paid over $100,000 per year. So I have been very blessed to have such great employees – both attorneys and non-attorneys.

My law firm is advertised on TV 400 times a day. When we get a client, we give that client "red carpet service" and we have gotten thousands of referrals to our office because of that great client service and because of the great results we get for our clients.

We also have another important reason for our success. We put our "heart and soul" into every case – no matter if the case is small or large.

Our law office has received many National Awards and we are very proud because my office started out as "just me." See the award list in my bio.

I drive two black Rolls Royce automobiles. They, too, help my image of success. One is a 4-door sedan Phantom. The other is a 2-door convertible. Those cars attract a lot of attention. People are constantly taking pictures of the cars. When I'm at the gas station, people want to come over and talk to me and ask questions about the car. I always welcome these conversations. People are always waving at me and shouting my name. It helps to be noticed. It's good advertising.

I purchased an easy-to-remember telephone number. The telephone number makes my advertising more successful and people remember my number. The number is 1-800-Call-Ken.

I absolutely love what I do. It's not work! I love talking to prospective clients and current clients and discussing strategy to enable us to help our clients through a very difficult time. Plus, I absolutely love the challenge of fighting insurance companies on behalf of my clients.

About Ken

Ken Nunn is the owner of the Ken Nunn Law Office, located in Bloomington, Indiana, which limits its practice exclusively to personal injury and wrongful death cases.

Ken is a member of:

- Million Dollar Advocates Forum and Multi-Million Dollar Advocates Forum. [Membership is limited to select attorneys who have won million and multi-million dollar settlements and verdicts. Fewer than 1% of lawyers are members.]
- National Academy of Personal Injury Lawyers – Top Ten Attorney.
- Rue Ratings BEST ATTORNEYS OF AMERICA – Lifetime charter member.
- American Association for Justice.
- Indiana State Bar Association.
- Indiana Trial Lawyers Association.
- Best Attorneys of America 2015.
- Top 100 Trial Lawyers 2015 – awarded to lawyers who have met or exceeded established standards of excellence in the practice of law.
- Nation's Top 1% by National Association of Distinguished Counsel, 2015 – for exhibiting exceptional virtue in the practice of law.
- Best Lawyers in America 2015, the oldest and most respected peer-review publication in the legal profession.
- Nation's Premier Top Ten Personal Injury Attorney.

Ken has been listed as:

- Top Trial Lawyers in America.
- Indiana Super Lawyer – awarded to lawyers who have attained a high degree of peer recognition and professional achievement.
- One of Indiana's Top-Rated Lawyers.
- AV Pre-eminent in *Martindale-Hubbell,* a rating system established in 1887. "Highest possible rating both in legal ability and ethical standards."
- 2012 Newsweek Leaders in Auto Accident Law.
- The Ken Nunn Law Office has been selected to be included in the "Best Law Firms of America" as reported by *U.S. News & World Report 2016,* based on a rigorous evaluation process by clients and leading attorneys.
- Who's Who of America, 2012.
- Lifetime Charter Member Best Attorneys of America.
- Kentucky Colonel by the Governor of the State of Kentucky.

- 2016 Top 100 Lawyers as listed by the American Society of Legal Advocates, member of nationwide organization of elite lawyers currently in practice.
- 2014 and 2015 Litigator Award: The nation's most coveted symbol of "litigation achievement."
- Lawyers.com 5 Star Award.
- Avvo Rating 9.6 Superb.
- Amazon.com Best Selling Author for: *Protect and Defend.*
- Amazon.com Best Selling Author for: *Dare to Succeed.*
- National Academy of Best-Selling Authors – recognizes individual authors who have achieved best seller author status after publishing a book.

Ken has been a guest lecturer at Indiana University, both to undergraduates as well as to students at the I.U. School of Law. Ken has also lectured at Indiana Trial Lawyers Association, and Ken really enjoys speaking to high school, middle school and grade school students.

Married for 53 years, Ken and his wife, Leah, have two children, Vicky and David, and two grandchildren. Vicky currently serves as a litigation attorney in the Ken Nunn Law Office.

CHAPTER 10

THE MESSAGE IN A SMILE: MAKING A DIFFERENCE ONE PATIENT AT A TIME

BY DR. JAYNE HOFFMAN

A smile is happiness you'll find right under your nose.
~ Tom Wilson

By all measures, my practice is a successful one, and for that, I am genuinely grateful. But numbers aside, it's what happens in my life each and every day when I enter my office that really lets me know that I've achieved success.

Imagine… you're face to face with someone who is so fearful of the dentist that they are shaking, almost crying. We're not talking a fragile-looking person, but a strong and burly man, who happened to have a horrific past experience that involved trauma to his mouth when he was a prisoner of war in Cambodia. You're talking with him and explaining what's about to happen, helping him to relax so the procedure that will make him healthier and happier, can begin. When that point arrives, he starts having flashbacks, consumed in terror and fearful of anyone even being near his mouth. You work with him, showing compassion and genuine caring for what is happening, and he understands this. And eventually, he relaxes. Together, dentist and patient get through the procedure and when it's done, he offers you a smile—a beautiful, heartfelt smile that's filled with gratitude for how you've helped him. *What you just "imagined" is what I experience frequently.* This is one of the most profound ways that my practice, Dr. Jayne Dentistry, delivers sedation dentistry (non-intravenous conscious sedation) to people in need with compassion and the type of expertise that comes from years of committed experience.

Finding a career that you love is golden, but finding one that is so impactful to others in a wonderful way is how you know you hit the jackpot.

The decision for me to become a dentist was easy. I'd been the only one in my family to have crooked teeth, and my father—a wise and respected physician—believed that my teeth would self-correct. So I waited, and waited. Finally, Dad admitted defeat and in my senior year of high school I got to get braces to fix the problem. Time passed by and then they were removed. I noticed something immediately wonderful, which started inside of me and worked its way out to my smile. I felt confident and healthy, more ready to take on the world—in an instant. You see, for many people, when we do not have teeth that are in good condition, we don't feel as good about ourselves. We hide our smiles and put our heads down if we begin to laugh. *No one should have to feel they need to do that.* Knowing this was profound for me, and I knew that I wanted to be a dentist that very day.

When I applied to dental school in the 80s, it was a mostly male-dominated field and although my grades and my motivations were excellent, the resistance was still there. It's hard to believe that was less than forty years ago! The Admissions Board at the university had said, "Why should we let you in when there are men who applied that will need to take care of a family some day?" *What a question, but I had an answer. It was simple: because I understood the value of dentistry in a way that many people did not from my personal experiences.* But furthermore, I had an amazing father who gave me wisdom that would carry me through my life. As a physician, he'd encountered many women who lived in tough situations, trapped by a lack of education and often not able to remove themselves from an abusive household. He always said, "I never want my daughters to be in that situation." And through encouragement and a focus on education and compassion, he made sure we set ourselves up so that would not happen to us.

Becoming a dentist was hard and joyful work.

I heard about a new approach to dentistry—sedation dentistry—and I was instantly interested in this. I understood people's struggles and concerns with the dentist, as they are as old as the field of dentistry itself (2600 BC, Hesy-Re, who is often called the first "dentist"). Anxiety is a part of what dentists deal with daily. *For me, I knew that if I was to be successful in helping these people move past those obstacles and onto better oral health, it made sense to find out how to make the experience as pleasant as possible for them.* So I went to work, being second in line at the dental practice that my husband and I took over from his father after he retired. Life was good and I felt myself getting into a groove. Then tragedy struck. My husband was killed in an airplane accident and there I was, left to not only offer dental services but run a business. It was not in my plan, ever. But I wasn't about to surrender and step aside, so I had to step up.

There were many learning curves, growing opportunities, and bumps along the way, but I knew that I had to dig deep and find a way to make it work. I had this passion for sedation dentistry and this tremendous capacity to be compassionate to those I met. Why not create a practice that aligned with those visions? *If I had to work it out, I knew that what I worked on would have to really align with the type of person I was and the type of professional I longed to be.*

Always loving education, I made sure that I went to get the training and services that would diversify my practice, making it so I didn't just offer sedation dentistry alone, but I would also offer other services that would help more people achieve their goals and personal satisfaction through a brighter smile and healthier oral hygiene. We all love seeing smiles, as they are contagious! Today, I help people with fluorides and sealants, bridges, crowns, root canals, tooth-colored fillings, Invisalign® braces, cosmetic bonding and porcelain veneers, digital x-rays, tooth whitening, dental implants, nitrous oxide sedation, and non-IV conscious sedation. Through these services, the people that I meet in the community I serve inspire me on a daily basis and their happiness becomes my happiness, too.

Out of all the skills that Dr. Jayne Dentistry offers, few are as impactful to someone's overall wellbeing as what sedation dentistry offers.

When you first get into dentistry you spend a lot of time learning the craft. You have to understand how to connect with patients, peers, and assess the proper actions with confidence. But I always sensed the need for more, and it was through the transformational changes that I played witness to in peoples' lives that it became really clear. What seemed like a mountain to someone could often be solved in a very unthreatening manner, and if it was more intensive, it was less frightening because we were a team that was going to get through it together. It's beliefs such as this that go a long way when you work in sedation dentistry. You can do so many thoughtful things without impacting business flow or quality of care, which is amazing. That's why we offer:

- Noise cancelling Bose headphones
- iPods with soothing music
- Chilled bottled water
- Coffee and tea
- Snacks
- Magazines
- Blankets
- Aromatherapy
- Neck pillows
- Hot/cold herbal wraps
- Wi-Fi
- Lip Butter
- Luxury lotions and hand scrubs
- BreathRX refreshing mouth rinse

Everything that is offered at Dr. Jayne Dentistry is meant to add to the experience and show patients that my staff and I are completely vested in their wellbeing. I cannot imagine having a practice run any other way. Teeth are so important—more than some people realize. When you have all your teeth you live an average of 5 – 7 years longer than someone who doesn't. Every day is such a gift and I want people to cherish as many days as they can.

Educating patients and the community in general about the importance of oral hygiene is also an important mission that is a part of the services I offer, and the volunteer work that I do in my Santa Clara community. Through dental exams you can actually screen for other medical conditions, such as diabetes, heart disease, oral cancer, etc. Many people do not realize this, but we can all agree that catching these types of susceptibilities and conditions early can make all the difference between prevention and proactive management. It's all too often that people only reach out to the dentist once something is wrong—they are already in pain.

Another milestone that would mark success for me is helping to teach prevention through regular check-ups. This is something I will always encourage, because everyone wins!

The area that I live in is very rich in diversity. It brought to light something that I had only seen through dentistry volunteer work in Mexico and Central America. You see, here in the US, we are extremely fortunate to have advancements in dentistry that make it a considerably more pleasant experience than it is in many other countries, to this day. Some people still have to get the type of dentistry that their government says they should receive and very seldom, if ever, does that mean even getting a shot of Novocain before a procedure. It's hard to imagine, isn't it! So through the rapport that my team and I build with our clients, we can help them have a better dental visit and quite often, we can also communicate with them in their native language. My staff is very diverse and they are a great asset to my practice. We've had times when there have been up to eight different foreign languages spoken fluidly in our office at one time. This is unique, and it has allowed us to have a stronger outreach to all communities within our larger Santa Clara community.

It's all these little details that don't take a lot of time or energy to initiate, but make a world of difference for people remembering what my practice has done for them. This is really significant because we are a small, private practice. *This says a lot and I know that the business practices that I've committed to are working, because we are consistently listed in the top 5% of private dental practices in the United States.* I'm so excited by this and it's actually spurred me on to my next step—growth and expansion.

When we help people we get to know them. Their fears are revealed. Their concerns are shared. To be a part of this is so rewarding to me; however, there are more people that need a dentist with my vision than who I have time to help. 24 hours a day is not enough! This is why an expansion of staff and like-minded dentists needs to take place. I've begun two initiatives to help people see the rewards that exist through practicing dentistry with the philosophy that I have proven can work.

1. **Teen mentor program**
   This program is going to be for teenagers who have an interest in dentistry as a possible career, showing them how an office works and giving them some insight into how powerful and personally motivating the world of sedation dentistry can be. We all want to make a difference and helping someone smile in appreciation and complete joy is a wonderful difference to make.

2. **Expanding the Dr. Jayne practice**
   I've never been clearer on the vision and outlook I have for the future of dentistry, in general, and my practice, in specific. Bringing on staff members who are aligned with the way I strive to make peoples' time in our office a positive experience will have a great impact, allowing me to not only serve my community better but to also expand the reach.

With one kind gesture you can change a life. One person at a time you can change the world. One day at a time we can change everything.
~ Dr. Steve Maraboli

I'd never say that I am the only person who has thought about dentistry in the way that I do, or even implemented it. However, I seldom come across anyone else who is as equally passionate and committed to the goal of wanting everyone to know and understand the importance of dentistry to the psyche and to physical health. Every smile has a message and a joyful smile is one that we always remember. This is the part of success that motivates me to give my best, day in and day out.

About Dr. Jayne

With over twenty years of service to the Santa Clara community, Dr. Jayne Hoffman has an amazing rapport with her patients and offers state-of-the-art dental services. Through her experience and heartfelt compassion, she strives to have every patient she helps recognize that their needs as a person and a patient are being met.

Since the day she had her braces removed as a teenager, Dr. Jayne knew she wanted to be a dentist. She noticed an instant shift in her confidence and felt healthier, loving how it felt to laugh and smile without embarrassment. This newfound awareness, combined with being raised in a compassionate, caring household let her know that the world of dentistry was just where she belonged.

Dr. Jayne received her education from the University of San Diego, graduating *magna cum laude*, and then attended the Arthur A. Dugoni School of Dentistry in San Francisco, California, where she received her Doctorate of Dental Surgery. She completed her residency at UCLA, focusing on the specialty of Intravenous Sedation. In addition, she received advanced training through the Dental Organization of Conscious Sedation.

Today, Dr. Jayne is a certified Preferred Provider of Invisalign® clear orthodontics and Lumineers® custom-made veneers. She continues to exceed the requirements for dental continuing education each year, wanting to serve her community better through intensive knowledge on how she can best help those who need dental services. Her professional affiliations include:

- Santa Clara Dental Society
- Santa Clara Chamber of Commerce
- California Dental Association
- American Academy of Cosmetic Dentistry
- American Dental Association
- National Organization of Women Business Owners
- Crown Council

It's in the spirit of service that Dr. Jayne operates each and every day. This gives her the greatest pleasure and she says, "The look of gratitude in a person's eyes, followed by that genuinely happy smile, gives me a feeling that I'll never tire of seeing. It's amazing."

Dr. Jayne's has a strong focus on how she can contribute to society and help others.

She freely offers assistance to many charitable organizations in her community and has spearheaded several programs, including *Dr. Jayne Treats for the Troops,* which is an alliance with three local Catholic schools where they work together to collect dental supplies, notes of appreciation, and lots of donated Halloween candy to send to Operation Gratitude, an organization that distributes contributions to U.S. troops abroad. She has also volunteered dental services in Mexico and Central America, as well as Polio vaccine services in Ghana. She also works closely with teens and displaced teens, helping them to learn proper dental care and works closely with dental education programs offered in schools.

In her free time, Dr. Jayne enjoys spending time with her daughter, Alexandra, and with her family and friends. She immensely enjoys attending concerts, traveling, wine tastings, and watching movies; especially with her dog Spice and her cat Chip snuggled up next to her.

CHAPTER 11

MENTAL FITNESS: DEVELOPING THE LEADER WITHIN

BY JANETTE MORÉ

Have you ever Googled for information about becoming a stronger leader? I just did—and came back with over 43 million results in under one second! Out in the real world, becoming and staying strong isn't so quick and easy. There are a lot of leadership programs out there, but few of them come to grips with our real lives, filled as they are with opportunities that don't materialize, relationships that don't work out, and good intentions that get sabotaged by our own foibles. How can we perform as strong leaders when our lives get messy—or even appear to be crumbling around us?

The good news is that emotional resiliency isn't magic. It's a quality you can develop in yourself, training for mental fitness the way you would train to strengthen your body physically. How do I know? I learned it the hard way, not from "Dr. Google," but from that greatest of all leadership programs—life.

Do you remember that kid who had no qualms about telling adults what you needed? That kid brave enough to walk up to the new girl and invite her to play? The one whom the teachers always seemed to pluck out of the crowd to lead the class project?

I was that kid. From day one, I was a cool, calm, confident child—the kind adults call a "born leader." As I moved through the high school and college years, I found that my peers would often turn to me for guidance and support. This was something I truly enjoyed—helping others do their best and achieve their goals.

My friends thought I was a leader, not because I bossed them around, but because I believed in them. They knew I could be trusted to keep my composure and a positive outlook no matter what the difficulties. For my part, I internalized the powerful sense of acceptance and significance this brought to my life. I assumed this was what leadership was all about! By the time I started my professional career, I was sure management was the natural place for me.

You guessed it—like many young professionals, I was soon frustrated with the leadership skills of many of my supervisors. Not only did they fail to motivate their direct reports, they actually went out of their way to create a wedge between the workers and management. More than ever, I wanted to become a supervisor. I was sure I had the leadership skills that would build a great team, with everyone working together towards a common purpose—no butting heads or mutual suspicion. One day, I vowed, “I’ll show ‘em how it’s done!”

Eventually, my dream was realized, and I entered the ranks of management. I was offered my choice of leading one of three product groups. I was so confident in my abilities, I chose the one area in which I had no experience. I had always enjoyed a challenge and thought of this as a fabulous opportunity. I also felt that this business unit had the greatest potential for growth, and therefore, my leadership skills and management style would have the chance to shine.

What I didn’t foresee was that there were other people in the group who already had their eye on my new plum position. When it was announced that I would be the supervisor of the group, it came as a total surprise to them. I wasn't prepared for dealing with the adversity that ensued. Mastering a new technology was enough of a challenge, but now I had to prove my competence while knowing at least a few of my new reports were rooting for my failure.

While this situation at work was unfolding, my personal relationships were also going off the tracks. I was a part-time single mother of two teenagers. I shared joint residential custody of them with their father, whose parenting style was much different from mine. I was also entering into a new relationship. None of my personal relationships was going particularly well, and therefore, there was no relief for me when I left the office. I found myself breaking down in frequent crying spells. This had never happened to me before! When, I sought help, I was told I was depressed and given a sample pack of antidepressants.

I'm sure many of the people in my life thought medication was a good idea. They were uncomfortable with my fragile emotions. I was too. Clearly, what I was doing wasn't working. I knew I could get through this rough period, and I still believed in my own skills and intelligence as a leader. The missing component? I was not what I now call "mentally fit."

As fate would have it, at about this time, I had begun attending the university to obtain a graduate degree in professional counseling. My loved ones couldn't believe I'd just added more stress to my life. But when I look back on it, I realize that my brain knew what I needed. I had always excelled in school and my new career direction gave me a much-needed sense of control.

Instead of antidepressants, I took a crazy leap of faith. I decided to implement the concepts I learned in my classes in order to improve my out-of-control relationships. This was the turning point, for it literally changed my life. Though I continued to struggle, I held fast to the belief that I did not have a mental illness. I developed a sense of hope that there were things I could do to improve my life. In spite of the unsolved stress in my life, I remained the architect of my destiny. It was in my power to create a happier future.

That was twelve years ago.

As I look back at how I persevered through this time, my success was due to the following six critical steps. I will now share my "secret formula" for mental fitness with you.

1. **Take Responsibility for Your Life**
   I had to take responsibility for my life. Certainly, I could blame my co-workers for making my life difficult. But when I was able to think rationally about my situation, I accepted that I had a choice in

how I responded to them. Because of my own limiting beliefs, I'd created the vision in my mind that others didn't respect me. And, as much as I didn't want to admit it, it had been my choice to be depressed. My depression was a coping mechanism that I hoped would cause the people in my life to change.

When I took responsibility for my life, I quit blaming others for my troubles and quit using my depression to get them to change. I was in charge of making my life better. This was very tough medicine for me to take, but necessary to begin my journey towards mental fitness.

2. Develop a Vision for Your Future

To muster the courage to make the necessary changes, I had to focus on what I wanted. I wanted to prove to everyone and to myself that I was a competent manager and that my leadership skills were effective. I wanted to regain confidence. I developed the vision of myself as a strong, confident, and well-respected leader.

3. Create the Placebo Inside Yourself

The placebo effect is a positive result that is attributed to a person's belief that a treatment will work. Our brains are phenomenal organs and can make incredible things happen when we believe in our own power to realize what we want.

I knew there was nothing actually wrong with my brain to cause my depressive episodes. I knew I was a good leader and that my management style was effective for building strong teams. Therefore, I would get through this difficult time. I could harness the power of my brain by believing in myself and releasing the limiting beliefs that sabotaged my success. I refused to accept failure as an option. These new beliefs created the placebo inside of me.

4. Build Emotional Resiliency

My situation at work had become overwhelming. When my boss suggested that I step down from my position, I agreed—willingly. That is not to say it was not difficult or painful. I had spent a tremendous amount of energy trying to fix my relationships with the team, and it is only natural to worry "What will people think of me?" Yet I knew this step was necessary to achieve my vision for myself.

Though I was still with the company, I like to refer to this time period as my "sabbatical." During this time, I prioritized my own basic needs. This involved taking care of my health and doing a lot of self-care, but also developing a sense of achievement and creating a support network. Understanding our own basic needs and getting them met is crucial to building emotional resiliency. It ensures that we have enough going “right” around us to create a type of safety net that is there for us during the inevitable, unplanned events.

I will be forever grateful to my supervisor for believing in me and allowing me to design my own job during this period. My assignments were activities in which I excelled. As a result, I received positive reviews and felt a sense of significance. I reinstituted a regular exercise routine. Taking regular walks was a great stress release for me, so I made them a priority. I also stayed in graduate school. I found the material very interesting and doing well in my classes helped me to feel a sense of accomplishment. Each of these activities was a positive experience and helped me to feel stronger emotionally.

5. Pay Attention to Your Feelings

Many of us are uncomfortable with our feelings, so we engage in activities that numb us to them. When we are mentally fit, we take notice of our feelings and physiology. They are our feedback as to whether the changes we’ve made are working. When our feelings are positive, that means we’re on the right track. When something doesn’t feel right, we can address the problem and make a deliberate decision about how to handle it.

When I started to believe that I was not qualified for my management job, my actions reinforced that belief. I was filled with self-doubt, I began feeling depressed, and I withdrew from my co-workers. The fact that I continued to feel worse, not better, was a signal from my brain that this coping mechanism was not working! Once I removed myself from the unpleasant situation and redefined my work, things began to change. I began to feel happier, which was my brain telling me that these changes were good for me.

6. Evaluate Your Progress

As we move towards our goals, we have to pause periodically and evaluate whether the changes we've made are working. If we find that we haven't progressed, it's time to regroup and try something else. I was absolutely amazed at how much happier I felt as I took charge of my life. If we believe it can happen, then it will!

As much as I wanted to change the culture of the business unit, I had to accept that it was beyond my capabilities. The simple changes I made during my sabbatical reaped huge benefits for me. I began feeling happier and more confident in myself. After a few years, I reassumed my management position and proved I was a resilient leader!

When I thought about what my next step would be, I decided to move on from the corporate world altogether. The next vision for myself was to tell the world about the importance of mental fitness; hence the name of my company, Mental Fitness Now. Today, my mission is to empower others by showing how they, too, can take charge of their success. Now you know my secret—so let's make it happen!

About Janette

Janette Moré is the founder of Mental Fitness Now and refers to herself as a Mental Fitness Trainer. She helps clients to believe in themselves and to navigate through the difficulties that are prohibiting them from becoming successful. Janette works with clients to move from feelings of helplessness and frustration to those of confidence and fulfillment. She facilitates this transformation by teaching clients a few basic principles that will equip them to better handle existing challenges and to seize new opportunities.

Janette's undergraduate degree was in chemical engineering and she spent over thirty years working in a technical capacity at two Fortune 500 companies. Before formally receiving a supervisory title, she naturally assumed leadership positions and was well regarded by her peers. Janette led numerous project teams and was often credited for transforming dysfunctional groups into higher performing ones. In her corporate career, Janette advanced to a position on a division operating board for the company.

The part of her career that Janette enjoyed most was providing support and encouragement to her peers and direct reports so they could identify and develop their potential. She found it rewarding to help others and applied to graduate school on a whim. She thoroughly enjoyed the material and completed the long journey to become a Licensed Professional Counselor (LPC). When the day arrived that she was eligible to take early retirement, Janette decided there was nothing more she wanted from her corporate life and jumped at the opportunity to begin a second career.

During her graduate program, Janette was attracted to the teachings of Dr. William Glasser and adopted Reality Therapy/Choice Theory as the basis for her counseling and coaching practice. Janette put this knowledge to the test in her personal life, which helped her to obtain a better understanding of the obstacles confronting her. As you read in her story, Janette successfully incorporated new behaviors that resulted in feelings of increased happiness and fulfillment, which transformed her life.

Janette prevailed in a male-dominated field and brings a wealth of knowledge and experience in helping her clients. From her own personal journey, she has gained a better understanding of human behavior, which has created a passion within her to help others. From this knowledge, Janette has developed a method for overcoming the inevitable distractions that occur. This method has worked for her and many of her clients, and it can work for you!

Janette offers a free 30-minute consultation for all new clients. This will give you an understanding of the benefits of obtaining mental fitness and how that often neglected secret can boost your career. She may be reached at: Jan@MentalFitnessNow.com or by calling 512-575-3579. Consult her website at: www.MentalFitnessNow.com for more information and insight into her beliefs and coaching style. Janette has succeeded in overcoming the obstacles in her life by becoming mentally fit and now she can help you to do the same.

CHAPTER 12

GET THE BEST VALUE AND EXPERIENCE FOR YOUR VACATION

– 10 TIPS ON HOW TO WORK WITH A TRAVEL AGENT

BY MARGIE LENAU

The family in the television commercial is having a great time laughing in the sunshine! *But that's not how your last vacation was. . .*

After carefully planning your vacation, the hotel wasn't what you expected, and you had to leave early because someone got sick. You thought you had the budget under control, but your credit card balance was much higher than you expected. After you came home, you decided that you didn't need any more stressful family vacations like that!

In addition to that, statics reveal one of our biggest regrets is not traveling enough.

Sharing time with friends and family and keeping in touch makes for a fuller life. My passion for travel led me to help others have unforgettable experiences together so they have no regrets.

I live in Michigan and we enjoy four seasons along the beautiful beaches of the Great Lakes. But the winters here can be brutal. When my children were growing up, we traveled to a warm place every year to take a break from the snow. We spent time together making unforgettable memories.

One of our favorite activities was a fishing excursion, where we caught a puffer fish, gar, small shark, and sea bass, and then came upon a Right Whale and her baby that were a little off course! Feeding the seagulls one day, my daughter ran from them with bread in her hands while masses of seagulls almost knocked her over. My son used the video camera to record sea life in a tide pool. We went horseback riding, visited historic sites, and heard ghost stories about homes we toured in Charleston. Some of our greatest vacations were spent at Theme Parks just having fun! Everyday life problems were left behind.

When it became easy to find vacation deals advertised online, many people began to DIY their vacations. I was one of those people! I was very careful to painstakingly look into every detail. I compared prices, flight schedules, tours, and searched for interesting places to visit. Friends would talk about their fantastic vacation deals and experiences.

I would ask myself, "What were they comparing their information to?" *People assumed the ads on the Internet were perfectly truthful.* The destination may look wonderful, but was it really like the pictures? This research took a lot of time and I was never sure if I was getting the best value. When the Internet became loaded with travel information in the 1990's, there were so many choices! Soon, friends and family asked me to help them plan their vacations. The more I searched, the more positive I was that there must be a better way.

How I got into this business

My dad used to have his own printing business and I grew up helping him in his shop. The idea that you could have your own business was familiar to me. I went to a local business college for Computer Science, but left to get married. After I had children, I was always trying new ideas to make money and help others make money.

We had used a Travel Agent to book my daughter's honeymoon, so I began to research how they worked. My brother-in-law introduced me to a man that was working on a large group traveling internationally. A local travel agency had software that would make the logistics of this large group more manageable. I knew this man made the wrong decision when he rejected their proposal, but I made valuable connections with the women there. I called the day after our final meeting, and asked to come in to discuss working with them. We talked a bit, then they handed me the information I needed to begin booking vacations. It became obvious very quickly that this was what I had been looking for!

I have to note that the face of a Travel Agent has evolved from what it was then to what it is today. More specialized and home-based agents are a common business practice. Travel Agents are now *Travel Consultants* and even more valuable to the booking process.

I knew this was how I wanted to help people, so I signed up with a few suppliers and began training and educating myself about their products. I started out slowly, but when my 30-year marriage ended, I was able to make Travel a full-time career.

TEN REASONS WHY YOU SHOULD WORK WITH A TRAVEL AGENT

1. **Travel Agents are trained and educated**
   Travel Agents know more about travel because they work with it every day, educating themselves with online certifications and in-person training. We are invited to see different resorts and destinations, not only by the Resorts themselves, but also by the Department of Tourism in other countries. For example, Sandals Resorts arranged a Caribbean Mega FAM (Familiarization trip) for Certified Sandals Specialists. We flew on their private plane to Exuma in the Bahamas, then to Beaches Resort in Turks & Caicos where I stayed in a 3 - Bedroom Villa. The next day, we toured the resort. That night there was a Chocolate party and entertainment, with a singer from the show, The Voice. On our last day, we traveled to Grenada to experience the new Sandals LaSource Grenada Resort. An Immigration Officer from the country we were traveling to was on the plane with us so he could process our papers quickly before we landed. In Grenada, they even had a parade to greet us as we entered their country! On another FAM trip, I toured every Sandals and Beaches Resort in Jamaica! This is just one example

of how Travel Agents educate themselves so they can make your dreams come true.

2. Travel Agents know what's new

Whether it is Theme Parks, Cruise Lines, or Tour packages, Travel Agents are trained online and in person to better help families. Most Theme Park vacations have many options and can be very confusing to plan. The help of a Travel Agent will give you more value and time to spend with your family. There are many experiences you may never know about without the help of an Expert. Options are constantly changing, from attractions, ticket options, dining, and Special Offers. *Travel Agents will help you choose what is best for your family because we know what is currently available.*

3. If you Dream it, you may be able to do it

The first question I frequently ask my client is, "What are your travel dreams?" Then we begin to make that fit their budget and time. A Honeymoon couple called to arrange their upcoming honeymoon. They said their dream was to go to Hawaii, but that would never fit their budget. They wanted me to quote Florida Resorts for them. I did discuss some great options in Florida, but I started looking at their dreams first. *They assumed* that Hawaii would be out of their budget. I sent them some ideas and they were shocked that they could afford to Honeymoon in Oahu! They received a travel gift and I made sure they were greeted with a traditional Hawaiian fresh flower lei when they arrived at the airport. So romantic! It was the Honeymoon of their dreams!

4. The DIY planner can work well with a Travel Agent

This is the person who thinks that no one else can plan a better vacation for their family. One client said I quoted a price for flights that was much too high. He booked his flight and then sent me his flight schedule. He had booked the wrong city in the wrong state! This person would work well with a Travel Agent because he would be able to make informed choices when presented with options he may not know about. *While looking for the least expensive room, you may over look an upgraded room that is just a few dollars more.* A Travel Agent may get you added value options like free parking, early check in, or late check out. *Many suppliers work only with Travel Agents, with options that do not appear online.* The DIY planner can have control over what is best for their vacation after looking over options that are presented to them. A Travel Agent may remind them that they need a transfer to the hotel or cruise port, and help them with a pre-night hotel so they can arrive in time for their cruise, avoiding problems like delayed flights. *There are benefits of working with a Travel Agent no matter the type of traveler you may be.* We are the Internet Interpreters and give unbiased recommendations.

5. **Advice for booking flights**
   The question I am asked most often is, "When is the best time to purchase a flight?" In reality, the best time to book is when you see a flight and schedule that you like at a price you like. And book directly with the airline. It's fine to look on the Internet to see what is available, but did you know not every flight and not every airline is on that search engine? Airlines sell the best value seats to first in line. The more seats sold, the higher the cost goes. In general, if you book close to your travel date, you will pay more than if you book early. But never book until you are sure when you will travel. Cancellation and change fees can amount to more than the cost of a new ticket. Global air passenger traffic increased by 6.5% in 2015, and the market will at least double within 20 years. Travel Agents understand the airlines better than the average consumer.

6. **Last minute deals may not be the value you think they are**
   Some of my wisest clients will book their vacation as soon as they confirm their travel dates, usually booking at least 6-9 months ahead. Compare that same vacation with a last minute booking for the same options and it will almost always be higher. I was talking with a hotel manager that was going on her honeymoon. She said they were going to wait for a last minute deal. I asked her, "If I came to you at the last minute and wanted a room at your hotel, what room would you offer me?" She explained how all of the best rooms would be gone and then stopped in mid sentence. "Oh! I see." She realized that a last minute deal is not always a good value. It's never too late to book a vacation, but your selection of flight and resort will be limited to what is leftover.

7. **The difference between a "Deal" and a good value**
   Travel Agents can save you money. A deal is what you perceive as

a good value. Whether it is a good value for your family or not is up for discussion. It may be worth spending a little more to include a dining plan, saving money while getting a better experience. A Travel Agent is a good judge of what else you can include to raise the value of your vacation dollars. A room upgrade may cost very little more for the amenities you receive. Do you need a kitchenette? Will you actually cook while you are on vacation? The room may sleep 5 people, but will you be on top of each other? Is free, in-room Wi-Fi important to you? Did you assume the hotel offered free breakfast and free parking? Is there a Resort Fee? A Travel Agent will help you figure out your total budget to get the best value. Sometimes, it's all about the marketing and may not be the best value!

8. Celebration Travel

We love a good Celebration! If it is your Anniversary, Honeymoon, Birthday, or Personal Triumph we want you to have the best! Have you seen Resort rooms with banners and decorations for an Anniversary or Birthday, sometimes with champagne and strawberries covered in chocolate? Travel Agents know how to arrange that! *I recommend trying a Suite with Butler service, especially for your Honeymoon.* Your Butler will take care of all the details, arranging special surprises! A Butler will unpack your clothes and take care of your room daily. Rose petals in your bath, setting your daily schedule, and making a personal phone to call your Butler with requests or questions is a great luxury!

9. International Travel and Passports

Always travel with a Passport. Travel Agents will tell you to renew early. Your passport should have at least 6 months beyond the dates of travel before it will expire to travel internationally. Don't forget that you need enough pages so that your passport can be stamped by immigration.

I recommend taking your passport while you are on a cruise that may not require one, called a “closed loop” cruise, in case of emergency. If you leave the ship while it is in a foreign port, and get back to your ship after it has sailed, you are stranded in a foreign country with no Passport. How will you get home?

10. We want you to be safe.

The first thing I think about when I get a request is that travelers stay safe so they can enjoy their vacation. With all of the arrangements made and documents in order, there is always a chance that something will go wrong. What if your flight is canceled or your luggage is lost with your medication or passport? What if you have an accident? Did you get a great rate because it was hurricane season? Travel insurance, gives you peace of mind. If you get a simple infection that sends you to a care center to be examined and get medication, many times this is all it takes to cover the cost of your travel insurance. If you travel without travel insurance, a Travel Agent can help you, but you will shoulder the cost. *We are your advocate and will give you personalized service.*

BONUS ADVICE:

Make your final payment early! Your reservation really will be canceled, even if you are almost paid in full! A Travel Agent will send you reminders, but it is ultimately your responsibility. Making your final payment a week early puts your mind to rest. Despite trying many times to reach a client for final payment, his stateroom reservation was automatically canceled. The only thing that I could do was put him with his other 2 friends that were traveling because the ship was sold out. Luckily, they had room for a third person. I worked with the Cruise Line to use some of his money to help secure the other room, but he did lose money. No one likes to see that happen.

Are you waiting for the perfect time, the perfect trip, or more money to make unforgettable memories?

To avoid regrets, travel often and travel now!

About Margie

Margie Lenau has a passion for helping families make unforgettable memories and strengthening relationships. She realized people were not traveling as much as they would like to. She saw that they needed encouragement and help planning their vacations so that they could spend time together. One of the big problems was the stress of planning, and not knowing if their plans would work well for their family. She saw how she could help with this.

Her story is that of a true Entrepreneur. Growing up in her father's printing business, she learned about owning a small business. She went to college for Computer Science, before getting married. As her family grew, she made money to help contribute to the family budget. She had a cleaning business to help support her children's school tuition, and developed a sales contact program that was used in car dealerships.

When it became easy to find vacation deals online, she quickly saw that there had to be a better way to book travel. After researching the complicated ins-and-outs of the travel industry, in 2008, she became an Independent Contractor for a local agency. These colleagues were very helpful in establishing her knowledge base. Soon, she formed her own agency, Wonderland Family Vacations. Starting out building her client list, her business quickly grew. When her marriage of thirty years ended, she became focused full-time on the development of her agency.

Margie has four children and four grandchildren. She has worked with Non-Profit organizations, and was a founding member of the West Michigan Turner Syndrome Society support group. She earned the Heart Beat Award from Families At Heart, a support group helping families with children with Congenital Heart Disease. Her second daughter has had two life-saving heart surgeries, and her son was born prematurely, so she knows the value of spending time together with family.

Margie has many certifications for travel products and destinations, and keeps current by traveling to familiarize herself with these products. She is a proud member of of the GIFTED Travel Network, a tribe of like-minded Travel Professionals, as well as CLIA, and IATAN. She has been interviewed on her local NBC affiliate about travel planning.

Margie is available to partner with other professionals who share her interest in travel. She holds Events to answer questions in person for their invited guests, as well as arranging specialty group travel.

You can connect with Margie at:

- www.WonderlandFamilyVacations.com
- www.twitter.com/MargieLenau
- www.facebook.com/WonderlandFamilyVacations
- MargieLenau@gmail.com

CHAPTER 13

PARENTING IS AN INSIDE JOB

– HOW LOOKING WITHIN CAN HELP PARENTS FIND THE KEY TO SUCCESS

BY SHA-EN YEO

"Are you happy, Mama?" 20-month old Hannah Tan asked her mother, Ling.

Truth be told, Ling was not. She couldn't understand how other parents showered unconditional love on their children, while she felt miserable about all the sacrifices she had to make. Parenting to her was not a nurturing journey, but a job filled with tasks and routines.

Mealtimes at home, in particular, were difficult. From a plump baby, Hannah had gradually grown thin. Her weight was something Ling took very personally: it became a direct reflection of her abilities as a parent. In a bid to make her eat and drink more, mealtime became emotional and mental tussles. The result? Ling screaming and Hannah numbly sitting at the table.

Things reached a peak when Hannah turned three and entered day care. Unable to supervise her diet and seeing Hannah get thinner each day, Ling grew increasingly antsy. After school one day, noticing that Hannah had barely drunk her water, Ling flared. She started throwing things around the room. Taking out the cane, she threatened to beat Hannah. Unlike her usual calm (and numb) response, Hannah started wailing loudly, fighting off the cane.

Feeling overwhelmed by guilt and thoughts of being a failure, Ling threw down the cane, ran to her room and sobbed desperately. Ling had reached her wits end. Then, like a light in the darkness, she felt Hannah embrace her and whisper, "It's okay Mama, I don't mind."

Hannah's stroke of kindness and compassion was a profound wake-up call. Instead of experiencing joy and fulfillment, Ling had been feeling ashamed and angry. She knew it was time for her to stop blaming her circumstances. It was time to do something about *herself.*

I met Ling when she was a student in my positive psychology class. We discovered that Hannah and my daughter, Sherrie, were the same age. I felt sad when she shared her story: her challenges are not uncommon. Over the last five years, I have spoken to many parents who struggle with managing their children. As a result, they are unable to find joy in parenting, and experience significant stress. As a mother, I know that parenting is a journey like no other. There is no manual and so much learning is on-the-job. It is a role that engenders great humility; like in Ling's story, the challenges can often result in exhaustion and helplessness.

What ultimately ends up being the solution is what Ling had to discover the painful way: parenting is an inside job! Looking within yourself is the first step to making the difference between success and failure. It starts by knowing yourself better, mastering yourself well, and finally, nourishing yourself wholly.

KNOWING YOURSELF BETTER

Knowing yourself better means focusing attention on parts of yourself you tend to gloss over: your thoughts, emotions, motivations, etc. Putting yourself in the spotlight may feel uncomfortable as you are probably used to focusing all your attention on your children (or everywhere else). The irony is that you may have lost sight of yourself while trying to figure out what makes them tick.

Three (3) Key questions to begin with:

- **What kind of parent do you want to be?** Articulating a vision of how you'd like to think, feel and act as a parent can help you be clear on how to interact with your children. For example, one day, my 7-year-old Sherrie returned from school crying, "Everyone says I am boasting about being school monitor!" She was crestfallen that her friends had misunderstood her excitement in sharing her accomplishment. Going back to my parenting vision: "Loving, calm and firm; guiding with wisdom" – I started off by acknowledging her disappointment, then asking her to relate the incident in detail. We talked about how many friends had actually made the comment, what her friends might be feeling and whether she felt she had actually been boastful. Through that process, she realized that not everyone thought poorly of her and that she couldn't control others' reactions. She felt extremely relieved. I told her I was proud of her and encouraged her to share her excitement with me.

- **What are your strengths and weaknesses as a parent?** When you know your strengths, you can leverage on them to feel more competent and experience more joy. When you know your weaknesses, you can begin learning how to manage them better. Empathy is one of my top strengths. I leverage this by trying to be aware of what Sherrie is experiencing, listening to her story and giving her a hug. That way, she knows I am not judging, or giving her a solution, and that her world is important to me. I get to understand her more deeply too. On the flip side, my weakness is forgetfulness – I often fail to remember what I say to Sherrie. This annoys her as she has to repeat herself. She gets most upset when I forget a promise I've made. To manage this, I key in reminders on my phone, and task her as the leader to remind me! She is a willing taskmaster and I am a happy follower.

- **What are your non-negotiable parenting values?** Values reflect your sense of right and wrong. Non-negotiable parenting values are ones you are not willing to compromise. Having these values can help you prioritize what is important to you, so you can make decisions more easily. One of my non-negotiable values is love: spending quality time being present with my children. This helps me maintain work-life harmony and sanity! No matter how much work I have left at the end of the day, I will not bring it home. Having it at home is a distraction and I could become resentful thinking about work left undone. Either way, I would not be focused on my children. How could I miss the satisfaction of seeing my 20-month old Zoey giggling with glee when her toy dinosaur (manipulated by my husband) creeps up on her from behind and gives her a surprise? Work can wait.

MASTERING YOURSELF WELL

Self-knowledge alone is insufficient to bring about considerable shifts in behavior and thinking; however, it is a great start. Knowledge gives you the option of being able to tweak how you think, feel and act. Mastering yourself means feeling in control of your thoughts, emotions and actions. It is the difference between staying calm in the storm versus becoming the storm itself!

Three (3) main areas to master:

- **Your thoughts.** You process more than 50,000 thoughts a day. Mastering your thoughts means being able to control the flow of your thoughts, what you pay attention to, and assessing whether they are reasonable before you act. Mastering your thoughts will prevent them from taking control of you! Just recently, Sherrie accidentally ran over Zoey's foot with her toy car. Zoey wailed because of the pain; Sherrie cried because she believed it was her fault. Having seen many near misses prior to this, my first thought was, "Why didn't Sherrie pay more attention to Zoey?" I could have easily accused her of being careless. However, I paused, and thought about Sherrie's intent: she didn't mean to do it. While Zoey recovered almost instantly, Sherrie was still sniffling. I reassured her it was an accident and that Zoey was fine. Being able to pause, pay attention to my thoughts, before moving into feeling or action, is a skill I have been practicing for the past two years. It has helped me notice a wider range of thoughts and be more intentional in selecting which thought to pay attention to.

- **Your emotions.** As a parent, you likely experience intense and varied emotions. Negative emotions can consume you if you let them. Mastering your emotions means acknowledging they exist, working through them by processing them, then realizing that you have a choice about how you want to feel. One day, when I returned home from work, Sherrie ran to hug me, and then promptly remarked, "You are so smelly!" Her candor would typically induce a laugh in me but that day, it was a trigger. I snapped at her, and she ran away pouting. I knew I had over-reacted but wasn't quite sure why. When I sat down to dig underneath the emotion, I recalled that earlier in the day, I had spent almost an hour searching for a cash machine to pay for my parking fee. As I walked round and round, I felt incredibly dumb for not having enough money on me. Sherrie's remarks had made me feel stupid all over again. Recognizing my folly, I apologized to Sherrie and we made up.

- **Your actions.** Your emotions and thoughts are less visible to your children. It is your actions that they ultimately observe, and respond to. Mastering your actions will make the difference between a positive or negative interaction with your child. Aristotle refers to this mastery as practical wisdom: *figuring out the right way to do the right thing in a particular circumstance, with a particular person, at a particular time.* My husband does this very well. Zoey is particularly fussy about eating her dinner. While I would be focused on feeding her quickly so she can go to bed, he would add in sound effects to liven up the process. Eating broccoli results in a 'Plop', cleaning her mouth is 'Zing zing' accompanied by swift wiping actions. What could have been a long draggy affair turns into a symphony and her dinner is finished with ease. The trick to mastering your actions is to be sensitive to the context and the preferences of your children.

NOURISHING YOURSELF WHOLLY

To love and support your children well, you need to keep your own pitchers full, so you can keep pouring as needed. Otherwise, you may be doing everything to make your child happy and well, but inside, you feel drained. It is incredibly difficult to draw fuel from an empty tank. Nourishing yourself wholly means putting self-care high up on your priority list, not just tending to yourself after everyone else's needs are met.

Three (3) focus areas for nourishment:

- **Be kind to yourself.** Treat yourself with self-compassion when you feel low or have made mistakes. This means comforting yourself with the care and concern you'd offer to your best friend. You won't trample on your friend when they are down, so don't do this to yourself. When Sherrie was 3-years old, my husband was posted overseas for three months. It was the first time I was alone without him, and I missed him terribly. On top of that, I was self-employed, just starting my business and clueless about almost everything! Sherrie kept asking for him, and I felt a guilty pressure for not being able to replace him. Many of those nights, I would cry myself to sleep, thinking about how weak and lousy I was. Upon hindsight, I could have treated myself more kindly and focused on all that I was doing to keep her happy. Now, when I notice that I'm overly critical of myself, I look in the mirror and say: "You are only human and you're trying your best." Then I give myself a hug!

- **Take good physical care.** Being physically well is not just about being healthy for the sake of it. It is about keeping yourself in tip-top condition, so you can play, support and enjoy being with your children. I learnt this the hard way three years ago. I had gone to Philippines to present at a conference and ended up returning home with a dreadful cough that lasted a month. Upon reflection, I noted that I had eaten lots of fried food, not gotten enough rest and hardly exercised. Coughing incessantly was not only painful; I was also irritable and tired. This meant that I had to limit playtime with Sherrie and was less tolerant of her little idiosyncrasies. Now, I am more sensitive to my physical wellness and make active choices to keep myself healthy. When I eat fish and chips, I eat fewer fries. I chase after Zoey at the park, instead of sitting down on the bench. Even though watching a movie at 11 p.m. sounds tempting, I choose sleep.

- **Do more of what you love.** If you have stopped doing the things you love to do since becoming a parent, you are not alone. You have likely turned your attention to what your children love to do instead. Doing what you love invigorates you, makes you come alive and reminds you of whom you used to be! Begin by listing down all the things you love to do. Next, schedule in your favorite activities in your calendar, just as you would your children's enrichment classes. For instance, I love talking with friends, playing badminton, savoring my food and being in nature. Every week, I make sure to have lunch with a friend and allow my taste buds to be tickled! Make no excuses for these pitcher-filling activities by planning ahead and ensuring child-care arrangements are settled. A win-win is to infuse these activities as a part of family life. Over the weekend, I suggest an outing to the beach or park. That way, I get to nourish myself while spending time with my children!

Going back to Ling - once she realized that everything originated from herself, she felt empowered to self-manage and not let external circumstances run her daily life. She began taking active steps to understand herself: reading self-help books, attending personal development courses, committing to regular yoga and meditation sessions. With heightened awareness, Ling began to see her thoughts, emotions and behaviours more clearly. Instead of obsessing and trying to reason everything out, she was able to pause and observe, before responding to a given situation.

She changed the way she talked to Hannah, encouraging her to try new things and not be afraid to make mistakes. Even when Ling had her own fears, she held back, allowing Hannah to explore on her own. What happened solidified that she was on the right track: Hannah started to resume her child's role, becoming more active and outgoing, just like any other child would be. Mealtimes turned to peacetime and Hannah, now 7-years old, is eating almost as much as an adult!

Lao Tzu's famous quote: *"The journey of a thousand miles begins with a single step"* is one I hold dear. Ling's parenting journey, like yours and mine, is an ongoing one. There will be situations you can prepare for and unexpected obstacles that come your way. What makes the difference between the success and failure of this journey is your humility to notice what's not working, your willingness to keep trying and your conviction to be better than before.

About Sha-En

Positive Psychology entrepreneur Sha-En Yeo is the first Singaporean graduate of the Master of Applied Positive Psychology (MAPP) program at the University of Pennsylvania. Sha-En has been featured on the national TV documentary *'Chasing Happiness'*, she appeared in *MyPaper*, Singapore's top executive newspaper, and shared her wisdom on national radio FM 938LIVE. Sha-En is the go-to authority for positive psychology in Singapore.

A Singapore Government Education scholar, Sha-En has more than 10 years' experience in the education sector. As founder of Positive Education, she has championed the need for well-being as a priority in schools, helped teachers reignite their purpose for teaching and empowered parents to reconnect deeply with their children. In her most recent role as the inaugural Wellness Director of Yale-NUS College, she established the foundation for de-stigmatizing mental health issues, increasing accessibility and lowering barriers for mental health support on campus.

Sha-En's greatest accomplishment and satisfaction is in parenting. Positive psychology has heavily influenced her parenting style and her children constantly motivate her to become a better person. Sha-En has a lofty goal: she wants to empower parents all over the world to take charge of their parenting journey, experience less stress and live more joyfully – ultimately to raise the next generation of flourishing children. She is currently writing her first parenting book.

Sha-En identifies most with being Peranakan Chinese. She loves spicy food, deep conversations and books by Brene Brown. Sha-En currently resides in Singapore with her husband and two beautiful daughters.

You can connect with Sha-En at:

- shaen@positiveedu.com
- www.positiveedu.com
- www.twitter.com/PositiveEduc
- www.facebook.com/positiveeducation

CHAPTER 14

WHY CAN'T I HAVE IT ALL?

– THE JOURNEY FROM DISCONTENT TO DESTINY

BY SHERRI SMITH

I believe I'm here for a reason and my purpose
is greater than my challenges.
~ Jon Gordon

Growing up, I watched my dad work at two government jobs and then retire from them when "that time came." My mom also worked at the same place for a long time; as did my sister and just about every family member I knew of. But for me…well, that was a different story. I was a teacher and I loved my students and connecting with them, but some other parts of my job left me feeling unfulfilled and discontent. I just did not understand why.

Never one to sit still, I would look for that "fulfilling" opportunity and then move on. But inside, I always thought, *Is it me? Why is it so hard to find satisfaction?* Over the years I'd heard of people who would master a job and then grow bored or discontent, and then they'd move on. I wished that would have been my case, but I knew that it was not.

With all the sadness and unanswered questions lingering in my mind about my professional potential, I truly felt like I was abnormal, perhaps even defective. Something was stopping me from finding happiness in my job, and I just could not determine what that was. How I envied those who could find their happiness and just stay at a job, because I did not even see that as a remote possibility.

I just wanted to find a career and stick with it, confident that would make the unstable feelings I had inside go away.

Evaluation mode was what I was always in. Finally, I'd determined that it was my environment, and a change of pace from teaching positions would really fill that unexplainable void I'd been living with for so long. So I went big, taking a leap of faith and accepting a position with a Fortune 500 company. I had to move hundreds of miles away from my home and to a new city.

My new role was a leadership role and I'd been shocked to get it, feeling that I really didn't have the experience necessary, but I was wrong! Being wrong never made me as ecstatic as it did when I found out I was hired. My hopes were soaring and my outlook was very positive.

Then life got real. Quickly, I felt that the company I had made a big move to be a part of wasn't really the best fit for me. Its culture didn't align with my values and ideas for the future I wanted, or my goals that I'd set for within the company itself. It was time to go back to where I'd come from.

Feeling deflated and falling into a slight depression as a result, I felt that I'd failed—again! I went back to teaching. I loved the people part of the job and would just have to make do until that dream job and I came face-to-face. And a few months later, we did. This time, my leadership role was even higher and I thought, Wow, now I'll be happy. It's finally my time.

Again, discontent set in. I was into this job for only a few months and I began to get burnt out, fatigued, and stressed. I loved most of what I did, but did not like some significant parts of the job (specifically the administrative aspects). With each passing day, I grew more tired and exhausted. The job was really taking its toll on me and I finally went to the doctor for a check-up. Something needed to change. And that's when my life changed forever. I learned I had cancer.

Grace and willpower got me through my cancer struggle and I knew I was blessed with a gift a year later when I was in remission. I'd made it and beat the odds! And finally, I was back to a healthy energy level. Now the biggest question: what next?

Yes, I was back in the game…rather, trying to figure out what my game was.

Admittedly, I was anxious to go back to work and my family was eager to have me stay at home. At home there was a more relaxed me, a stress-free person who could really contribute to my family's wellbeing as a homemaker. And I really loved that role. But again, I suddenly got bored, but it was worse, because this time I felt guilty about it. I loved my family so much and it made me feel awful to know that I still wasn't content, that I wanted something more.

I knew that I should be happier than what I was. The thoughts of why nothing was ever good enough tortured me. Why am I never content? Am I that picky? That ungrateful? What! So I went back at it. Being at a crossroads I had to find out what it was that I was seeking. So, I threw myself into hobbies and classes to seek answers. Still…something wasn't right. I felt so lost.

In a chronically leaking boat, energy devoted to changing vessels is more productive than energy devoted to patching leaks.
~ Warren Buffet

Everything does happen for a reason and our attention is drawn to certain things because we are meant to be witness to them. For me, this type of moment happened one day when I was going through my Social Media. I saw one of my friends who always posted happy thoughts and looked genuinely happy, too. I was curious. What was her secret? She'd mentioned something about Jack Canfield and I was curious. I went to his website to learn more, as I didn't know a lot about him. I saw that he had a "Train the Trainer" program and its description instantly drew me in. I wanted to know more so I took action—inspired action—and signed up.

I've always loved personal development and that was one of the reasons why my struggles to find that content place in life had been so frustrating. Not figuring it out was torturous. Previously, I'd held back on personal development-based seminars simply due to cost. But I was at a turning point in my life and I said, "I'm jumping in, all in," and I did. I viewed it the way someone would view a down payment for their dream home—it was an investment in their future. I still had no idea what I'd do with this training, exactly, but it did not matter.

Nobody was more shocked than me when I came across my soul purpose from the seminar.

Suddenly I saw it. My destiny and my soul's purpose. I had that "aha" moment! All those years I'd spent trying to do something that wasn't congruent with my heart. It was over, and now the training that started out as a task to develop another set of skills to use, instead, became a bootcamp for my soul.

I called it bootcamp because I was in this intense, life-changing situation where I had to dig deep down and challenge my limiting beliefs that I had previously thought were removed from my life. Then I stretched beyond my comfort zone. I knew that I needed to work with people in some capacity—they are my "why" and that what I did had to be built around this. Knowing this freed me—both emotionally and mentally.

One of the most powerful moments of my bootcamp for the soul was when I was being led through a guided meditation that referenced what I am not:

- My job
- My experiences
- My past
- The narrative that I or anyone in society says I am or have to be

I could change my story! This was such a powerful moment and I began to cry, realizing that I'd been holding myself hostage all those years. I'd been comparing myself to others and society's standards, paying little to no attention to who I was, rather the roles I identified with. I didn't have to pick career or home. I didn't have to pick success or failure. The nagging questions about why I could never feel thankful or grateful had been dissolved.

Learning that it was okay to not love everything was so liberating. It 'sucked' to have to travel so much and be burnt out mentally and emotionally, so I wasn't present for my family when I was there. Likewise, it sucked when I was watching everyone outside my four walls have a job and contribute to lives that they seemed to genuinely appreciate.

From that moment on, I resigned from my old life and redesigned a new one, using another set of rules.

No, this is not the beginning of a new chapter in my life; this is the beginning of a new book! That first book is already closed, ended, and tossed into the seas; this new book is newly opened, has just begun! Look, it is the first page! And it is a beautiful one!
~ C. JoyBell C.

Taking responsibility for how I wanted my life to look and deciding that I didn't have to go back to the corporate world or sacrifice time with my family to experience success changed everything. I had other contributions to make that were aligned with me and purpose driven, and I was also aware about the important take-away lessons from my journey thus far:

- I would find a way do the parts of my past careers that I embraced doing.
- I would subcontract out the parts of my past careers that I did not like to do.

Those two simple points of awareness changed my life in a rapid and wonderful way. My family dynamics became instantly better with both my husband and my children. I was more filled with joy than I'd ever remembered being. And I created the place I was meant to be. Today, I own my own consulting firm and I'm a People Strategist. When I am "working" I love it, because I feel the excitement and have energy and drive for a greater purpose—to help others. People are my business.

My heart is the compass that guides my life.

Today, I meet so many people that are in that place that I'd been in for so long. They're struggling to figure it out and are eager to feel content and fulfilled. They often ask how I finally made the change. Well, it wasn't easy for me to connect the dots that showed me what was missing, but thankfully I did, and I am always grateful to share what I've learned with others. I want everyone to feel this energetic joy that comes from living your soul purpose. So, today when people ask me about my success, here's what I share with them:

1. *When you are deciding something, if it isn't a "hell yes!" then it's a no.* If you have to deliberate on if you want to do something to the point where you are talking yourself into doing it, don't do it. Take inspired action only. When you don't know all of the answers, but the universe winks at you, pay attention! It's a sign telling you to take action—just like I did with Jack's training.

2. *You don't have to have all the answers.*
When things begin to get confusing, go back to the basics. Take your temperature. What I mean by that is use your heart as your barometer or compass. If it doesn't feel 100% right that is a caution flag. Your alert—get back on course!

3. *Play big.*
This is the toughest bit of advice, I'll admit, because it takes a mindset shift that can be hard for many people—at first! For me, it was really tough. I had to stop focusing on a career as a job you work at for a long time, collecting a 401(k), and then retiring. Just because my parents did that didn't mean that was what I should be doing. It was their story...and that was okay. My story was meant to be different because that mindset did not work for me. No one else can take the actions to change our narrative besides us. I found meditation to be quite helpful during this part of the process as well, because all the whispers of the universe came to me, helping me to unfold my thought process to discover my relative truth.

Everyone has the ability to have it all, so long as they know what their "all" is.

One thing that's truly incredible about finding the destiny that you were meant to be aligned with is how everything that you've gone through becomes clear. You can see how you really had the hints about the answers you may have needed all along, but you just didn't bother to take note of them. This is okay. This happens to everyone and I'm yet to meet the person that knew from the beginning. Our journey to our soul's purpose will never be a straight line, because life is like our heartbeat—it has ups and downs, but an incredible amount of strength to keep moving us along.

About Sherri

Sherri Smith is a People Strategist, Coach, Trainer, and Author with more than 20 years of combined experience in human resources management, training and development, and education. Sherri has the proven ability of understanding others and developing their talent. She has held Human Resources leadership positions for Fortune 500 and mid-size companies.

Sherri's empathic, down-to-earth nature, professional background and life experience provides her the versatility of perspective and depth of insight to connect with people of all personalities, ages, and backgrounds. Her natural ability to nurture relationships results in long-term solutions and successful outcomes.

Sherri is a certified Success Principles and Methodology Coach, and hold certificates from Cornell University in High Performance Leadership, Change Leadership and Managing for Execution. Furthermore, Sherri holds a Master's degree in Human Resources and Management, and a Master's certification in Elementary Education. She serves on the committees, and is a member, of the Society for Human Resource Management (SHRM) and The Chamber of Commerce. Sherri's passion is working with participants at the homeless shelter providing personal development and esteemed-based workshops and employment coaching and training.

You can connect with Sherri at:

- Sherri@smithadvisorypartners.com

CHAPTER 15

SUCCESS IS A CHOICE WE MAKE

BY VICTORIA LEE HUFF

It was almost a usual Sunday for this family of three. . .Sundays at their house began with fresh-roasted coffee brewing and Nina slicing up the maple pastries that she carefully selected from Kroger bakery the day before, while her husband Jim sat quietly reading the newspaper. He would paraphrase some of the latest and most intriguing top news stories as Nina would stand there listening intently in her blue gingham print apron tied around her waist carefully protecting her Sunday clothes. Jim always made a point to pay close attention to the top stories and current events. He was never short on starting a conversation and although he only had a high school diploma with his name on it, he could speak about every current topic trending in the news.

Jim was a born leader back in the 1930's. He was the youngest of a large family who were rich with love but the times they were living in made it difficult for them to make ends meet economically. So, Jim began delivering papers with his brothers at age 4 and pumping gasoline at a local station during his high school years. He was a born leader as he loved music although since his family could not afford music lessons, he learned to master a baton and led his catholic high school band as a drum major. After high school, during the Korean War, he served as a Corporal in the United States Army in the 82nd Airborne Division for parachute assault operations. And, Jim had such a genuine smile, the one that made you actually feel his happiness and want to share it.

Sunday was important to him. It was a day of rest from his manually intensive blue collar job at the local gas company. Sunday was family day usually spent at home in the morning, while the sounds from the family stereo resonated throughout every nook and cranny of their duplex which some may refer to as half-a-house or a twin single. This wasn't the average size of stereos today or even the 80's boom boxes. In fact, it may have been 1000 times larger compared to the size of the smallest music player today. There was an AM/FM radio, 8 track and vinyl record player all strategically encased within a large maple colored wood credenza that took up one entire wall of their modest dining room. Jim was very proud of that big purchase they made when they moved out from a part of town that had a high crime rate and the site for many protests of that era.

Often times when there was upheaval on the streets, Jim would hastily pull the blinds and direct his wife and daughter to the back side of their apartment away from the windows so ranting people carrying the signs could not see them. Moving to the suburbs was living out his American dream. Jim was grateful that his long work hours afforded him and his family the opportunity to move to a neighborhood with a church close by and a good school to educate their only daughter.

It was a ritual for him to enjoy listening to the stereo sounds every Sunday morning. And, when the windows were open in the warm weather, even the neighbors within this coal mining valley town enjoyed the music of the Glen Miller Orchestra and Barry Manilow. Sunday was Jim's day of rest. A day to just be with family.

Then, in the afternoon, all three of them would climb in the 1970 orange pick-up truck to take a ride along the many country roads in West Virginia and go visiting. Most of their relatives were living within a 10-mile radius because back in those times, families did not move too far away from one another. Instead, they stayed in close proximity of each other so they could get together for Sunday meals. On some Sundays, they would travel south on Route 7 to visit their cousins Viola, Ray and their dog Misty. Today, they were traveling north on Route 7 to visit their friends in Wellsburg, which was about 30 minutes away.

Two pig-tailed girls, one blonde and the other brunette, were introduced by their parents a few years ago. Some of their times together consisted of playing with the classic wood alphabet blocks, placing colored rings on a plastic tower and watching the vintage Fisher Price television entertain them. Other times, it was the musical schoolhouse clock that taught them how to tell time the old fashioned way, turning the handle till Jack popped up out of his box, which taught them about consequences, and listening to the many fairy tale stories read to them by their parents. Both girls were always tickled pink as they listened intently to the same tales they had heard many times. Although looking into their glimmering eyes as they sat cross-legged in front of the reader, you would think it was the first time they heard about Princess Cinderella's fairy godmother turning her carriage back into a pumpkin as the clock struck 12. Both bright-eyed girls continued to enjoy those stories as they grew, even more so than before. After all, life is way too short and can be so overwhelming at times not to still believe in fairy tales.

As the years went by, the girls enjoyed reminiscing about those tales especially when the handsome prince sweeps the princess dressed in her beautiful gown, sprinkled with magical pixie dust and wearing those sparkling, iridescent glass slippers, off her feet. They get married and ride off into the sunset together and live happily ever after. . .Perhaps those stories represent the eternal hope of triumph required to overcome life's challenging times. And, what girl doesn't sparkle from the inside out after being sprinkled with magical pixie dust? Here's the good thing, that magical pixie dust doesn't expire and has no age restrictions, therefore as long as you still keep a sprinkling on hand and believe, of course, it will start your day out on a joyful note. So be sure to never allow your supply to completely dwindle away. Now, there may be times in life when it's difficult to see the sparkles or feel the soothing dust as it gently falls upon your skin, although the magic it offers will never leave you. And, if your best girlfriend's is missing, kindly offer her some of yours.

So that particular Sunday they travelled up north so the two girls with pig-tails could listen to an extra special story book that appeared to be written just for them. They were excited for their time together as always. Their ears would be listening to this story for the first time ever. And, if the girls only knew how many months prior to this day their parents had been talking about the details and planning this day. They were waiting for the appropriate time to talk with their girls about this. . . The girls' parents were filled with excitement and nervousness as they anticipated how they would feel as they told their beautiful daughters the story. While the adults sat in the kitchen sipping on sweet tea, their girls dressed up in their princess gowns and the sparkling slippers in the TV room. Then, it was time, so both pig-tailed princesses sat on the edge of the sofa as they gently bounced up and down in anticipation of what words were going to jump off those storybook pages. Would they hear about a prince and a princess? What about a fairy godmother? What possibly could these little girls be learning from this storybook?

Soon after both girls announced they couldn't wait any longer, their parents joined them in the TV room with faux wood panel-covered walls and began taking turns reading pages from this book. On the front cover, there was a family of three. One mom, one dad and one little pig-tailed girl.

So the story they heard sounded something like this. . . Sometimes throughout their vast kingdom, difficult decisions must be made very carefully to allow happiness and promote goodwill throughout all the land. Sometimes princesses are wrapped carefully in warm blankets and marked with "extra special delivery." For there were only a limited supply of extra special deliveries. When the stork saw those markings, he carefully knew exactly which well-deserving parents were ready and waiting to receive their new baby girls.

Both of the pig-tailed girls sitting on the sofa learned that they had not only been marked as an extra-special delivery, but they were also chosen from all the other babies in the land. That is when both girls learned they were both special and chosen because they were adopted by a mom and dad who promised to love to them to the moon and back, forever and ever.

Throughout the years after that special Sunday, as one of those pig-tailed girls, I remember many times sitting on my daddy's lap as he read me that same story. As time went on, my hairstyle evolved from pigtails, to the Dorothy Hamill, and then the big hair held in place by Aqua Net hairspray, although my memories always gently reminded that I was chosen. That word and the way my parents presented it to be, resonated throughout my being and gave me great comfort throughout life's challenging times.

We have all been chosen to be here for a reason. All things begin and end with you. We each arrive and depart this world alone. Therefore, it's important that we know why we are present and what we can do to fully embrace each challenge and every phase of our lives.

Success Tip 1: Be true to yourself. Do not succumb to what you think others want you to be. Instead, stay true to who you were chosen to be . . . Identify your passions so you know why and what purpose you were chosen to fulfill. What is your story? If you don't have a clear one to tell, ask your loved ones and write your story. Remind yourself of who you are and what you represent each and every day. What makes your heart sing? When do you feel most alive?

Success Tip 2: Be mindful of your words and how they affect others. Choose your words carefully. Negative words really don't make us feel any better and probably cause more stress. Hurtful words are like boomerangs. Sure, you may feel good and powerful temporarily in that moment. However, when you are speaking them to others, they come right back at you. Omit words like 'hate' and 'no' from your vocabulary. Instead choose other less harsh words to express your feelings. Remember, once those harsh words are heard, they really can't be taken back even when you ask nicely.

Success Tip 3: Be intentional with your actions. Stay fully present in each moment. Do your best to just focus on the task at hand instead of multitasking your list within your mind. That tends to create anxiety.

Success Tip 4: Be humble in your actions. Don't feel as if you have to 'over talk' or outdo the person next to you. All of us have our strengths and weaknesses, as well as gifts to share.

Success Tip 5: Be kind to yourself and one another. It's contagious. Be mindful that as you are kind to others, you must also be kind to yourself. Make wise choices.

Success Tip 6: Be part of the solution, not the problem.

Success Tip 7: Believe in yourself. If you don't, no one else will either.

Success Tip 8: Be intentional. Stay in the present. Create and embrace experiences with those chosen people in your life. Remind yourself not to take those special people or the experiences for granted.

Success Tip 9: Always have a back-up plan or be ready to create one on the fly. If the electricity goes out, be sure to eat the ice cream in the freezer before it melts.

Success Tip 10: Practice daily gratitude. Be grateful, not wasteful. What experiences are you thankful for and why? Who was involved and how did they make you feel?

Success Tip 11: Do your best to find one good thing to appreciate about those people in your lives. Focus on that positive attribute instead of magnifying the not-so-good ones. And, the other stuff you don't like, just simply excuse. Don't take on their issues though. Their issues will drain you and take you away from fulfilling your true purpose.

Success Tip 12: Choose happiness. Look on the bright side of things. It's the best alternative. Dwelling in the not-so-good is not productive and will not move you forward. It will hold you back and keep you stuck.

Success Tip 13: Create your legacy and live it every day of your life. What makes your heart sing? What family rituals do you remember from your past? Which ones would you like to instill in your children? What do you stand for?

About Victoria

Victoria Lee Huff is an Executive Success Coach who helps women reclaim and reignite their personal, spiritual and business powers within to elevate their game to a higher level. She believes as passionate women caring for many at work and home, we must take our turn to stand on a pedestal to recognize and celebrate our achievements, reclaim our power and propel ourselves forward to an even higher level of success.

Formerly a seasoned corporate sales executive earning a multiple six-figure income, Victoria walked out of that lucrative role to follow her passion and pursue her dreams of creating a new extraordinary life with more purpose, passion and of course, freedom. In 2008, Victoria began building a multiple award-winning private duty caregiving agency in Plainfield, Illinois. Her agency has been evaluated by the stringent guidelines of the Home Care Standards Bureau. Her agency diligently maintains high care standards and business practices to uphold the A+ rating for the last 3 years. She is the Executive Director and committed to providing quality and compassionate care to our elderly, new moms, and special needs community members. She also has several articles published on a variety of topics relating to elder care. In addition, Victoria is a national member of the distinguished group of Certified Senior Advisors.

As a speaker, Victoria's genuine and no-nonsense approach to achieving health, wealth and happiness will prompt you to take action and create a plan so that you don't look back upon your legacy and say you wish you would have or you wish you could have. . .

Another trending topic she speaks about is embracing our role and duty to care for our aging loved ones as well as our children and in some cases, our grandchildren.

Victoria trains executives and small business owners with her compassionate ways of embracing every moment in our lives, instead of simply enduring because every phase of life is meant to be enjoyed.

Victoria was orphaned at birth and raised by loving parents in Wheeling, West Virginia. This small town girl grew up in a traditional, modest and blue collar family. She cherishes her childhood days and enjoys carrying on many family traditions. Victoria is a proud advocate for both adoption and eldercare. She is committed to giving back to our worldwide community by volunteering through several organizations with her children.

She is an avid runner, Xtreme workout fanatic, a black belt, a fairy tale believer and a single mom who enjoys spending time at home and traveling adventures with her two children and their four-legged canine, Charlotte Rose.

CHAPTER 16

BUILDING YOUR OWN ROAD TO SUCCESS: PETER DIAMANDIS' QUEST TO CHANGE THE WORLD

BY JW DICKS & NICK NANTON

It's been our honor in recent years to be able to work with space pioneer, physician, engineer and entrepreneur Peter Diamandis, founder of the X Prize Foundation as well as co-founder of Singularity University, Space Adventures Ltd., International Space University, Planetary Resources, Human Longevity Inc., and the Zero-Gravity Corporation.

Last year, we were grateful to get permission to tell his story in our Emmy Award-winning documentary on Peter's life and work, *Visioneer*; now, in this exclusive excerpt from our new book, *Mission-Driven Business*, we're proud to be able to offer this illuminating interview with Peter – and how his passionate commitment to his mission enabled him to create exciting new challenges that have engaged the entire scientific community, as well as such private sector legends as Richard Branson and Tony Robbins.

Among the many, many honors he's received, Peter Diamandis was recently named one of Fortune magazine's "50 World's Greatest Leaders" – and with good reason. Armed with an unshakeable belief in his cause, Diamandis spearheaded private industry's entry into space exploration, despite a lack of significant money and resources.

Peter likes to say, "The best way to predict the future is to create it yourself." To that, we'd like to add, "The best way to experience success is to be committed to your passion."

In Peter's latest best-seller, *Bold: How to Go Big, Create Wealth and Impact the World* (co-written with Steven Cotler), he discusses at length the importance of having an MTP (Massively Transformational Purpose) – which is the equivalent of being Mission-Driven in our book. We asked him to speak a little bit more about his own personal MTP and how it spurred him on:

I grew up inspired by the Apollo program and by Star Trek. My heart and soul really connected with that, and I feel very lucky to have had that inspiration. However, I grew up in a family that was very much a medical family and urged me to become a doctor. I remember one day telling my mom I wanted to be astronaut and her response was, "That's nice son, but I think you need to be a doctor." She said it in a very caring way, and I ended up pursuing medicine to make my family happy - but also, because I realized if I wasn't a fighter pilot, the next career that had the highest acceptance rate in the astronaut core was a physician. So I rationalized that and went that route.

But the passion of wanting to go into space never left me. When I went through MIT, when I went to Harvard Medical School, I got to meet a lot of astronauts, and I realized after some time that my chances of becoming one were relatively low because of the acceptance rate. Even if I did get accepted, did I really want a career as a government employee? I'd only get a chance to fly once or twice in my career, and I'd have to do what I was told. That wasn't what I wanted for myself. I ended up channeling that frustration into building a series of entrepreneurial efforts in the space arena and, finally, starting the XPRIZE foundation.

For me, space was my guiding star, it inspired me, it woke me up in the morning, it ultimately drove me to start a dozen space companies. My mission and purpose in life has been to open the space frontier and make it accessible to humanity. I've added to that mission and purpose.

In 1995, Peter founded the X Prize Foundation, which offered a $10 million prize for the first entrepreneurs who could successfully launch a private aircraft into space. Here, he discusses how he analyzed the incentive competition that motivated Charles Lindbergh to perform the first solo flight across the Atlantic, a contest that announced it would award the winner $25,000 – and how he realized that he could put the principles of that early 20th Century competition to work nearly a century later.

As I read Lindbergh's story, I made notes in the margin. I was amazed by how much money the teams were spending to win $25,000, some as much as $100,000. I remember totaling it up at the end, and being astonished that it was nearly $400,000 or 16 times the prize purse. Equally incredible was the fact that Lindbergh appeared to be the least qualified guy to win the competition given his short flying career at the time. I was fascinated by the idea that by offering up an incentive competition, a winner was automatically selected and financially rewarded.

I thought about that prize and its implications. A $25,000 purse commanded $400,000 in team expenditures and ultimately gave birth to today's multi-hundred billion-dollar aviation industry. And, as I finished reading Lindbergh's book, I started thinking about a prize to promote spaceflight and wrote down in the margin, "XPRIZE???"

My thinking at the time was that perhaps a prize could be used to develop private spaceships for the rest of us. I had long since given up on the idea that I would actually travel to space as a government astronaut. But...if I could create a prize to encourage the creation of a new generation of private spaceships, perhaps that would be my ticket to space. Since I had no idea who would be my prize sponsor, I used "x" as a place holder, and thus the origin of the name XPRIZE.

A few months later I wrote up my XPRIZE idea. I then wrote an article that appeared in National Space Society magazine and was invited to give testimony in Congress about it. The year was 1994. It was during this testimony that I first met Doug King, who was about to become president of the St. Louis Science Center. One evening, over dinner, we started discussing the XPRIZE; Doug said, "You have to come to St. Louis. St. Louis is where you'll find the funds to support this vision."

Once the fourth largest city in the United States, St. Louis had descended to number 40, and was eager to regain its reputation as an aerospace leader. So, with my good friend and partner Gregg Maryniak, I traveled to St. Louis and met the one person that Doug believed could raise the capital, Alfred Kerth, who was one of the great thinkers and promoters of St. Louis. In my first meeting with him he got so excited he stood up and shouted: "I get it. I get it. Let's make this happen."

We met that evening at the Racquet Club for scotch and he laid out his vision. We would create the NEW Spirit of St. Louis organization that would follow in the footsteps of the original. The New Spirit of St. Louis (or NSSL) would be a group of 100 St. Louisans who contribute $25,000 each to provide the seed capital to launch XPRIZE.

On March 4th of 1996, we held another meeting at the Racquet Club, at the same table where Lindbergh himself had raised his original $20,000. That evening we raised about $500,000 from twenty St. Louisans who pledged to join NSSL. About two months later, on May 18th, we used that seed funding to boldly announce the $10 million prize competition - albeit without actually having the $10 million in place!

That day, hundreds of press outlets reported on the story and gave credibility to my idea. People got it; people believed it and it was a brilliant launch. But the hard work was just beginning - the work to fund not only the $10 million purse, but also the operation of the foundation itself. As bullish as I was, pitch after pitch failed to turn up a title sponsor. I presented to well over 150 CEOs, CMOs and philanthropists, everyone from Fred Smith of FedEx to Richard Branson of the Virgin Group, but the audacity of the prize and the chance that someone could die in the attempt, stalled our search for a sponsor.

The New Spirit of St. Louis Organization added members slowly $25,000 at a time and it was those funds that allowed us to continue operations. These funds helped us continue along but ultimately were not enough to fund the purse. It was then that two friends of mine told me about the idea of a 'hole-in-one insurance policy', the notion that one could buy an insurance policy to underwrite the prize.

Here is the way it worked.

We had to set an end date to the competition. We selected December 31st, 2004. We would buy an insurance policy and pay a multimillion dollar premium. If someone were to win the prize by making the two flights to space within two weeks before that deadline, then the insurance policy would pay the ten million dollars. If no one pulled it off, then the insurance company would keep the premiums. We were basically placing a large Las Vegas bet.

Of course, the insurance company would also be betting that the efforts of Diamandis and his supporters would come to nothing – and that nobody would come knocking on their door to actually collect the $10 million prize. So the insurance company did the necessary legwork to assure themselves that no one would succeed at the XPRIZE mission.

The insurance underwriter hired a consultant to evaluate all the teams registered for the competition. They approached companies like Orbital Sciences, Lockheed and Boeing only to verify that they did not intend to compete. The big players were somewhat dismissive of the idea that a start-up entrepreneur could build a private spaceship and fly to space.

Luckily the insurance underwriter took the bet. All I had to do now was come up with a three-million-dollar premium payment. The problem was that I didn't have three million. What I did instead was negotiate with the insurance company a series of progressive payments. The XPRIZE foundation would make a $50,000 payment every month for a year, and then make a $2.6 million balloon payment at the end of that year. The insurance underwriter was effectively giving us runway to raise the funds. They didn't feel they had anything to lose - their expectation was that they would take our money and never have to pay anything out.

The first couple of $50,000 payments we made from funds we had raised. I made the next payment personally - and then we were out of money. Every month for the rest of that year-long period, Gregg and I would need to go and raise the money. It was not an easy task. I remember many Monday mornings knowing that I only had five days left to raise $50,000 or the competition was over.

Of course, the biggest challenge was being able to manage that $2.6 million due at the end of the year. If we had so much trouble raising $50,000, how would we manage an amount 52 times as large?

I*t was at this point that I met my guardian angel, who came to me in the form of a magazine article. I was in my Santa Monica apartment on a Saturday afternoon, catching up on some reading when I flipped through a copy of a Fortune magazine issue featuring the "Wealthiest Women under 40." One of those women was named Anousheh Ansari and as I read her write-up, I stopped dead in my tracks. I read it over and over again in disbelief.*

"It is my dream to fly on a sub-orbital flight into space," Ms. Ansari was quoted as saying.

Yes, Anousheh, like me, had grown up watching Star Trek *and dreaming of becoming a space explorer. As I read further I learned that Anousheh, her husband Hamid, and brother-in-law Amir Ansari had just sold their third company called Telecom Technologies to Sonus Networks for over a billion dollars. That was when I knew I had found our sponsor.*

We flew down to Dallas to meet Anousheh, Hamid and Amir. We presented the XPRIZE vision and expressed our great desire to have them underwrite the purse and the operations of our first prize. According to Anousheh, they were sold within the first 10 minutes. I waited two days to hear from Hamid who called to say yes, that they would do it, that they would fund the operations and fund the remaining insurance payments. Shortly thereafter we announced the purse had been fully funded, and was now being re-named the Ansari XPRIZE, named in their honor.

Now, the only question was, could anybody win this before the December 31st, 2004 deadline?

Of course, there was still a major piece of red tape that Diamandis had to cut through – and the way he accomplished that impressive feat was surprisingly easy. But only because, once again, someone had responded to the power of his mission and wanted to be a part of helping it come to fruition.

In 2003, a year before the prize was to be awarded, in a meeting with Marion Blakey, the FAA administrator, and Patti Smith the associate administrator, I explained how the current FAA rules did not allow for private spaceflight. In order for the competition to be won in the U.S., the rules would have to changed, or teams would need to fly from outside U.S. territories. In her southern drawl the Administrator responded with, "Well then, we'll just have to change the rules, won't we?" True to her word she worked with Patti Smith to write regulations that ultimately allowed for private spaceflight to blossom.

The XPRIZE was to be collected only after two spaceflights had been accomplished – and the deadline was coming up fast. It wasn't until six months before the time would be up, on June 21st, 2004, that the first space flight was attempted. As it wasn't carrying a full load of three passengers, it didn't count as one of the actual flights required to win the prize, but it proved to be an invaluable and successful trial run.

The first official qualifying flight finally came three months later on September 29th – and the date for the second and final qualifying flight was set for October 4th, the anniversary of the USSR's launch of Sputnik, the first satellite ever to fly into space launched in 1957.

It's hard to fathom how much work went into reaching the October 4th 2004 milestone. That day has been, and always will be, a special day for me. I remember leaving my Santa Monica apartment at 2:00 AM and driving 2 hours out to the Mojave Desert to meet up with my team. Through the night tens of thousands of people descended from around the world to be there for the historic event. With me that day were my mom and dad, my soon-to-be wife, Kristen and all of my closest friends. What I remember most vividly besides the ocean of people who had gathered, was the lineup of close to one hundred satellite news trucks camped out to watch and see whether Burt Rutan and Paul Allen could win the $10 million Ansari XPRIZE.

In the pre-dawn hours, the carrier airplane WhiteKnightOne was being fueled and SpaceShipOne was being readied. The pilot on this X2 flight was Navy fighter pilot and SpaceShipOne test pilot Brian Binnie. Brian would go on to become our Charles Lindbergh. A tall, thin man with a generous attitude and a strong supporter of XPRIZE over the years, we could imagine no one better to carry the torch of commercial space on that day.

Just after sunrise, WhiteKnightOne's twin Williams FJ44 jet engines carried SpaceShipOne from the Earth's surface on an hour-long ascent to 60,000 feet. Our high-magnification TV cameras watched from the ground and broadcast the image to both the TV stations and large Jumbotron screens for the crowd to see. Edwards Air Force Base, a mere 50 miles away, watched the spaceship's flight on its radar, helping us measure its exact altitude to determine if we had a winner.

It was a magical moment when Brian's voice boomed out over the loudspeakers "Release, release, release." Seconds later SpaceShipOne was released from WhiteKnightOne, then a few seconds later its hybrid engine ignited and Brian was thrown back into his chair as multiple Gs hurled the ship upwards towards space. Brian flew a picture perfect flight. The vehicle not only exceeded the 100 kilometers required to win the $10 million but shattered the X15 altitude record set some 40 years earlier.

The winning of the XPRIZE was, of course, a pivotal point both in the advancement of Diamandis' mission as well as its ultimate expansion. The event ended up bringing many important and influential people into his orbit, people who were energized by his ambitions and, even more importantly, his ability to transform those ambitions into reality.

Another vivid October 4th memory was having the XPRIZE capture the coveted Google Doodle real estate. On the Google homepage, soon after the winning flight was completed, was an image of SpaceShipOne flying over the Google logo, next to it a small flying saucer with two green aliens observing the flight. That Google Doodle later lead to my addressing a room full of 4,000 Googlers at the Googleplex on the Ansari XPRIZE, and a subsequent lunch with Larry Page, Google co-founder (then co-President and now CEO). During that lunch I presented an impromptu invitation for him to join the XPRIZE Board of Trustees (which he happily accepted).

His participation, along with Sergey Brin, Eric Schmidt, Wendy Schmidt, Elon Musk, Jim Gianopulos, Arianna Huffington, James Cameron and other notable figures who subsequently joined the XPRIZE Board of Trustees breathed new life (and capital) into XPRIZE, fueling our commitment to use prizes to take on the world's grand challenges and create large-scale incentive competitions where market failures existed.

What motivates these kinds of prominent business leaders and influencers to work with Diamandis and join in his mission? He sums it up in one word. . .

PASSION.

I think having my true passion shine through when I'm on the stage, or when I'm communicating, brings people to me. It's about speaking from my heart. It's being authentic in what I truly believe and having that come through. Whenever I don't...it fails. Whenever I do, people gravitate towards it.

It's that we have common aspirations, passions and interests to do big things in life. Google co-founder Larry Page once said something to the effect of, "I have a simple metric, a question I use now that says, "Are you working on something that can change the world, yes or no." It's the experience of most successful people in the world that, when you revolutionize one industry, you're not satisfied ever again with incremental change, you're looking to do big and bold things in life. So you're attracted to people who do equally big and bold things.

As Diamandis said earlier, his initial space mission has led him to embrace other important pursuits in which technology has the potential to solve pressing world problems. The more he can do to make that happen, the more he will do.

It was only after I had some success with space that I expanded my mission beyond that. I went into a larger orbit, if you would, beyond just the grand challenge of space and into even bigger challenges. If you can take on private space flight, you can take on a lot of other seemingly-impossible goals. I don't think it's the case that you have to have only one mission in your life, I think it's important to have something that you build on and grow with.

We are entering a point in history where entrepreneurs are now capable of doing what only the largest companies and governments could do before. Forty years ago, only a government could build a spaceship. Today, a small team of 30 engineers powered by exponential technologies can do it. In the same way I believe that there is no problem that cannot be solved, that entrepreneurs powered by technology can take on any challenge and find a solution, I believe that we've entered a day and age where we can stop complaining about problems and start solving them. That's how you can impact the lives of a billion people.

But finding that initial MTP (Massively Transformational Purpose) is something that I think is ultimately one of the most important first steps any entrepreneur, any CEO needs to take on. Whenever I talk to people now, I say, "Do you know what you would do in life if you didn't have to work, if you had all the time and energy and resources in the world? Do you have a mission? Do you have a purpose in life?" That's one of the most fundamentally important things.

Peter Diamandis doesn't just talk about thinking big and doing big things – he actually finds the ways to turn intangible ideals into reality. By kickstarting the movement towards private entrepreneurs taking on mankind's biggest challenges, he's opened up many more potential pathways to progress than have ever existed before.

So, how can you challenge and change the world? How can you create a mission that will attract the rich and powerful to your side – and engage the imagination of millions?

It's a tall order – but it's also a guaranteed recipe for building your own Road to Success!

About JW

JW Dicks Esq., is a Wall Street Journal Best-Selling Author®, Emmy Award-Winning Producer, publisher, board member, and advisor to organizations such as the XPRIZE, The National Academy of Best-Selling Authors®, and The National Association of Experts, Writers and Speakers®.

JW is the CEO of DNAgency and is a strategic business development consultant to both domestic and international clients. He has been quoted on business and financial topics in national media such as *USA Today, The Wall Street Journal, Newsweek, Forbes, CNBC.com*, and *Fortune Magazine Small Business*.

Considered a thought leader and curator of information, JW has more than forty-three published business and legal books to his credit and has co-authored with legends like Brian Tracy, Jack Canfield, Tom Hopkins, Dr. Nido Qubein, Dr. Ivan Misner, Dan Kennedy, and Mari Smith. He is the editor and publisher of the *Celebrity Expert Insider*, a monthly newsletter sent to experts worldwide as well as the quarterly magazine, *Global Impact Quarterly*.

JW is called the "Expert to the Experts" and has appeared on business television shows airing on ABC, NBC, CBS, and FOX affiliates around the country and co-produces and syndicates a line of franchised business television shows such as: *Success Today, Wall Street Today, Hollywood Live*, and *Profiles of Success*. He has received an Emmy Award as Executive Producer of the film, *Mi Casa Hogar*.

JW and his wife of forty-three years, Linda, have two daughters, three granddaughters, and two Yorkies. He is a sixth generation Floridian and splits his time between his home in Orlando and his beach house on Florida's west coast.

About Nick

An Emmy Award-Winning Director and Producer, Nick Nanton, Esq., is known as the Top Agent to Celebrity Experts around the world for his role in developing and marketing business and professional experts, through personal branding, media, marketing and PR. Nick is recognized as the nation's leading expert on personal branding as *Fast Company Magazine's* Expert Blogger on the subject and lectures regularly on the topic at major universities around the world. His book *Celebrity Branding You®*, while an easy and informative read, has also been used as a text book at the University level.

The CEO and Chief StoryTeller at The Dicks + Nanton Celebrity Branding Agency, an international agency with more than 1800 clients in 33 countries, Nick is an award-winning director, producer and songwriter who has worked on everything from large scale events to television shows with the likes of Steve Forbes, Brian Tracy, Jack Canfield (*The Secret*, Creator of the *Chicken Soup for the Soul* Series), Michael E. Gerber, Tom Hopkins, Dan Kennedy and many more.

Nick is recognized as one of the top thought-leaders in the business world and has co-authored 30 best-selling books alongside Brian Tracy, Jack Canfield, Dan Kennedy, Dr. Ivan Misner (Founder of BNI), Jay Conrad Levinson (Author of the Guerrilla Marketing Series), SuperAgent Leigh Steinberg and many others, including the breakthrough hit *Celebrity Branding You!®*

Nick has led the marketing and PR campaigns that have driven more than 1000 authors to Best-Seller status. Nick has been seen in *USA Today, The Wall Street Journal, Newsweek, BusinessWeek, Inc. Magazine, The New York Times, Entrepreneur® Magazine, Forbes, FastCompany.com* and has appeared on ABC, NBC, CBS, and FOX television affiliates around the country, as well as on CNN, FOX News, CNBC, and MSNBC from coast to coast.

Nick is a member of the Florida Bar, holds a JD from the University of Florida Levin College Of Law, as well as a BSBA in Finance from the University of Florida's Warrington College of Business. Nick is a voting member of The National Academy of Recording Arts & Sciences (NARAS, Home to The GRAMMYs), a member of The National Academy of Television Arts & Sciences (Home to the Emmy Awards), co-founder of the National Academy of Best-Selling Authors, a 16-time Telly Award winner, and spends his spare time working with Young Life, Downtown Credo Orlando, Entrepreneurs International and rooting for the Florida Gators with his wife Kristina and their three children, Brock, Bowen and Addison.

Learn more at:

- www.NickNanton.com
- www.CelebrityBrandingAgency.com

CHAPTER 17

THE WISDOM TO EMBRACING SUCCESS

BY RONNIE SINGH

MY REALIZATION OF THE INNATE WISDOM ON HOW TO BETTER DEAL, MANAGE AND EMBRACE SUCCESS.

Growing up in India, I was schooled and educated in the finest institutions. I was very fortunate to be born in a privileged Indian family with loving parents who were successful in whatever they set out to do.

My journey of learning the wisdom of embracing success led me to my first profession as a tea taster with a prestigious company in Kolkata, India. At that point, I felt I was set for life as the salary and perks were much more than any 23-year-old in India could ever dream of. By the time I reached my mid-thirties I had already had my share of so called 'worldly successes' with the accolades, achievements, money and social recognition. However, I started experiencing strange anxious emotions arising from within, I realized I was becoming negative in the way I looked at people, relationships and life in general. I was no longer inspired in what I did, I couldn't pinpoint where this uneasiness was arising from, but it was influencing me as I had begun to lose purpose in life.

Then one day, while I was sitting alone and introspecting, I suddenly had a realization that my life goals had evolved from wanting outward success to seeking purpose and fulfillment within. I felt that outer success had not fulfilled my need for self-worth, I now needed to look deep within into my belief structure instead of trying to experience worthiness on the outside.

It was then that I started probing deeply into ancient Indian philosophies related to the mind, experimenting with all kinds of meditations, yoga and practicing metaphysical mind techniques. I fortunately stayed on the course of reeducating myself. I ultimately started experiencing the essence of fulfillment arising from within. I'd like to describe that feeling as a sensation of emotional freedom. I noticed that I was becoming happier and my mind started seeing things differently, so I began writing down my experiences.

I soon quit my profession and went about sharing the knowledge and tools to help people experience what I had experienced. Over the past few years, I have been working as a Personal Development and Emotional Freedom Coach and the journey of life has taken me to different corners of the world in which I spend my time educating and guiding people on how they can truly enjoy a fulfilling and successful life.

In my profession as a coach, I feel 'success' is once again rubbing shoulders with me. However, this time over, I feel I am wiser and better able to enjoy my success because I have re-educated myself to see things differently. Today, I support my clients in better dealing, managing and embracing success with the help of seven esoteric concepts, which I like to call the **"Seven Laws of Wisdom for Embracing Success."**

In this chapter I look forward to sharing my perspective of these seven esoteric concepts, and I am sure once you read this chapter, it will inspire you to introspect on how you too can better deal, manage and embrace success in your own life.

WISDOM CONCEPT NO. 1

LEARN TO PRIORITIZE HAPPINESS OVER SUCCESS

During the initial years of my career, I believed that professional success was the most vital ingredient to happiness. I did everything in my power to prioritize all efforts towards professional success, and as time went by, I started to feel disconnected with who and what I am. This was when I first started experiencing emotional anxiety. I started to realize that despite 'having it all', I felt a strange emptiness within myself and I couldn't make sense of that. Then one day, it suddenly dawned on me that I first needed to address happiness before I could truly enjoy my successes. Only happiness could help me fully appreciate this gift of life. Without happiness, success had completely lost its value and novelty to me. That realization turned my life around.

Today, I teach a practice which entails addressing our inner needs of emotional fulfillment and happiness. I personally prioritize this daily practice before I set out to go about my everyday duties, no matter what comes into my life, this daily practice of happiness keeps me emotionally uplifted.

I can truly say that now I enjoy my successes much more because I prioritize being happy. Creating an environment of happiness is the key to enjoying and embracing success and most importantly it's what we as humans deeply strive for.

WISDOM CONCEPT NO. 2

LEARN THE ART OF MIND MANAGEMENT

When I look back at my formative years, they were very beautiful. However, I was unable to appreciate those beautiful moments, as I had no awareness about keeping focused on the beauty and goodness of what life was offering. Instead, my mind was busy dwelling on the trivial things which were pre-dominantly negative. It's only when I learnt and practiced the art of managing my mind that I started experiencing life very differently. You may have heard about many 'successful individuals' suffering from stress and anxieties that lead to substance abuse and sadness. What use is this kind of success?

Unfortunately, the root of the problem is that most of us lack the knowledge to better manage our minds. I do wish **'mind management'** could be taught as a subject in school, as without it, we humans are heading towards a mental and emotional breakdown. I use several techniques to better manage my mind. These techniques have helped me easily dissociate from dwelling on negative thoughts, allowing me to choose which thought I would like to spend more time with. Today, I share my knowledge of mind management with my students.

WISDOM CONCEPT NO. 3

LEARN TO BECOME GRATEFUL FOR EVERY NEGATIVE EXPERIENCE WHICH COMES YOUR WAY

Like most people, I was living with the illusion that to be successful I needed to segregate myself from negative people and negative experiences. Only when I started going deeper into metaphysical studies did I realize, that all the negative experiences which came into my life, were there to teach me something about myself. That's when I started positively seeing the higher purpose of life. The most fundamental realization was that *to better enjoy and hold onto success, we need to remain open and in acceptance of our immediate reality, with the readiness to positively learn from all the negative experiences coming our way.*

With this realization, it's fundamental to reframe all past experiences by looking for the positive lessons in them. As a result of this understanding, I learned to see the higher purpose in which I could perceive that every negative experience coming in my life was my greatest teacher. Negative or bad experiences are simply our guide to maturity, tolerance and learning to evolve to do things differently, so that we can align our lives to our higher purpose. Practicing gratitude towards our negative experiences inculcates emotional stability and instills an indomitable courage to face challenges in life with an open mind.

WISDOM CONCEPT NO. 4

LEARN TO EMBRACE IMPERMANENCE IN LIFE

From a young age, I was conditioned to believe that I needed to create a life in which there is some form of stability and permanency. Well, life decided to help me change that kind of thinking and after going through many tumultuous experiences, I came to the realization that my emotional pain was in many ways related to the belief that I could create some sort of professional, personal and relationship 'permanence' in my life.

Many of us are conditioned to believe that we can create permanence by being, believing, behaving or following a certain way of life. Nothing can be further from the truth because the moment you try to create an environment of permanence you also start to subconsciously create anxiety and fear towards its opposite, which is impermanence and change.

Life by its very nature is evolving, changing and is always in a state of flux. If you look back at your own lives, you will see that every person, relationship, situation and circumstance has evolved and changed in some form or the other. So whatever may be your situation, just remember to embrace impermanence so that you can better accept and adapt to the experiences coming your way. Embracing impermanence will ultimately define the essence and the quality of your feelings during periods of success.

WISDOM CONCEPT NO. 5

LEARN TO ACCEPT THE POLARITIES IN LIFE

Over the years of seeking and trying to understand why one person can remain focused and defiant in his/her quest to success while the other will subconsciously squander away whatever chances/opportunities they have, I came to the realization that to enjoy success I needed to accept both the polarities of negativity and positivity in everyday living. To be successful doesn't mean that we will transcend negativity, it actually means that we will learn to accept both the positive and negatives coming into our lives as part and parcel of enjoying success. Personally, for many years I had remained resistant to this wisdom and in turn suffered emotionally.

It doesn't matter what culture, religion, education or environment you come from, if you want to enjoy and experience the true essence of success, then you need to learn to remain open to accepting both the polarities of good and bad, positive and negative, and right and wrong coming into your everyday life. All life's precious moments that you are spending rejecting a polarity, are moments you are subconsciously being affected at an emotional level. To be able to truly enjoy success, one needs to embrace the polarities of life.

WISDOM CONCEPT NO. 6

LEARN TO FIND BALANCE BETWEEN EFFORT AND SURRENDER

From a young age, I was conditioned to believe that to succeed and achieve my goals, I needed to both mentally and physically push my limits. Today, I have discovered a simpler and yet more effective way to manifest and achieve things. I teach this formula to my students.

The formula is that we need to balance our physical and mental effort with an emotion of surrender. This refers to the understanding that whatever we set out to achieve, at a deeper level we need to cultivate an attitude of surrender, especially during periods of maximum effort. The surrender can be in the form of an emotion, faith or devotion to a higher power. One doesn't necessarily need to be religious to benefit from this. A person can benefit by simply surrendering to something of value.

Just as our bodies recuperate when we surrender to a good night's sleep, the same way our spirit grows in strength when it connects to an emotion of surrender. It's a very powerful technique providing effectiveness and humility in effort. Those who understand and apply this wisdom experience positivity and emotional stability in their journey to better attain and enjoy success.

WISDOM CONCEPT NO. 7

LEARN TO LET GO OF TRYING TO CONTOL OUTCOMES

Once you have deeply understood and incorporated the previous six esoteric concepts related to the wisdom of embracing success, only then can you reach the higher understanding of the seventh esoteric concept.

The Seventh law of wisdom is **'letting go of trying to control the outcome.'** Initially, it may seem strange and difficult to comprehend, but if you remain aware, you will realize that most human anxieties are caused by trying to be in some form of control. Maximum stress is caused by trying to influence the end result or outcome.

Learning to let go of the outcome allows you take your power back. It does not happen by simply deciding to. In fact, this understanding comes after cultivating a discipline related to self-introspection, awareness and experiential realization. Today, with conviction I can affirm, that the reason I maintain emotional stability and truly feel worthy, enjoying every moment of outward success, is because I have transcended that place of trying to control the outcomes associated with my efforts. I have realigned my beliefs to focus on being inspired in the moment, instead of trying to control future outcomes.

Well, I hope this chapter was insightful and got you to contemplate on how you too can benefit from these seven esoteric laws/wisdom concepts. You may have noticed these seven concepts of wisdom are a simple guide for letting go of control, rigidity, and becoming open to accepting the polarities of life. I believe every personal experience coming our way is directing us to our higher purpose to reach **Ultimate Freedom.**

About Ronnie

Ronnie Singh is a master coach specializing in personal development and guiding people to experiencing emotional freedom. His philosophy and approach is metaphysical, and he has helped transform the life of thousands of people who have benefitted by working with him in both private and group settings. Today, Ronnie's signature coaching programs are in high demand as they are deeply introspective, assisting people to find solutions to their life's problematic issues.

Ronnie was born and brought up in India before moving to live and work in Europe, the Middle East and Africa. He works with people from different social, ethnic, religious and cultural backgrounds and imparts tools and techniques to guide people to transcend their critical mindset in order to ultimately help them connect to a higher state. Ronnie believes that emotional fulfillment can be experienced when knowledge and practice are combined together. He explains that every person has an individual journey in life, and if they are on the right path they can experience fulfillment and freedom from attachment to negativity.

Ronnie's mission is to educate and assist people from all parts of the world to transcend negativity and embrace a life aligned to their true calling and higher purpose. He believes we can experience happiness and fulfillment by continuing to evolve, learn, accept, adapt and grow in life.

Ronnie's life story is inspirational, he draws parallels between his younger years and a boat lost at sea. He explains how he felt he had no idea which direction or path his life was going. That inspired him to start searching and seeking for purpose and fulfillment, which ultimately led him to study various ancient and modern philosophies relating to the mind and emotional fulfillment.

After years of learning, research, introspection and experimenting with different tools and techniques, he reached clarity. From his own transformational experiences, he now believes that every person has the potential to transcend their life's nibbling problems. However, for that, he feels we individually need to take responsibility and be ready for change.

Ronnie explains how negativity is a magnet for misery, and emotional issues such as stress and anxieties are just a mere symptom of a deeper emptiness, which needs to be addressed before it turns out to become an uncontrollable Frankenstein.

Ronnie is well versed with various philosophies, concepts and coaching techniques ranging from:

- **Ancient Indian philosophies (Advaita Vedanta, Yogasutras)**
- **Neuro-Linguistic Programing**
- **Metaphysical experiential laws of the universe**
- **Time line therapy**
- **Subliminal programing**
- **Subconscious communication**
- **Reeducating and reprograming the mind**
- **Passive awareness techniques**
- **Emotional freedom technique**
- **Awareness and breath meditations**

Despite his hectic schedule, Ronnie is able to balance his life and divides his time for both his passion to help people and spend time with his family. He has a loving wife and son.

You too can transform and benefit from Ronnie's private sessions or signature coaching programs. If you are interested in knowing more about Ronnie, then simply visit:

- www.ronniemastercoach.com

Facebook fan page: Ronnie Master Coach
Twitter: Ronnie Master Coach
YouTube channel: Ronnie Master Coach

CHAPTER 18

BELIEVE IN YOURSELF

BY MARYANN CASTELLO

I had my last corporate "job" for seventeen years. Every day, I would go into work and do the best I could to do my job functions perfectly and satisfy all my customer calls. I worked very hard and was eventually promoted to a management position. I took on everyone's stresses and would find resolutions to staff problems. I was the person who had to keep the peace for everyone, find resolutions, make suggestions, and do corporate training. Even though I liked what I did, I realized it was not my passion. It was my only known way of life, so I continued to do it every day.

During my time of employment, I eventually did not feel like myself. My health started to deteriorate and I did not know why. I just kept the same day-to-day routines and expected a miracle that one day I would wake up and everything would be perfect. Back in the year 2000, I had my life scare. Most days I would feel dizzy, endured temperature change fluctuations, palpitations, extreme fatigue, undesired body changes and panic attacks, just to name a few. I went to my medical doctor and was diagnosed with hyperthyroid. I was prescribed medication and followed the directions explicitly. After a couple of weeks, I was still not feeling well. Then it happened, the SCARE! I could not breathe, literally. My throat was closing. I started to panic. What if this was the last time I would see my family, friends, life, etc.? I was brought to the hospital emergency room three days in a row. The result was that I was experiencing a severe allergic reaction to the medication I was taking! I followed all the doctor's protocols to the letter and to my dismay, my symptoms kept deteriorating until I was unable to take most allopathic medications.

I knew I had to find another solution. I knew deep down inside there had to be another way. Then it happened! What I believe was divine intervention. I was lead to wonderful people that explained holistic modalities to me and I decided to give it a try. It turned out to be the most important decision in my life. I followed all the recommendations given to me and I started to notice relief of some of my symptoms. After a couple of months, I had almost complete relief. In fact, I had more energy, more desirable body changes, no palpitations, no temperature change fluctuations, or panic attacks. I felt like my old self again, but even better!

Through this experience, I realized that I had complete control of my body. If I was having a bad day, then I felt that way physically. If I was having a great day, I felt like I was on top of the world! There you have it, I thought. I am in complete control of my physical, emotional, mental, and spiritual self. I am empowered to be in constant awareness of my own body and am able to recognize any changes that I was experiencing, and was able to adjust various holistic modalities to achieve complete homeostasis.

I was fascinated at the thought that I can control what happens in my life. What if I could? How would I want it to be? I started to research this philosophy with teachings from Dr. Wayne Dyer, Louise Hay, Esther and Hicks, and Neville Goddard, to name a few. I discovered that everything I researched pointed to exactly what I experienced. So it got me thinking. What do I really want? I decided to journal my thoughts:

October 13, 2003

- *I want a job that will see my value and reward me accordingly.*
- *I want to be a mentor to my peers and help expand their job knowledge.*
- *I want a home life where I am not the one always shouldering the responsibilities.*
- *I want to be happy and healthy.*

October 20, 2003

- *I still want to be employed by people who see my value and not treat*

me as if I do not know what I am doing.
- *I want my old life back where I work corporate during the day and sing gigs at night.*
- *I want to make more money.*

November 30, 2003
- *I don't like that my job functions are not defined and I keep getting in trouble for trying to do the right thing.*
- *I do not make enough money for all the hours I put in at this job.*
- *I want to be healthy again!*

When I started to read my journal I realized that I was not journaling every day and that my thoughts were progressively getting more negative. I was frustrated and tired. Could I really empower myself and take charge of my life? This seems like too much work, I thought. I would rather take it easy and just relax on the couch and watch television. I felt like giving up.

I went to bed that night and had many dreams and started to get a vision of how I saw my life. There it was! Right in front of me in panoramic view! It was everything I dreamed of. I woke up and knew I had to get to work right away to achieve my vision. I wrote in my journal every day. I recited affirmations every day. I meditated every day. I made a vision board and studied it every day. After a few weeks, I noticed some things were changing for the better. I DID have the power to change my thoughts that would change my life! I went to work during the day and went to school at night. I did not have much free time, but I knew it was all going to be worth it in the end. I stayed true to myself and worked on all aspects of myself – physical, emotional, mental, and spiritual. I've planted the seeds and I knew if I continued I would keep growing until I achieved what I wanted. My journal entries looked more like this:

June 21, 2012
- *I am entering a career that will fulfill my every need and want. I am rewarded for my efforts on all levels.*
- *I am feeling healthier and have more vitality than ever before in my life. I'm alive!*
- *I am attracting abundance in all aspects of my life.*

June 22, 2012

- *–I am fulfilling my passion by helping others achieve their good health and goals.*
- *–I love all the numbers I see in my bank accounts that continue to grow effortlessly and easily every day.*
- *–I am elevating to my highest good each and every minute of every day.*

June 23, 2012

- *–I have my own business where I see clients on a regular basis and I am able to provide solutions to any of their concerns.*
- *–I am expanding my bank accounts every day and my prosperity is increasing.*
- *–I am elevating to new heights beyond my wildest dreams!*

I did not deviate from redefining my healthy lifestyle, my studies, or my new goals. I finally saw that I could open my own business and help others in the process. So I did just that, but on a very small scale. I worked my full-time corporate job and saw clients only two to three times a week. My main goal was to make a difference in each and every client's life. I realized through the process that I did not have all the self-confidence I needed to be able to make this into a full-time business. I still needed to work on myself. I did just that. I continued with all my meditations, affirmations, vision boards, and prayer.

I was vacationing with family when I received a call from a gentleman, Guy, who needed to seek help for his wife, Donna. He explained she had cerebral palsy and was not able to walk. She was confined to her wheelchair. I asked him if I would be able to call him in a couple days as I was on a family vacation and did not have my calendar with me. He said okay, but he kept calling me almost every day until I returned home. As it turned out, I did see his wife and we had a wonderful session. She followed all recommendations and she got better little by little. The next time I saw her, she was able to walk using canes instead of being confined to a wheelchair. That was the first blossom from my seeds that I planted.

As it turns out, I received the second blossom from my seeds shortly after. Donna gave me a referral. Her referral changed my life, literally. He was Grammy Award Winner, Producer and Arranger, Tony Camillo.

Not only did we share a passion for healing, but for music too. He took the time after his session to hear me sing. As he listened intently and I was sweaty from nerves, he said "Let's work together." My "a-ha" moment! I was on cloud nine. He then referred a medical doctor, Dr. Otto Jorgensen, who believed in the healthy lifestyle principles that I did. We realized we could combine our efforts. Dr. Jorgensen then referred someone he knew, Ryche Chlanda, who was a singer, songwriter, guitarist, producer, and arranger for sessions. Everyone offered to work on my album together. I could not believe what was happening right in front of my very eyes!

From all of the events that took place, I decided I wanted to open my own business on a big scale. Was I scared? Of course I was, terrified in fact. I had everyone pushing me to go for it. How do I go about it? Is this even possible? I started to make to-do lists and went to work. Before I knew it, with my group of cheerleaders, I was able to work through all the self-doubt that I was experiencing. I would dream about it. I would FEEL myself owning my own business. As I started to believe this was all possible, I spoke with a chiropractor, Dr. David Seeley, who graciously agreed that I could open my business in his office. I was elated. It was happening.

As we had the grand opening, I believed I can do this and more! I wanted to continue on my pursuit of helping others. More and more opportunities were finding me!! Everytime my phone would ring, it was another way I was able to be recognized for my accomplishments and other opportunities would be presented. Before you knew it, I've become a successful holistic health practitioner, a licensed massage therapist, a recording artist, television and radio personality, a co-author, and a business woman who could speak with people who would like to invest to assist her in her own product line!

I sit back and recognize how fortunate I am. My tree finally blossomed in its entirety. I have regained my health and feel better than I ever did. It has been a very long process, but my healing journey equipped me to see life experiences from different perspectives. I have met so many wonderful people along the way that cared enough to help me when I make mistakes, but were there to see me elevate above them. Has it been an easy road? No. I had to make many sacrifices in order to find my life's purpose. I had to BELIEVE in myself and FEEL myself experiencing the life I wanted. I thought about an acronym for FEEL:

F – FOCUSED
E – ENERGY
E – EMULATING
L – LOVE

If you focus all your energy emulating love, then that is what you will always get back in return. What you focus your mind on, is what you attract to yourself. I always wanted to attract positive loving and healing experiences into my life. It took me many years to discover I had the power within me the entire time to change my life. You do too! Start today. It can mean the difference between your ultimate successes or maybe not reaching your full potential.

Use the following six steps to change your life:

1. **ENVISION YOUR VISION**
   Start to think about the qualities you would like in your life. What career would you like to pursue? How do you see your home life? Do you want a relationship? Do you want to start a family? Ask yourself any question you would like to help design your vision.

2. **WRITE IT DOWN**
   Keep a journal and make entries daily. Use affirmations that are always in the present tense and do not have any negative words. Keep them short and repeat them daily.

3. **MAKE A VISION BOARD**
   Supplies Needed: Poster board, glue, scissors, markers, magazines. Get your favorite magazine and clip out pictures that you saw in your vision. Arrange and glue them on your poster board. You can use the markers to write anything you want to emphasize on your board. Put it in a location so that you see it frequently.

4. **MEDITATE DAILY**
   Sit in your favorite chair, on the floor, or lay on your bed. Face the palms of your hands to the ceiling. Close your eyes. Inhale through your nose slowly and exhale through your mouth slowly. Repeat and concentrate on your breathing. You will notice your mind will

drift off. See where it goes. See if you see anything from your vision board. If you do, take the time to see it and let it resonate with you.

5. **FEEL IT**
   This is perhaps one of the most important steps. Keep your focus on your vision and feel it inside of you that you have already achieved your vision. Notice all your body sensations and how they make you feel when you see your vision. Take a moment to concentrate on the feeling.

6. **BELIEVE IN YOURSELF**
   This is the secret. When you believe in yourself you can accomplish anything you put your mind to. Nothing is impossible. When in doubt pivot your thoughts to positive uplifting thoughts and you will achieve your goals.

So go in peace, love, and most of all…….

BELIEVE IN **YOU**RSELF!

About Maryann

Maryann Castello is a Board Certified Holistic Health Practitioner and a NJ State Licensed Massage Therapist. She is a healing force. Her multi-disciplinary approach to the healing arts provides comprehensive results. She specializes in clinical nutrition and various forms of massage: medical, Swedish, shiatsu, reflexology, and chair massage. As a Reiki Master Teacher and Practitioner she also incorporates *jin shin jyutsu* and chair energy work. She believes in educating others and teaches clinical aromatherapy, fragrance, and detoxification classes at the Academy of Natural Health Sciences. She serves on advisory boards for public schools Departments of Special Services and is an ordained minister practitioner.

Maryann is a graduate of the Academy of Natural Health Sciences and various other institutions. She is the CEO and Founder of Neos Zoe LLC, "New Life Through Balanced Living." She is a TV and Radio personality who has been featured on Spotlight Television, Danny Coleman's Rock on Radio, and currently hosting her own radio show, along with Co-Host, Frank MacKay, as an expert in various holistic modalities. She was selected as one of America's Premier Experts™ and has been quoted in *Talk Nation Magazine* and *NJ Discover* with Calvin Schwartz, on creating healthy lifestyles. Maryann also has been named the VIP Woman of the Year 2015-2016 from the National Association of Professional Woman.

Maryann is a professional singer who has worked with Grammy Award Winning Producer and Arranger, Tony Camillo and Singer/Songwriter, Guitarist, Producer and Arranger, Ryche Chlanda. She has an upcoming Meditation DVD Line and her radio show can be found on iTunes, Sound Cloud, Blog Talk Radio, and Frank MacKay Media.

It is Maryann's desire and mission to help each individual to achieve complete homeostasis by educating them through her teachings of various holistic practices to empower themselves through their healing journey on the physical, emotional, mental and spiritual levels. She is committed to her own personal growth and continuing education to keep her on the frontier of innovative holistic solutions for achieving optimal health, harmonious living and lifestyle choices.

Maryann Castello, HHP, LMT, CL.N, CL.A, F.C., Dt. Sp.

You can connect with Maryann at:

- Maryann@NeosZoe.com
- www.facebook.com/NeosZoellc
- www.twitter.com/NeosZoe

CHAPTER 19

GOOD IN DEED®

BY KELLY SMITH PARKER

Serving our purpose can be a rocky road that is always under construction, but in the end, we become masters of the good we wish to see.

Anyone who has achieved their goals understands one immutable principle: there are roadblocks that will make the course bumpy and daunting. However, that same road is also lined with green light moments that are simply indescribable, providing exhilaration and satisfaction not found on the safer, more traveled road.

I would love to say that I chose this less traveled terrain intentionally, but it would be more accurate to say that it chose me. Long before I knew that I wanted to help others with my life, Good In Deed® was percolating inside of me. A combination of the right people, the right jobs, and the right timing has always encouraged me on my path and guided my way forward.

For this, I am thankful. Beyond words.

In a world where a small percent of the population—by their own admission—get to do what they love to do every day, I am grateful that I can do just that and use my gifts and talents to their fullest. Quite honestly, all my gifts and talents need to be used to their fullest, so I can accomplish my mission: to spur on good deeds like wildfire.

I have unbridled anticipation for the continued road ahead as success is not a destination, but a journey. It is the faces of people that I've helped along the way, including men, women and children, that inspires me to set off on the road each morning and accomplish my mission to do good by the end of each day.

THE SEEDS OF GOOD IN DEED®

When you work hard for the things you care about, your work matters.

I was fortunate to grow up around people who were "doers." They worked hard, honored their commitments, and always showed up. My father was a successful ophthalmologist who helped launch the Doheny Eye Institute in Los Angeles. My mother was a pediatrician at Kaiser in Los Angeles. They worked passionately for the people and things they cared about, and they knew that their work mattered personally and professionally. This philosophy drove them, and they shared it wholeheartedly and vigorously with my younger brother, Matt, and me. We drank in their stories and enthusiasm, knowing that we too wanted to do work that matters. In fact, we couldn't understand why anyone would choose otherwise.

Knowing what you want is different from knowing how to accomplish it. While I was sure that I was destined to live a life of purpose, I still sought out that ONE THING that would make it happen. When I turned sixteen, destiny called.

The Doheny Eye Institute is an organization that helps the blind see. After I turned sixteen, I was looking for a summer job. My Dad suggested I would be a good fit for an opening at Doheny. Lee Jackman, the head of Doheny's fundraising department, who also became one of my lifelong mentors, gave me the summer job based on Dad's recommendation. My life would be forever changed.

SOMETIMES YOU START A TASK AND IT BECOMES CRYSTAL CLEAR THAT YOU WERE PRE-WIRED TO DO IT

The first day of my internship was transformative. If this wasn't that ONE THING, it most certainly was what the ONE THING was supposed to feel like: good. I loved the work and was good at it too. In between school and activities, my years would be intertwined with fundraising at Doheny. Then one day in 1994, with my Communications degree in hand, Lee had a position open up in her office and she asked me if I'd like to become a full time employee. Yes please! I was sure that my Dad had something to do with that decision, but when I told him about it, he didn't even know I was a candidate. It was then that I knew I had earned the job without his assistance, on the merit of my own work and I readily accepted.

Sometimes we move so fast that we miss important and significant road signs. It is only in retrospect that I recognize Good In Deed®'s mission began right there, even though it did not fully form until two decades later.

THE WORKS OF GOOD IN DEED®

Every now and then all the little streams in our life, seemingly unconnected, merge into a raging river of purpose.

In 2006, we were living in a family-friendly neighborhood in Orange County, and I had just watched *"The Secret,"* a film about setting a specific vision for your life and then claiming it. Starting with those seminal days at Doheny, I had always dreamed of founding my own charitable organization and this film was the ultimate green light to go after that dream. My nearly twenty years in non-profit and charitable work would be the blueprint to do this. I wanted my company to look different than all others. I envisioned a company that would widen and enrich the circle of givers and receivers. With the vision, the foundation, the Advisory Board and the roadmap in place, *Good In Deed®* began its grassroots works in 2006 and would receive an officially registered trademark on March 11, 2014, its official birthday!

During my career in fundraising, I saw a trend. Many notable charities in a community would hold a fundraiser and those who could afford to buy tables or tickets attended. This classic model can work well, and a lot of good happens because of these events. It just wasn't the road Good In Deed® needed to take.

The question we asked ourselves was this: *Would we rather have ten people give a thousand dollars each or would we rather have two thousand people give five dollars each?* For us, the answer was clear, and we intentionally set up our organization on the good deeds of the average person. If someone could not afford a ticket or table, we wanted to show them the vast opportunities to support good works in the world of charity. To us, every person can be "wealthy" to the extent that they are able to help others and change lives. Their "wealth" can be shared through dollars, talent and time, as long as they know about the endless ways to share it.

So we decided to create an online portal that would inform and connect people with opportunities to help charities. We wanted to be the matchmaker for good works and to become the "global site for giving." Our online structure involves and requires plenty of research and effort. I personally spend most of my time researching the needs of organizations and individuals that I read about or hear about. We then alert the community about those needs via our website, newsletter, and social media platforms. Each day we need to balance the mission for those in need while not being too aggressive with potential supporters.

The result: the work of *Good In Deed®* is not passive but rather active, engaged and alive in the community. It is action that inevitably touches the lives of all who participate in both giving and receiving. People may not always recognize how they can participate and it is our mandate to provide opportunities for every person to become an agent for change. Our job includes being the matchmaker for a need, sounding the alarm for help, and mobilizing the community to do good. These are not actions we have to do; these are actions we get to do. It's a privilege.

THE FRUITS OF GOOD IN DEED®: A SITE TO SERVE, A HUB TO HELP, A PORTAL WITH A PURPOSE, A CAUSE FOR ALL CAUSES

More people are willing to give than we often recognize.

"It is more blessed to give than to receive." We found this statement to be absolutely true. We have also found a great willingness by people to give, if you just have the fortitude to ASK. People are generous and kind at heart; they just need to be nudged, nurtured, and equipped to give. It is this group of people that *Good In Deed®* is seeking: our congregation, if you will, to do good.

We have built a website called GoodInDeed.com and have several social media platforms set up. Our website includes several "Community" webpages listing ways to do good, blogs of do-good stories, testimonials, our mission and much more. We do our best to share the joy in the faces and hearts of those being served. There are testimonials, like this one:

> *MotelChurch is an all-volunteer organization that plants churches in rundown weekly motels to bring hope to the people living there. Every weekend people living in those motels come to the parking lot where MotelChurch volunteers provide a warm breakfast, encouragement and friendship. We first heard about Good In Deed® from one of our volunteers who was familiar with their work. After a few emails with Kelly and Amy it was obvious that they and the Good In Deed® organization were pretty amazing. We asked for their help in producing our annual Thanksgiving brunch, which brings a wonderful Thanksgiving feast to people living in motels around Southern California. Our goal was 70 turkeys, which would allow us to serve all of the motels where we served. Good In Deed® graciously sent out a wonderful email to their donors and within a week or two we were blown away – they had hit the goal. When we received the checks we could only marvel at the gift they were providing to the homeless and working poor people struggling to survive in small motel rooms. Having a regular meal on any day is a blessing for so many people. But, getting a full-blown Thanksgiving meal with roast turkey, mashed potatoes and gravy, veggies and even pumpkin pie – well, for many people they suddenly felt like they were no longer stranded in a motel with strangers, they were home among family. Thanks to Kelly, Amy, Good In Deed®, and their many donors who gave so selflessly so that the less fortunate among us could have a great Thanksgiving! You are living examples that we are not supposed to just say that we care about others, we are supposed to do something about it.*

And, this:

> *Project Hope Alliance is ending the cycle of homelessness, one child at a time, right here in Orange County. Kelly contacted us in August of 2015 to ask how she could help. At the time we were launching a new pilot program for our kids called Bright Start, and were in need of art supplies for 19 of our volunteer mentors to use in mentoring our children. Her response was, "Would you accept a check to go towards these needs?" and "When would you like it?" This response was amazing for me to hear! Then in November,*

she contacted us again to inquire what kind of funding we might need for our holiday events. We throw a Cookies with Santa party for the families we serve where Santa comes to read a story and pass out gifts for each child. Kelly not only provided the funding for all of the gifts, she surpassed the goal. At every turn, Kelly has been able to meet our needs with an enthusiasm and dedication of which every non-profit dreams. She has quickly become an ardent supporter of Project Hope Alliance and continues to further our mission through her hard work.

We are grateful for and humbled by success stories like these. They emphasize an undeniable truth: in spite of great wealth existing in our world, our country and in our communities, the needs are enormous. We keep working on ways to spread the word to do good to a wider audience.

Looking forward on our roadmap, we have developed a plan for a *Good In Deed*® app that would allow people to easily discover lists of ways to do good. This is a costly and intensive part of our road to success; however, we believe that it will exponentially increase our global impact. The needed funding, time and dedication is worth it. The *Good In Deed*® app is a critical task on our to-do list, and we are committed to its completion.

Another action on our continued road to success is to bring *Good In Deed*® stories to a broader audience. By compiling a book and publishing it, we hope to inspire others to do good. The idea is not to pat ourselves on the back for all that we have accomplished, but rather to encourage and spur on others to do the same in their communities. Stories are powerful: they allow us to see what's possible and what can be achieved. We relate to stories and often think, *if they can do it, I can too.* A book that helps someone see their vital role in the lives of others is indeed a powerful secret to their own success.

Additionally, we envision *Good In Deed*® chapters around the world, a network of life-changing do-gooders. This network would collectively:

- Collaborate on what has worked for givers and receivers;
- Identify causes and donors for those causes;
- Solve problems within communities across the globe;
- Bless more people in need;

- Multiply givers to receivers;
- Share inspirational stories of changed lives.

After a lifetime in charitable work, I personally am still visualizing what's next, *Good In Deed*® 2.0, 3.0 and on! I see these visions as sure road signs that I am exactly where I am supposed to be; my assigned seat in my car of life, if you will. When I drive by people without homes and warm coats, I want to step up. When I see a person who has slipped through the cracks of society and needs a helping hand, it is clear my work is not done. I believe everyone has the right to food, clothing, and shelter. My work over these many years shows me there are so many who have very little or none of that basic trio that so many of us take for granted.

Until this is resolved, I have work to do. We all do.

When people see or hear about devastation, they sometimes think to themselves, "What can one person really do? What can I really do?" From what we see every day, the answer lies in an individual action which then spurs on collective action. Good deeds, no matter how small or large, are truly transformational for the receiver and the giver. We continue to move purposefully on the road before us that is full of these opportunities to do good. We stand ready to make a difference as instigators, encouragers and servants.

And that is good. *Good In Deed*®.

About Kelly

Kelly Smith Parker has a big idea, and she's not intimidated by what it's going to take to accomplish it. "If someone isn't laughing at your dreams, then your dreams just aren't big enough," she says.

Born in San Francisco, California, to an ophthalmologist father and a pediatrician mother, Kelly has always been a doer, seeking to better the lives of others, as her parents did, through their professions. From the age of sixteen, she has been deeply involved in all aspects of charitable work, always with the end desire to change lives through her efforts. She is a graduate of the University of Southern California, and her professional career includes Senior Development Officer positions at Doheny Eye Institute in Los Angeles and The Harker School in San Jose.

In 2014, she launched her online philanthropic organization, *Good In Deed®*, and for the past two years she has been working tirelessly to meet the philanthropic needs of those in her community and beyond. Her dream of turning *Good In Deed®* (**www.GoodInDeed.com**) into the "global site for giving" and becoming a ubiquitous force for good in our world is progressing nicely. The #DoGoodInDeed community is changing the world's landscape through its actions—doing good deed by good deed along the way. She is certain that she is exactly where she needs to be, and she is persevering fearlessly and passionately, moving forward with purpose in every step taken to make this dream a global reality.

In her message of inspired action, Kelly says, "I believe everyone should have access to food, clothing, and shelter. But my work every day tells me that so many among us still do not have access to those three fundamental things that most of us take for granted. I want to change that. And do so much more."

Today, Kelly lives in Orange County, California with her husband, John, and their two sons, Cole and Austin. Outside of her mission to do good in this world, she also enjoys baking, exercising, hiking, paragliding, parasailing, snow skiing, snowshoeing, traveling, and zip lining. Kelly is philanthropic with her personal time, as well, by volunteering at her sons' school, in her community, and at her church.

You can connect with Kelly at:

- Kelly@GoodInDeed.com
- www.GoodInDeed.com
- www.twitter.com/DoGoodInDeed
- www.instragram.com/DoGoodInDeed
- www.facebook.com/DoGoodInDeed

CHAPTER 20

I AM HAPPY

– HOW I CHANGED MY MIND AND FOUND SUCCESS, WEALTH, HEALTH AND HAPPINESS!

BY CRAIG HAGEN

There is a crack in everything, that's how the light gets in.
~ Leonard Cohen

Nineteen years ago, a light as bright as the sun appeared through a crack in the wall I'd built to keep the real me hidden from the world. For decades, I'd put tremendous effort into making sure people didn't see the real me. My wall became stronger as the real me became weaker.

But then the light that had shone through that crack shattered my wall, and I was able to live the life I have today as the real me. By the time I was 32 years old, my wall's exterior displayed a character who was happy, confident and successful; a man married to a beautiful, intelligent woman; a man destined to be a Congressman, Senator or Governor. But that wasn't the real me.

On the inside of my wall was the *real* me; terrified I would someday be revealed for *who I am.* From inside that wall, I saw no way out. I was trapped. My light had dimmed to where I'd thought of extinguishing it myself. I thought of ending it all. Ending the acting. Ending the pretending. Ending my life. Fortunately, and I mean very fortunately, that beautiful, intelligent woman had the courage to do something. She saved my life. She divorced me.

She cracked my wall.

Of course, I was devastated. It was the end of my performance. I thought for sure everyone I knew would reject me because of *who I was, who I am.* I had no idea where to turn. I had no idea what to do.

A few weeks later, a beautiful light began to flow and shatter the wall for good.

I was in Northern Norway, above the Arctic Circle, attending my best friend's wedding. I had just witnessed this most beautiful expression of love and happiness in their marriage ceremony. I was standing on the shores of the North Sea around midnight, the waters and sky illuminated by the midnight sun. It was a view of nature unparalleled in its beauty. It was simply breathtaking. The night sky looked like anything other than the night sky. It was hazy and slightly orange from the glow of the sun that would never entirely disappear on the horizon. Light shimmered on the surface of the water. The air was charged with electricity so powerful it felt like time stood still. The beauty all around me captivated me and *I felt a part of it.* I felt an energetic connection, as though the beauty I saw before me was also inside of me. At that moment I knew the beauty I saw before me was inside of me. It was *the real me*, the true me.

I felt elated and peaceful at the same time. I knew I would never find happiness - true happiness or anything else I wanted - by living a life based on what others thought of me. That is when I accepted who I was. I loved myself for *who I was, who I am.* I knew then I, too, would have the happiness and the love my friend and his wife had. All I had to do was accept me for me, change how I thought about myself and love myself. As I did this, my light began to burn brighter.

When I returned home from Norway, I returned as the real *Craig*; not Craig the actor, the politician, the performer, the perfect boy, but the real me. I was working on accepting myself and loving myself, and was committed to being the best me; the real me; the "me" who is a proud, gay man.

I've spent the last two decades on the journey of loving myself and it has made all the difference in my happiness. As I've accepted and loved myself, my light has grown stronger and brighter and clearer, and now it is my privilege to share that light with you.

Do you ever look back on a part of your life and wonder, 'Who was that? I can't believe that was me. I can't believe I said that or did that.' I look back on the first thirty years of my life that way.

For some time, I felt guilty about those years. I felt guilty and ashamed of who I was or, rather, who I thought I should be, trapped behind my own wall. Not anymore. Today, I know I came into this life for the very experience of living those years and learning those lessons in order to live my life more fully than I ever dreamed possible.

Despite my best efforts to fortify the wall protecting me, that crack appeared and, although, at the time I was devastated and mortified, I can now look back on that moment as a great gift, a turning point in discovering my true self.

There were cracks that appeared before this time, but I didn't recognize them. It's often said of miracles that it isn't until after they've happened that one can see them. Today, I know miracles are happening all the time. I expect them to happen and, most importantly, I know I have the power to see them and so do you!

CHOOSING HAPPINESS INSTEAD OF CHASING HAPPINESS

Your thoughts are powerful. Choosing to embrace those thoughts that positively reinforce whatever it is you desire—to be happy, no matter where you are, no matter what's going on—can change your life. When a crack appears and the light shines through, embrace happiness and become the most powerful person in your life.

Our power to be happy is within us all the time, even when we're unaware of its existence. Our power to be happy—to do, be or have anything we want—exists in the thoughts we think.

Happiness doesn't come from anyone or anything outside of you. To find your happiness, you have to reclaim your power from whomever or whatever you've allowed to lay claim to it: your parents, your boss, your job, your school, your government, your church; whomever it is that told you something about yourself or how to live your life that simply doesn't make you happy.

Who have you given your power to? Does your job have your power? Are your efforts focused on doing things you don't like to do; things that don't inspire you or make you happy; or, even worse, things that make you feel physically or emotionally ill?

Does an intimate relationship have your power? Are you staying in a relationship where the love is gone? Are you staying married for the sake of the kids, or in an abusive situation? Does society have your power? Are you critical of yourself, the way you look, your body, your weight because you're not a cover model or actor or actress?

What about money, does money have your power? Do you believe there is never enough or that it goes out as fast as it comes in?

On any subject, do you have thoughts that are causing you to feel anything but good? What thoughts make you feel stressed, angry, jealous, bad? Do you generally look outside yourself for the cause of these feelings? Is it because of what someone said or did?

Whenever you look outside yourself for the cause of how you feel, you give your power away and you become a victim. If you want to be happy, to be successful, to do, be or have anything you want, then you have to accept responsibility that you are responsible for your thoughts and the feelings you choose to have about those thoughts.

Here are four easy steps to happiness, success, wealth and health – the four steps to be, do or have anything you want.

We have already established that you must accept responsibility for your thoughts and how you feel. Find a quiet place, someplace where you won't be disturbed. Take a deep breath and relax. Take a couple more deep breaths; connect with how your body feels; if you feel tightness anywhere in it take another deep breath and, as you exhale, feel those muscles relax.

When you feel as relaxed as you can, when you feel calm, begin these four steps.

Step 1. Take an inventory of your thoughts

Examine your thoughts on subjects important to you. When you think about these subjects, do you have positive or negative thoughts? Do you feel good or bad? As you do this, don't judge your thoughts and feelings, simply observe them. What are your thoughts about some of these subjects: money, career, health, relationships or others?

Step 2. Identify the underlying beliefs

Many people think beliefs come from experiences. However, they are the products of your thoughts. As Abraham-Hicks says, "A belief is a thought you keep thinking." The thoughts and beliefs to which you hold most tightly—those you feel the strongest about, and think and talk about often with a great deal of passion—bring about the experiences in your life. In other words, you get what you think about, whether you want it or not. What are some underlying belief patterns supporting the thoughts you think?

I'll give you an example. Growing up in my family, my father was fond of saying, "Money goes out as fast as it comes in." The reality was, in fact, that it did. Every time my dad made some money, there was an expense that appeared as if from nowhere. When I was in my early 30's, I was making $100k a year and yet I had no money. One day, while agonizing over paying bills and the balance in my checking account, I heard my dad's voice, "Money goes out as fast as it comes in." I realized I'd subconsciously created a belief system about money that was creating my reality. At that moment, I took responsibility. First, I acknowledged, and was deeply thankful for the money I did have. I earned a lot of money and I was thankful for that. Secondly, I vowed to remind myself of that every day, multiple times a day. Every time I was going to spend money, talk about money or think about money, bills or expenses, I thought about how blessed I was with an abundant paycheck, even when there were more bills than income. That began a pattern of thought and affirmations that very quickly changed my finances from debt to prosperity.

Step 3. Create new thoughts

Have you ever wondered why you think the thoughts you do? A citation from the National Science Foundation suggests 12,000 to 50,000 thoughts per day. Even more daunting is research that suggests 95% – 98% of those thoughts are the same ones we had the day before.

When we don't understand that our thoughts are our own and nobody else's, we tend to look outside ourselves for the cause that defines how we're feeling or what's happening in our life. If we're not happy, we especially want to blame someone or something for the way we feel. This is how we give our power away.

I don't just mean literally; I also mean figuratively and unconsciously. When we accept, without making a conscious choice, those rules that parents, church and society are famous for proclaiming, we give our power away.

In addition, if we do think the same thoughts day after day, then we have a deep well of pre-programmed concepts about ourselves that are constantly, and unconsciously, running through our thoughts. These thoughts can tend to be negative and, therefore, don't contribute to our happiness and well-being.

So, how do you change them? First, by becoming aware of them and, second, by choosing positive thoughts that reinforce what you want in your life.

One of the easiest and most effective ways to do this is by creating affirmations. Affirmations are conscious thoughts you choose to positively reinforce what it is you want to do, be or have. Thoughts like, "I am happy;" "I am blessed with an abundance of money;" "I am well;" "I am surrounded by loving people;" are all affirmations that, when consistently chosen, create a belief system that will bring about the experiences you want in your life.

Step 4. Pay attention to your emotions

Throughout this chapter, I have mentioned feelings. I use the term here synonymously with emotions. Many people believe feelings or emotions are the result of something that occurs outside of us. In reality, they're the result of something we think. They are a gift. They tell us how we're doing in life. When they're positive, they reinforce the thoughts, beliefs and actions we're taking in pursuit of those experiences we want to have in our life.

Pay attention to your emotions because they are the indicator of how you're thinking. When you feel bad, it's an indication you should choose a better feeling thought about the subject. Emotions are not responses to external stimuli they are the result of the thoughts you choose to think about a particular subject. When your emotions are negative that's your indication you are thinking thoughts about that subject that are taking you away from your happiness.

CONCLUSION

When the cracks appear and light begins to shine through, you will see the path toward living your true life. CHOOSE THE THOUGHTS AND BELIEFS that create a life in which you can be, do or have anything you want.

About Craig

Craig Hagen grew up on a cattle ranch in North Dakota knowing his future would be anything but ordinary. His journey became extraordinary in 1990, when he became the youngest person in the United States ever elected to a state's Executive Branch. The front page of *USA Today* declared he had "beaten the father of North Dakota." Craig's no stranger to doing what others said couldn't be done.

After eight years in elected office, Craig entered the private sector, creating a successful career in senior management at two of the world's most recognized Fortune 500 companies, AOL Inc. and Electronic Arts Inc., the popular video game company. Craig currently serves as the Global Head of Government Affairs for Electronic Arts.

Through all of the challenges and opportunities he's experienced through the years, Craig has learned that the path to success, wealth and happiness is determined by what you think and believe, more than where you went to school or who you work for.

This philosophy has led him to study meditation, energy medicine and energy psychology with some of the world's foremost experts. He advocates that your thoughts impact everything, from your relationships to your income to your physical health. Learning and applying his ideas will enable profound change.

After speaking to large and small audiences and working with individuals, he has helped others realize that their ability to do, be or have anything they want begins and ends in their mind. His strategy for success is about the thoughts you think, your emotions and taking action, and it works as well in the living room as it does the boardroom.

Contact Craig about a speaking engagement or working together by emailing him at craig@craighagen.com or calling 954-560-5228.

Craig, his husband Ben Arvizo and their furry, four-legged children, Saka and Jericho, live loving and peaceful lives in their homes in Florida and Nevada.

CHAPTER 21

A SUCCESSFUL BUSINESS DEVELOPMENT PROGRAM

BY CHRISTINE SPRAY

Vision is the art of seeing what is invisible to others.
~ Jonathon Swift

Our life experiences often frame our story and our path to success. For me, that meant growing up without a father. He passed away before I was born and the lessons that I may have learned from him never came to be. Fortunately, my ability to recognize what I did have to work with and develop within myself to make the best out of everything, is something I'm eternally thankful for recognizing.

From an early age, I had a strong ambition to be the best at whatever I did. That desire helped me with my performance in sports and on the job. Everything interested me and I loved to learn, absorbing wisdom from managers and actively seeking out ways to learn about business from every angle. The words of one of my boss's drove me: "Get out of marketing and into business development; marketing is a cost center and the first thing to get cut when times get tough. By being good at business development, you'll always have a job, make plenty of money, and be a profit center for the company." I took that advice to heart, being promoted to management by my early 20s as I was paying my way through eight years of college. I gained insight and experience with the many hats I wore, including marketing, sales, business development, human resources, operations, finance, and most importantly—the golden nugget—how to generate revenue.

Today, so many businesses are missing the business development process that leads to increasing revenue. If a rainmaker leaves or retires, the business often does not have either the people or processes in place to develop other personnel into those coveted rainmakers. New business is developed by building relationships with current clients, new clients, centers of influence, vendors, partners, and organizations. Business development activities could include public speaking, serving on boards, targeting specific businesses and industries, executive cold calling and strategically networking. Developing a program that fosters both business development activities and accountability among key professionals provides the platform for professional service firm's growth and success.

Create caring and robust connections between every employee and their work, customers, leaders, managers, and the organization to achieve results that matter to everyone in this sentence.
~ David Zinger

INCREASE REVENUE PROGRAM™

The Increase Revenue Program™ is a model that can be used in-house across diverse industries and factors in each employee's unique ability as valuable assets to the organization. Many businesses find themselves in troublesome situations when it comes to revenue growth from just the slightest change in their organization. Perhaps the founding partner who brought clients into the business retires, or perhaps a great revenue generator moves on to another opportunity. Instead of these things creating chaos in a business, why not give the possible rainmakers in the business the processes they need to help them all have a role in generating revenue based on their personalities and strengths?

Companies can increase their organization's revenue by:

- Identifying Dangers: lack of time, focus and a plan
- Capturing Opportunities: increase revenue, market share and awareness
- Maximizing Strengths: knowledge, talent, and reputation (internally and externally)

With the **Increase Revenue Program™**, companies can professionally develop their people and organization to maximize revenue opportunities.

How to Create Value	Description	How it Creates Value	Proof of Commitment	Deliverable
I. Individual Revenue Assessment™	50 Question interview with each person responsible for developing new business	Benchmark for the individual and organization about what is taking place currently and uncover areas of opportunity for new business	Meeting with management team	Summary of action items from individual meetings, completed assessments, six month training program with topics identified
II. Business Process Review™	Power Point presentation understanding the five drivers of growth	People recognize the role they play in each of the five drivers	People become champions of each driver	Champions create committees and action strategies for implementation
III. Business Development Program™	Monthly group training and one-to-one coaching	People receive tools and resources to implement immediately in their day to day business	People realize and recognize the return and rewards of their new activities and the way they build relationships	The people and organization are focused more on generating business faster with accountability
A. Proven Business Development Tools	Interactive exercises, handouts and examples on proven tips that work	People can implement the tools and resources immediately	Deeper relationships are formed with clients, prospects and referral sources	Increased revenue from new business, from existing clients and centers of influence
B. Action Strategy Model™	Document with business development action strategies	New business development activities	Metrics and commitments are established	Action strategies are tracked and reported regularly

How to Create Value	**Description**	**How it Creates Value**	**Proof of Commitment**	**Deliverable**
C. Accountability Partner Plan™	Information for serving as an accountability partner	Each person is responsible for ensuring the other person is making progress	Bonding, energy and success is created among each team	Internal support with a vested interest in progress and success
D. Activity Tracking Model™	Excel spreadsheet with new business development activities identified	Creates momentum, accountability and competition peer-to-peer and firm-wide	People report at the monthly meeting what worked, what surprised them, what they learned and successes	A tool that identifies, tracks and serves as an accountability tool for building an effective pipeline
E. Revenue Tracking Model™	Spreadsheet with new business opportunities identified	Creates momentum, accountability and competition peer-to-peer and firm-wide	People report the leads in their pipeline	A tool that tracks new opportunities in the pipeline and related revenue
IV. Committee for Growth™	Internal group focused on new business development	Group meets monthly to discuss action strategies, processes; builds momentum and accountability	People look forward to meeting; track activities and leads, report on accomplishments	People see, hear and recognize that their success is tied to their activities; they learn from each other
V. Personalized Strategic Plans	Document used to create short-term and long-term goals	Creates daily, monthly, quarterly, annually, three-year and five-year goal setting	Action strategies are created in each of the goal sections by and with each person	Each person has a plan that is created by them; they have immediate buy-in and responsibility to meet their goals

How to Create Value	Description	How it Creates Value	Proof of Commitment	Deliverable
VI. Employee Ownership Model™	Investment in people, plans, training, goals, and professional development	Empowerment, rapport, trust and support	Excitement, energy, verbal and actions are more open about business development	The firm is helping each person identify and reach their goal; people buy-in and think more like owners
VII. Long-Term Growth Plan	Strategic individual plans and group training	Camaraderie and buy-in	Interest and willingness to learn more	Increased revenue per person; increased revenue per practice area and increased total revenue for the organization; established rainmakers on the team; employee retention

By nature, people want to make contributions to help them grow as a person and lend value to their work environment. It's when they don't know the process on how to add value, particularly revenue generating value that they give up. Through the model, the path from a technical service provider to a more immersed interest in business development with success can become a tangible reality. The model works for people, whether they are shy, analytical, outgoing, or creative.

BUILDING A BUSINESS DEVELOPMENT PROGRAM

"Employees are a company's greatest asset—they're your competitive advantage. You want to attract and retain the best; provide them with encouragement, stimulus, and make them feel that they are an integral part of the company's mission."

~ Ann M. Mulcahy

When the goal is to help a business maximize their revenue-generating potential, it is important to give a clearly defined answer to what business development is, exactly. Business development includes:

- Meeting assigned sales goals for bringing in new business to the organization.
- Conducting personal lead generation activities as required to fill the pipeline with new name opportunities and attain sales quotas, including cold calling, seminar or trade show participation, and networking in the local community.
- Developing and maintaining required expertise in assigned services and products to independently qualify prospects for appropriateness of fit.
- Managing the sales process, which includes developing, qualifying, and managing all prospects through the sales cycle.
- Generating and qualifying sales leads and then meeting with prospects.
- Bringing appropriate colleagues with more expertise and specialized knowledge into the sales process at the appropriate points.
- Providing specific information for proposals to be generated by the sales person, including completing prospect information, engaging and servicing detailed, and any special terms and conditions.
- Maintaining pipeline and forecast information, as well as prospect contact information and status in the organization's contact management database.
- Responding to requests for information from prospects with appropriate documentation, using the sales person when available and appropriate.
- Transitioning closed engagements to the appropriate person.

Coming together is a beginning; keeping together is progress;
working together is success.
~ Henry Ford

When I look back on it all, I'm grateful for those words of wisdom from that manager long ago that showed me that marketing and business development were two distinctly different things, one expendable and one meant to be sustainable. As life's experiences have helped lay out this wonderful process that has been so effective for such a wide range of businesses, I take such great joy away from what I do for businesses day-in and day-out. It never gets old, because people are originals who can do great things if they're given the best tools to succeed.

Business development is about building relationships, not selling products or services. There is a strategy to success and building one relationship at a time is where it starts. When we think of our own lives and the businesses we choose to give our patronage to, we tend to be drawn to and motivated by positive relationships that are rooted with authentic individuals contributing to their business's success, therefore their own success. It's a joy to help people develop this mindset through the business development process and the results are the true benchmark of success.

About Christine

Christine Spray is a nationally-recognized business development keynote speaker, best-selling author, consultant, trainer, coach and Professional EOS Implementer. Christine serves as a CEO and business advisor with a passion for helping people and companies grow.

Best-Selling Author with Steve Forbes: ***SuccessOnomics - Doing Business in Today's Economy*** Best-Selling Lists and Rankings: #1 Direct Marketing, #4 Marketing, #5 Marketing & Sales, #11 Entrepreneurship, #12 Small Business and Entrepreneurship, and #91 Business & Money

Best-Selling Author with Brian Tracy: ***Transform - Your Life, Business & Health*** Best-Selling Lists and Rankings: #6 Direct Marketing, #13 Marketing for Small Business

Founder & President – Strategic Catalyst, Inc.
Christine Spray launched Strategic Catalyst, Inc. after working in public accounting and industry in senior leadership roles with start-up, restructuring and growth responsibilities. She recognized that by aligning business goals with marketing, human resource and business development strategies, organizations could leverage new business opportunities for far greater results. With more than 20 years of experience, Spray has created proven programs for management in the area of new business strategy by implementing Revenue Growth Assessments, Business Development Programs, Strategic Business Development Plans, and Accountability Models. Spray is a graduate of Coach University's Two Year Program and EOS Worldwide.

Founder & President – National Business Development Association
Christine Spray launched the National Business Development Association (NBDA) to fill the need for a national trade association to provide best practices to individuals whose primary responsibility is generating business for their organization. NBDA provides a vibrant learning community where members can stay on top of industry trends and continually hone their skills through targeted professional development. Members of NBDA strongly believe in order to be a successful business development professional, you must focus on others and their needs before focusing on yourself. You will find this philosophy at the center of everything that is taught at the NBDA.

Master Chair & National Speaker – Vistage International
Christine Spray serves as Chair and National Speaker for Vistage International, the world's leading chief executive organization; its affiliates have more than 16,000 members in 16 countries. In her leadership role, she leads C-level executive discussions to help companies implement more efficient processes and programs that reduce costs, increase profitability and foster enhanced growth.

Spray enjoys giving back to the community where she serves and has served in the following roles:

- Founder and President, National Business Development Association
- Former Chair, Women Energy Network's Advisory Council and Executive Group
- Former Board Member, Women Energy Network
- Former Committee Chair, Emerging Women Leaders Greater Houston Partnership
- Former Committee Chair, University of Houston Alumni
- Former President, Association for Accounting Marketing
- Former Co-Chair, Kay Bailey Hutchison Texas Governor Race
- Former Nominating Chair, Leadership Council American Lung Association
- Former Board Member, Houston Health Charities of Texas
- Former Board Member, Houston Strategic Forum
- Former Board Member, MIT Enterprise Forum
- Former Board Member, YMCA Camping Services
- Former Delegate, American Society of Women Accountants
- Former Chairman, Small Business Committee GSWCC
- Former Co-Chair, Shaker Committee GSWCC

Spray has been recognized for the following:

- Houston Hero Award,Houston's Entrepreneurial Independence & Leadership
- 50 Most Influential Women, Houston Women Magazine
- Rookie of the Year, Vistage International
- Chair Excellence Award, Vistage International (3 years)
- Entrepreneur of the Year, Houston Technology Center
- Top Ambassador, Greater Houston Partnership
- Lifetime Member, Greater Houston Partnership

CHAPTER 22

HOW TO RECOGNIZE AND REMOVE SUCCESS BARRIERS

BY DR. TAMIERA HARRIS

REMOVING SUCCESS BARRIERS

Often times we wait until something bad comes up before we try to fix the issue. If you are doing it this way, then you are not working smart. As a Researcher and Project Manager, I was trained to build-in mitigation strategies to identify risks early so we can put the best solution in action in a timely manner to avoid missing timelines or important milestones. This completely goes against my think positive mantra, but it works for one specific reason. Although you are considering what's the worst that can happen; you are also confidently putting forth solutions to address those concerns so you can achieve the goals you set forth.

As an Entrepreneur and Business Owner, I have had to sit down and write out how I would overcome some of the barriers I faced when it came to resources, time management and completing projects, all while trying to stay positive and keep the faith. I am a fighter when it comes to my goals and like the great Muhammad Ali, you won't take me down easily. In fact, you won't take me down at all. When my back is up against the ropes, I am using that rope for support; I am observing the situation and planning my comeback. There is less emphasis on the barrier in front of me but more focus on how I will get past it and come out victorious.

FIX YOUR ATTITUDE AND IMPROVE YOUR BUSINESS

Your attitude has a significant effect on the outcome of a situation and can make any aspect of your life more difficult than it may already be. In life, attitude is everything since it will not only dictate the mood you are in but also affects those around you. Any attempts you make to become sucessful are greatly influenced by your frame of mind. Your mindset has the capabilities to alter your performance for better or worse. Whether you're running a business or working for an employer, it's important to put your best face forward so you can create a peaceful, collaborative work environment.

We are the masters of our own destiny. Therefore, we need to hold ourselves accountable for whatever happens in our life. Today is the outcome of what we did yesterday, and tomorrow will be the outcome of what we are doing today. This is the kind of thinking that successful people use to take control of the situation. It's positive thinking and it requires being proactive in order to achieve the kind of results you expect.

FEAR CREATES NEGATIVE THINKING

When most people approach goals or projects they are cautious. Some are dealing with trust issues, while others are contemplating what to do next and if it's all worth it. It is too easy to stay in our comfort zone, so we have to learn how to break through some of doubts that cloud our mind. For example, you put two investors in a room and one might say that now is a terrible time to buy real estate properties based on the market trending in the sellers favor. While those who are willing to take the risk might say that now is the best time to buy because of that same reason. It is all in the way you think and how you process information. Are you just talking, throwing out statements, or do you have real historical data to suggest one way or the other is better when making business moves?

Whether it is the fear of the unknown, success or failure; that emotion has the ability to prevent you from acting in a logical or beneficial way. This fear could be something that has been instilled in you since childhood, making it difficult to recognize since it has become a 'part' of you over your lifetime. Remember emotions are just that and often they impede our ability to think clearly or intelligently. When it comes to running a business, you have to believe in what you have determined to be the best course of action for your goals and be confident in your decisions as you share that information with people. Manage your goals like a project that is time-specific and helps you remain accountable for the actions you set forth.

THREE STEPS TO ELIMINATE NEGATIVE THOUGHTS

1. Stop attaching too many thoughts to negative outcomes without proper planning of risks and solutions.
2. Develop a strong belief system that no barrier in this world can stop you from achieving your goals.
3. If the outcome turns out to be different than you expected, firmly believe that God has something better planned for you. Just call it a Spiritual Intervention.

Another strategy I use to eliminate negative thinking is to work out my plans backwards. Once you have your business or any goal written down, then you will break it down further until you get to the first step. This is a great process since it helps you envision your goal as if you already achieved it and then breaks down all the steps or milestones needed to make that happen. This is a great motivational strategy since some people will take years to complete their goals, which is ok, but you can decrease the time it takes to complete your goals by simply using strategic practices to manage the goal-like project milestones. This is how I complete my goals faster. In the next section I discuss these efficiencies that I have implemented and how I use them to manage my goals, teams and clients.

BUSINESS MANAGEMENT EFFICIENCIES

This might be the most valuable piece of advice you get, in any type of economic times, good or bad. Efficiency is the key to success and helps to manage costs. Every dollar spent needs to be accounted for and every action taken should have a documented result. This applies to every facet of your business, from the recruiting and hiring of new employees to the final distribution of your product or services. When recruiting, use on-demand recruiting software to be more efficient. During the hiring screening phase, streamline the interview process and screen resumes more thoroughly. Check all references and make sure that the applicant you are about to hire is who they say they are and actually can perform what they are assigned to do by incorporating performance reviews.

One of the best ways to run a company stress free and with high quality outcomes is to make sure everyone has a specific job. In a perfect world, everyone will do that job to the best of their ability and things will run smoothly. Unfortunately, although this is a great efficiency, it is still not perfect. Cross training your employees so someone can step in when an employee is unable to perform the assigned tasks is necessary. This is also a great way to mitigate staffing issues and to avoid quality issues in other areas of your business. You don't want to have overlapping responsibilities, but you also don't want lost production or missed business opportunities. Make sure when you enter a new employee into your job applicant tracking system, that you list additional skills which can be helpful to your company. They may come in handy when you're in a pinch and need to do more with fewer people.

MANAGE YOUR GOALS LIKE A PROJECT

1. **Develop positive relationships with key Stakeholders.**
2. **Face the Client and manage the Team.**
3. **Do your research and evaluate the competition.**
4. **Define the process and follow the defined process.**
5. **Enhance your expertise through continuing education and workshops.**

To keep your projects running smoothly and on schedule, look to these best practices listed above which can be related to any business. Do you want to walk in the office with a smile when working with a client or customer or would you allow your attitude determine the outcome of your day? The effort you put forth to develop a positive approach to work is a significant aspect of setting up positive relationships.

When it comes to managing clients or customers to avoid confusion, it is important that the central point of contact is one designated person or department. This could mean setting up a customer service department or having a project manager, coordinator or other assigned personnel that can manage stakeholders. While most roles are not expected to have a comprehensive understanding of every specialty within a business, cross training is necessary especially for small businesses.

When implementing goals, you will need to define the processes using specific guidelines. To avoid conflicts, it is best to define the project management methodology early, notating how the processes will be outlined to carry out the requirements needed to bring more goals to completion. Then you can make sure your entire team is able to complete tasks per the guidelines that were established for those goals.

The key to ongoing project management success is to insure your knowledge and skills are as comprehensive and current as possible. The best way to achieve ongoing success is through professional education or training. By undertaking training that is relevant to your work, you'll bring greater value to the business while increasing your expertise.

You can have greater success completing business milestones by putting in place a supporting plan and taking action to achieve those tasks. To aid in completing tasks, you could consider outsourcing some job functions to help reduce costs, but don't forget to take good care of any employees you might eliminate. Generous exit packages create goodwill and increase loyalty from those who remain.

WALKING BY FAITH

Education or finances alone will not help you reach the goal. Unless you believe in yourself, you will not be able to take the first steps towards embracing your next business venture or collaboration among your colleagues and peers. I believe that Christ is in me and he is greater than any obstacle. I can also do all things through Him who gives me strength. These are some positive affirmations I live by as I am creating my goals and completing projects.

As I walk down this road to success, I will not let fear creep into mind. I will speak confidently of my goals and dreams and will work hard to achieve them. Negative thinkers are not welcome in my space. They cannot travel where I am going because this journey is personal. I will be available to support those who support me and I will not be intimidated by someone else's success. We can all prosper and become the success we imagine if we can recognize and remove the barriers that we might face along the way.

Today, as you are reading this chapter, I want you to imagine that big goal. I want you to be honest with yourself and identify some issues or risks that might affect that big goal. Then I want you to write down how you will work around that obstacle. For every goal you write down today, I also want you to assign an action to it and a due date. Then I want you to write out the next actions in a sequential manner from the top, starting with your Big Goal, breaking it down to the first day you start working towards that goal. Keep these goals in clear sight and check them off as you achieve them. Instead of focusing on a specific date that you picked randomly, I want you to look at every step that is expected and plan realistic timelines.

We all have something that we are good at and can do that thing with no problem. This is where you want to become an expert and develop your niche. This chapter is meant for you to be able to sit down and get more done. I use these strategies to manage my jobs and businesses. If you are ready to take your business and brand to the next level, start assigning tasks and get your support system together to help you focus on completion. On the road to success I had to walk by faith. I had to believe that although I had never witnessed successful Entrepreneurs, Business Owners or Millionaires growing up, that I would be all those things. Do not let your situation become an obstacle to what you want to do in life. Dream big and take small steps towards your goals.

About Dr. Tamiera

Dr. Tamiera Harris helps her clients create the lifestyle they have imagined. Tamiera was raised by her grandmother and grew up in North Philadelphia. She was determined to be successful and used her education and go-getter mentality to climb the career ladder. Tamiera is professionally trained as a Researcher and Global Senior Project Manager with experience managing large Clinical Trials for Pharmaceutical companies. She completed her undergraduate degree at Villanova University and a MBA and PhD degree from Keller Graduate School of Management and Walden University.

While Tamiera was busy pursuing her education goals, 15 years ago she began helping clients move from entry level jobs to six-figure careers. It started out as a side hustle until she fell in love with the career services field and added it to her goals. Tamiera is the author of *Sparkle Girl: How to Make Money as an Entrepreneur When You're Broke*, a Career Coach and Motivational Speaker. Tamiera's coaching strategies are centered on her philosophy of dreaming big and taking small steps towards your goals. Tamiera's desire is to help her clients acquire generational wealth and financial literacy.

Dr. Tamiera Harris is the Founder and CEO of Black Career Coach™, a nonprofit organization that helps clients overcome obstacles in the workforce by providing strategies that promote career growth and development. Recently, Tamiera launched Sparkle Girl University. Under Sparkle Girl University, Tamiera teaches online courses where she educates women on setting up profitable businesses using many free or low-cost resources. She is also the owner of 'Styles by Sparkles'. 'Styles by Sparkles' mission is to help women unleash their inner sparkle. 'Styles by Sparkles' provide hair, clothing, shoes, jewelry, accessories and opportunities to make money from home as a Sparkle Girl Consultant. Tamiera is also the founder of 'Sparkle Girl Conference', which helps women emerge as experts in their fields by creating the platforms needed to gain experience, the resources to make money and the networks to grow their businesses.

As a first time adoptive mother, Tamiera launched 'Baby Sparkles Biz' which is owned by her daughter. Baby Sparkles mission is to educate and empower children to embrace their individuality and to go confidently after their dreams. Tamiera recently released a Christian book coauthored with Tamia called *Baby Sparkles Goes to Church*. It is designed to be an interactive book to spark dialogue between parents and their children as they learn about church, prayer and family traditions. Baby Sparkles Biz also provides Clothing, Shoes, Accessories, Natural Hair Baby Sparkles Doll, Books and Educational products.

Tamiera is married to an amazing man of God and is a Christian woman of strong faith and determination. She credits her success to God and her ability to remain positive when faced with difficult situations. Tamiera is following God's purpose for her life and has been successful in helping celebrities and thousands of people reach their career and business goals.

You can connect with Tamiera at:

- www.drtamierasharris.com
- www.blackcareercoach.org
- www.stylesbysparkles.com
- www.babysparkles.biz
- www.sparklegirlconference.com
- www.facebook.com/DrTamieraSHarris
- www.twitter.com/drtamieraharris

CHAPTER 23

LIMITLESS LIFE

BY JUDY KOSEDA

If you can tune into your purpose and really align with it, setting goals so that your vision is an expression of that purpose, then life flows much more easily.
~ Jack Canfield

I like to use the following analogy: Aligning with our highest purpose, making wise choices, being in the flow, living the Law of Attraction, experiencing true satisfying success beyond our simple comprehension of what is possible, is like tuning into our favorite radio station. If we want to have the perfect sound from our favorite station, we need to aim the dial just so; to the intended station to align with the frequency that will give us the results we want. The further away from our perfect station, the more RFI we will experience.

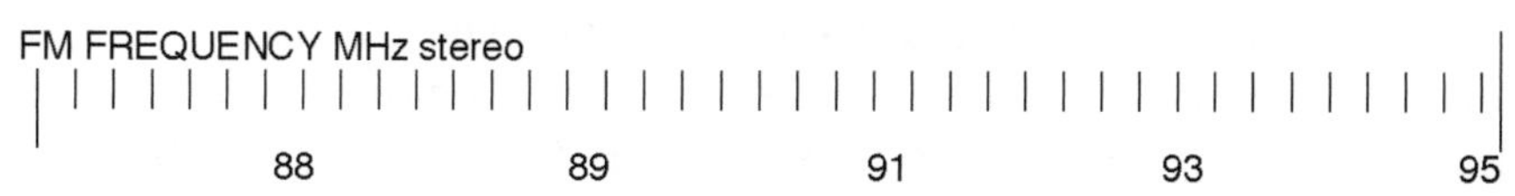

The further off we are vibrationally from our divine purpose, the more discomfort is experienced. Too far to the left, past RFI, beliefs, values, attitudes are in the way; too far to the right, future paced RFI in the form of negative thoughts, self talk. RFI are always blocks needing to be cleared. Aligning with our highest frequency we find ourselves in the resonance of pure potentiality.

The good news is the RFI in our lives is our High Self's way of letting us know we are out of vibrational alignment with our highest good. With awareness, we can then recognize the RFI for what it is, choose to let go of what no longer serves, and realign ourselves. This is the single most important thing we can do to accelerate toward success.

As a child, growing up with strict Catholic upbringing, I felt oppressed, misunderstood and alone. My inquisitive mind questioned everything including religious beliefs. Not as disrespect, but a genuine desire to understand. The nuns in school reported to my parents that I was impudent, my father, horrified at my questioning the church and religion, also rejected the 'evil' ability I had of knowing ahead of time what was going to happen. He often referred to me as a 'devil child'. Growing up I felt like a freak, and struggled with shame, doubt and confusion. I learned to keep to myself and pretend to be normal. I so longed for someone who was like me that I could talk to. I so wanted to understand.

We can judge our progress by the courage of our questions and the Depth of our answers, our willingness to embrace what is true rather than what feels good.
~ Carl Sagan

One rainy afternoon, the 7 year-old me, was hiding in my room, crying. Mum came into my room and asked why I was crying. I blurted out all of my feelings of shame, hurt, loneliness, through blubbering sobs. Wiping the tears from my eyes and taking me by the hand said, "Come with me." She led me into her bedroom and sat me on her bed. Pulling out a pretty box from the back of her dresser drawer, and put it on the bed between us, she opened the box, and made me promise that this was our secret, because dad wouldn't approve. She pulled out a book, and began to read to me. That book was *Cosmos* by Carl Sagan. I was in awe of those beautiful words. It was like coming home. The gift was a profound inner knowing that each of us in this beautiful 'Comos', is a unique and integral part of something far greater than individual self, and that each of us brings our own unique gift to the world.

Mum taught me to be independent as I child, that translated into keeping to myself. From an early age, I learned to be responsible for myself. I was driven to understand. I loved learning, studying what ever books I could get my hands on, and found solace in science, spiritual books, and meditation. Life was lonely, and I certainly wasn't a happy camper. As a teen, my music and poetry were decidedly dark and moody. Other kids at school were cruel, saw me as weird, nerdy and not cool. I decided I wanted to be popular and figured I could 'fake it till I made it' and merge into the mainstream of 'normalness', make friends, have fun, fit in, be cool. What ever it took!

Fast forward, March 1976, I had just started working my first full time job. My dad, ever frugal, 'convinced' me to purchase a used car instead of a new one. After all, I was just getting started in the work force, and a used car was good enough. I was a little afraid of buying used because I didn't know anything about cars, and I was worried I would inherit someone else's problems. I certainly didn't want that! My dad reassured me that if I bought from a dealer, they have to do safety checks on the cars before they're sold and I would have nothing to worry about.

I went ahead as he suggested, and bought a used Ford Maverick. Five days after I bought the car, I was on my way to work, and the brakes went and I narrowly missed plowing into the fender of a truck in front of me. Shaken, I took the car back to the dealer. They acted like it was no biggie saying, "Yeah. That could have happened any time, nothing we missed during the safety." I was upset, but dad assured me, "It happens all the time."

A week later, I was getting ready for work, and was feeling really unsettled and considered calling in sick. I headed out any way, and with every mile I drove, I was feeling more and more anxious. I really wanted to turn around and go home, but I kept going. As I was merging onto the highway the steering completely went on the car and I watched in slow motion as the car headed toward the center guardrail, bounced off, spun around and headed straight toward the other guardrail toward a 40 story drop into a river below. The last thing I remember was saying, "Oh God." . . . that's when the transport truck hit me. The gas tank exploded, and car engulfed in flames, I remember hearing a voice screaming "open your seatbelt, open your seatbelt!" the back of my head was on fire, smoke and fumes were choking me, I couldn't see, just felt for the buckle and managed to push the release button. There was a loud roaring in my head, then everything went black… And then everything was luminous white….

When I came too, I was in the hospital. I had been in a comma for several days. Severe burns, head injuries, broken jaw, ribs, collar bone, dislocated shoulder, punctured lung, blood clots in my ear canal, 64 stitches on my face. I was a mess. The doctors told me I had died on the way to the hospital, that they brought me back and I was lucky to be alive. The road to recovery was a long one, but the experience of passing over was a transformational one. Letting go of fear of death, I knew I could show up, and be who I am, and have the courage to follow my intuition. The more important learning was, what you focus on, you attract.

Even when you think you have your life all mapped out, things happen that shape your destiny in ways you might never have imagined.
~ Deepak Chopra

How many times have you sat safely within the narrow confines of your life, comfortable in your current thoughts, beliefs and expectations? Then, out of the blue, something shocking happens that completely destroys your picture of peace and harmony. There is a sudden realisation that your comfort was based on a foundation of false thought, belief and action. This is a humbling, frightening experience.

Fast forward ten years, I had fallen in line with tradition, finished school, got a job, got married… all the stuff you're 'supposed' to do. I became what everyone else thought I should be. I even married an atheist to make sure that all that woo woo, hokey pokey spiritual stuff didn't interrupt my normal life. I'd built up a strong, capable confident 'persona'. Life was outwardly good. Inwardly I felt empty. The relationship with my husband was turbulent. Life certainly does bring us teachers, sometimes in the form of our greatest tormentors. After 15 years of emotional abuse, the marriage was over. I remember the day he said to me, "I'm not happy, I want the old Judy back," and I numbly replied, "You killed her." I didn't know it at the time, but that truly was a gift.

You can't heal what you don't acknowledge.
~ Jack Canfield

I called it my year from hell. Within the course of 12 weeks, my marriage ended; I lost my home, my best friend to cancer, and then two months later, lost my job of 15 years. My world came crashing down around me and literally everything was gone. The experience shook the foundation of my sense of security and forced me to question my strongly-held beliefs, perceptions, attitudes and behaviours. It was an event that penetrated to the core of my being, affecting me spiritually, mentally, emotionally and physically. Ambitions built on false premises had to break down in order to make room for true ones.

Once we hit rock bottom the choice is ours. We can revert to the self-defeating, restrictive behaviour, or reach for transformation. When we are ready to align with the High Self, we become aware that our true security and strength lies within ourselves and our relationship with the Universe, and not in some false belief system or artificially-created world. Through transformational experiences we grow stronger, wiser and more serene as we develop a completely new perspective on life we did not even know existed.

The most important aspect of crisis is that with any destruction there comes creation. My experience was an awakening and about inspiration, freedom, reality and the release from bondage. It was a raw truth and honesty that came through a shocking and impactful life event, and represented a necessary experience, that forced me to get out of my comfort zone, wake up, shatter illusions, and finally reveal my true inner self.

Living our purpose requires awareness by attuning to our internal and external RFI. This doesn't have to be painful or difficult. Discomfort comes from resistance against the external forces pushing us to align more to our true selves. With deception and illusion destroyed, we are free to embrace new opportunities and move forward into a more positive psychological state, where we can align clearly with our highest potential.

We can't become what we need to be by remaining what we are.
~ Oprah Winfrey

In the aftermath of losing everything I held dear, came the freedom of letting go. I was ready whether I liked it or not. No going back, only forward. All I could think of was, "If I find a place to live, I will be OK." My intention was to have a place in two weeks. I was empty, open, and looked squarely in the face of my reality. I let go and followed my inner guidance. Instead of me falling apart, by letting go, my life began falling into place like a beautifully choreographed dance, one so profound, I could not have ever imagined.

A condo came my way, and despite it being offered for sale instead of rent, I went for it anyway, asking if the owner would be willing to rent to me. The realtor said, "Slim chance, not going to happen." Within 24 hrs, the owner had accepted. He was desperate for money coming in as he had to move to the US, and keeping two homes was more than he could manage. The condo had been vacant for a year. Timing and price were perfect.

Settling into the condo, I was unpacking boxes, putting books onto the book shelf and asking myself, "Well Judy, now what?" If you could do anything you wanted, what would you do? This is your time. The teaching certification binder I was putting on the shelf, fell down onto the desk below, and opened onto the page of a guest speaker who talked about self empowerment and NLP. I felt compelled to call her, although two years had passed, and I wasn't sure if she was still teaching or even at that number. I called anyway. Much to my surprise, she answered the phone. Yes she was teaching and had a Master's course starting in two weeks. Excited, I asked how much the course was. My heart sank when she said $5,000. I told her I'd get back to her. I certainly didn't have that kind of money. The only thing I was certain of, was feeling strongly this was something I had to pursue.

As I went to bed that night, I prayed, if the course was for my highest good, then I am open to receive guidance. I woke up at 3 a.m., knowing exactly what to do, so I jumped out of bed and wrote it all down. I could barely wait to go to work! My intention was to bring this proposal directly to the president of the company first thing in the morning.

With unwavering confidence, I went directly up to the president's office that morning, paperwork in hand. I'd never even met the man before, but I walked into his office, smiled, said good morning, shook his hand, and calmly delivered my proposal. The company would sponsor my tuition, and in return, I would provide training for the management team. This training would help the company meet the financial targets for the year, and here's how. He smiled and said, "Absolutely." I handed him the paperwork, and he approved it on the spot. I thanked him, and left his office. It was surreal! Never in all my life, had I had such an experience.

Experiential knowledge of being connected to that greater power that we are all connected too, was the turning point. Life since has been filled with wonder, excitement, joy and adventure. My passion became my purpose, my purpose became my life. I've gone on to share through teaching, motivational speaking, writing and coaching, what I've learned and methods I've developed such as AIM™, and Tools for Modern Mystics™, to help hundreds of men and women from all walks of life succeed at what matters most to them by living with awareness, intention and momentum.

Simple as 1-2-3, you too can start right now!:

1. Ready: ready, willing, motivated
2. AIM: A= Awareness: being totally tuned in; guidance is always available
I= Intention: absolute clarity on what you want
M= Momentum: take action now, keep moving
3. Fire: ignition, passion, fuel

TO YOUR MAGNIFICENT SUCCESS!

About Judy

For more than 20 years, Judy Koseda has been coaching entrepreneurs, educators, corporate leaders, men and women from all walks of life to create the life they desire, and she can do the same for you! Co-author of *The Road to Success Vol. 2,* with Jack Canfield, Judy is widely recognized as a leader in peak performance strategies.

Judy was born and raised just outside Toronto, Canada and had anything but a simple life. Three major transformational life experiences, including a near-death experience changed her entire life and every single part of her understanding of the universe and our existence. We all have a divine purpose. The more attuned we are to our purpose, the more limitless life becomes. Tragedy set her on a path, in pursuit of true human excellence, and achieving a limitless life both personally and professionally. Mentored and coached by many of the world's leading experts in personal and business success methodologies, and having experienced first-hand the profound effects these methodologies can have, she has dedicated her life to the success of others. Judy helps her clients tune in to their purpose, get crystal clear on what they want, discover what's holding them back and guides them to action to achieve their vision.

Her personal motto is: "Your path to joy, and living your ultimate life experience starts with knowing who you really are and what you really want. Our purpose in life is to show up fully as we are, and share our unique gifts with the world."

Through personal one-on-one sessions, group coaching, motivational and keynote speaking, Judy uses proven psychological and strategic mind technologies including NLP, EFT, Meditation, Cognitive Behavioural Therapy, Hypnotherapy, Past Life Regression, Success Principles, The Law of Attraction, and tools she has created herself, such as the "Success Frequency", and "Tools for Modern Mystics and Successful Business Men and Women" to help her clients achieve their goals and find fulfillment in their lives. Judy has many years of experience providing corporate training, has taught personal development classes at the Learning Annex in Toronto, and has been interviewed on the topics of Leadership and Success Principles for TV as well as Forbes e-magazine publication.

A practical and insightful coach who ignites the imagination, she works with clients to join the world's most fulfilled and successful men and women, whether you want to be the best salesperson in your company, become a leading architect, score top grades in school, lose weight, buy your dream home, make millions, or just get back in the job market. She'd love to hear what you want for yourself, your business, your career, your family, your future and discover how you can have your limitless life quickly and easily.

For consultation, Judy can be reached at:

- www.judykoseda.com
- www.mylimitlless-life.com
- https://www.facebook.com/JudyKoseda/

CHAPTER 24

THE SECRET: IT'S EASIER THAN YOU MAY THINK

BY PAUL CAWLEY

The one thing I really found that inspired me was a philosophy that was actually larger than the world I lived in. It was universal and I gravitated toward it like it was the sun. I don't know if it was the sun, but it sure did shed some light.

The Law of Attraction is the secret that I'm talking about and want to share with you. It works for anyone who wants it to work for them and is accepting of all, only staying away from those who fill their lives with negativity. For some, they naturally understand the Law of Attraction, attuned to its instinctive nature. But for most, they have to retrain their thinking and learn about it in order to receive its guidance. It is worth the effort, because it creates a harmonious personal revolution—one that I've experienced and know that others can too!

Buddha is credited with saying, *"What you have become is what you have thought."* This is the key to the Law of Attraction, because at its core, it gives us the insight that we are all products of our thoughts. If we wish for good and act with good intentions, good will find us. And the opposite is true, as well. Negativity never leads to positive results, they are polar opposites in the ebb of life. While there is no way to guarantee it, I feel most confident that this path would have been impossible without my ability to tap into the right thoughts, patterns, and actions to achieve this.

When the book *The Secret* gained international attention, it brought a spotlight to the Law of Attraction for many people to benefit from. It helped them realize something different in regards to their roles for their destinies. Through its words, a better understanding of the important principles that lead to success were formed. The thoughts many people had about success were something like this:

- "They have got to be the luckiest guy in the world."
- "Nothing ever goes my way."
- "Well, that's them. That could never happen to me."

All three of these statements have one thing in common—they hand over our destiny to everyone else. We are our own destinies! Feeling deprived and not worthy just doesn't attract good things. We must learn how to attract what is good, because this is what success is based on.

IN ORDER TO ATTRACT ANYTHING, YOU MUST FIRST BELIEVE THAT IT IS POSSIBLE

It doesn't work to hope for something that you think is impossible. It's not motivating and the negative part—the impossible—is such a strong emotion to battle against. Exhausting, really. In order to help me start achieving everything that I was leery of, I switched to an "it is possible" mindset, and from there, I did this exercise. I encourage you to try it, as it really helps to cultivate the type of awareness that it does take to achieve heartfelt, soul-aligned, success.

- Get a pen and a piece of paper and write down everything you would ideally want in life. Maybe it's related to finances, health, job, travel, etc.

- Put a number between 1 to 10 next to each item you wrote down, placing a 1 by the items you feel you have the lowest chance of obtaining within one year and a 10 by the ones that you feel you likely will obtain within a year.

Know this when you are done…the number that you put next to each item is your belief in that item coming true. How do you measure up to the "possible" as compared to the "impossible"? In the end, only *you* can gauge how much you believe in your desires. And if you're like a great number of people in this world, you could use a bit more belief in your life. To achieve this, you must start developing your "belief muscle." As this grows stronger your 1's will move up and become closer to 10's. It's quite incredible, and it's how I was able to obtain success in many areas of my life, including success in various business endeavors. I believed in myself and my intention was good—to help others through what I knew was a good use of my gifts and insights.

Today, when people ask, "How did you do that?" I have the answer, and I am really excited to *not* keep it a secret. I want everyone to know what I've learned, and with some good grace, they can live it, as well. This is a set of beliefs, thoughts, and philosophies based on the Law of Attraction that helps people who seek it to harvest happiness—both professionally and personally—that make people wonder what your secret was. And you will know that it is not luck!

1. **Feel Good Now**
   People always tell me that they'll feel good after they get a new job, a raise, or find a relationship that satisfies them. What about now? Now is all you have. So stop getting it backwards. The Law of Attraction states that "like attracts like." This means that if you are unhappy or worried, the universe is going to give you more to be unhappy and worried about. Embrace that you can be happy right now and that happiness will come to you, bringing you a great many wonderful things. This all has to do with our vibrations in our world—positive vibrations bring positive outcomes; negative vibrations bring negative outcomes. Accentuate the positive!

2. **Be Grateful Now**
   Every day should be a day where you acknowledge what you are grateful for. Maybe it's your spouse, the smile from your children, your day at work, your dog with its happy expression and wagging tail—whatever it is, acknowledge it and appreciate it for how it makes you feel! The universe also acknowledges gratitude and as a result, it sends more to you for you to be grateful for. That's how great gratitude feels!

3. **Practice Forgiveness**
   You must forgive yourself for where you fall short and grant forgiveness to those who do you wrong. This is necessary. A way

to make this tough process become easier is to write the person's name that needs forgiveness on a sheet of paper, along with the statement: I forgive you. This is simple, yes, but it does dissipate the negativity that's flowing from you just a bit, if not completely. It is so liberating!

4. **Accept Responsibility**

   It's hard to believe that you are where you are due to your own choosing. Casting blame and fault on others is counterproductive to changing your outcome. Honest reflection into your past decisions usually reveals that you could have chosen a different path. Perhaps you ignored the better path because it didn't fit into what you "thought you wanted" or you ignored your gut instincts—which are in direct communication with the universe. Own up and move on!

5. **Act "As If"**

   You must feel that what you want is already in your possession. When you believe that you have already attained something, it is no longer impossible. It is achievable and it inspires you to take the actions to make your "as if" become your "here and now." So visualize that first substantial paycheck that you are longing for, feel what it's like to hold it, imagine taking it to the bank and depositing it, and put yourself in that situation where you are doing what you choose to do because you can. Claim it!

6. **Use Powerful "I Am" Statements**

   The statement "I am" leaves you with a choice. Do you follow it up with something negative or choose something positive? This choice makes all the difference in your outcome. Positive statements are the affirmations that help you bring your desired outcome into fruition. For example, instead of saying, "I am overweight" you would say "I am attaining my ideal weight."

7. **Be Generous**

   Generosity comes from the heart while it also helps others. There are few things that feel better than that. When you offer that donation like you have extra money to give, you are subconsciously acknowledging that you have enough money. Caution: this does not mean emptying your account. You can be responsible and act from your heart. Think of the powerful stories of good things happening to people who gave their last penny to someone who they felt needed it more. Generosity is a gift we can all offer!

8. **Stay Clear of the Timeline Trap**
   Avoid impatience and don't accept that you are just an impatient person by nature. It's a developed habit, not a hereditary trait. There is great joy to be attained by experiencing the satisfaction of knowing that something good is coming your way. Enjoy that feeling and draw strength from it!

A great way to give yourself a reminder of all these points of awareness and the power of the Law of Attraction in your life is to create a dream board (also known as a vision board). Fill this piece of poster board or bulletin board with all types of things you want in your life—that ideal job, a better financial picture, a great house, a genuine smile—anything. Add in quotes that inspire you and positive "I am" statements that help remind you of what you seek. And if you really don't want it, this is a good way to make adjustments. Our desires can change over time as we learn, grow, and become more aware.

THE LAW OF ATTRACTION IS ALWAYS IN MOTION, MAKING GREAT IDEAS COME TO YOU

It's amazing how new ideas tend to find you at the most unexpected times when you are creating an internal/external environment that draws on the Law of Attraction. You want to be aware of these moments when they happen and find a way to record them. Even a wonderful, compelling idea or realization can get lost in the chaos of life. The best way that I've found to capture these thoughts is to have a pen and a piece of paper handy at all times. I keep this by my night stand and also in my car. I type notes on my computer when I'm by my desk. I also take advantage of my built-in recorder on my phone. Anything to help me remember good ideas and points of awareness—and you can sense these things—is something I do. The results have been greater clarity and vision in:

- Solving problems
- Tapping into new ideas
- Awareness of the goodness in my life

It's imperative to cast out good vibrations to our never-ending universe, because change doesn't just happen in our conscious minds. It is also an activity of the subconscious, working in mysterious ways without us even realizing it. This is the main reason that all changes of habits and healing of negativity begin from within. It's our power center with the universe.

The things I share are my passion and I've experienced the rewards that happen as a result. I want to give back to the world that has given me so much and let other people in on the secrets to creating the personal platform that leads to successful thoughts, visions, and outcomes. I can think of no greater gift to leave this world. To me, this is the epitome of success.

As you go out and begin to attract the wonderful things that the universe is waiting to deliver to you, I wish you joy, happiness, and the excitement of pursuit in achieving all the things that you desire. There's no one better equipped to chart your destiny than you. And you can do it!

It is my wish that the ideas presented in this chapter can give you a basic understanding and roadmap to implementing the Law of Attraction into your life.

About Paul

Paul Cawley is an entrepreneur, speaker, and author, who has been involved in various businesses including martial arts studios, real estate brokerage, appraisal, mortgage, title, investing, as well as consulting, and publishing. He describes himself as a lifetime learner, one who is constantly seeking new ways to improve himself, and pass this knowledge onto his clients.

This is accomplished through learning from the best leaders in respective fields, and using his own personal experiences in business and the self-improvement field. In addition to the conscious relay of information, he also utilizes his experience as a certified instructor for the National Guild of Hypnotists to install this new information on a deep subconscious level of understanding to the client, to take them from where there are now, to where they want to be.

Thru the information contained in his chapter, you will learn the principles he utilized to go from a frail kid to becoming not only fit, but attaining a master level black belt rank in karate and opening his own karate studios. Then parlaying that early success to much larger and successful business and personal achievements.

Paul is in the process of coauthoring an audio program with the legendary Brian Tracy. These audios recorded in an interview format, will supply the listener with the valuable insights gained by Paul and Brian, through their many years of experience in the business and personal development arena. The information is cutting edge and will eliminate the learning curve, and put you on the fast track to success and prosperity!

Being from a small coal mining area in Pennsylvania, it seemed times were tough, but the people were tougher. A lack of opportunities, and persistent challenges, brought out the best in most of them, and he would like to personally thank everyone he had the opportunity to learn from, teach, meet, or have the pleasure to call a friend.

You can contact Paul at:

- www.PaulCawley.com

CHAPTER 25

PARTNERING FOR PROFITS

BY ELMER DAVIS, JR.

J. Paul Getty once said, "Be open-minded concerning the vast opportunities for mutual benefit." While the idea and the value of collaboration is nothing new, the scope of ventures that abound in today's world is nothing short of astounding.

Partnering up via joint venture involves two or more businesses (or like-minded) persons pooling expertise and resources to achieve a particular goal. The risks and rewards of the project are shared. This can be motivated by a number of reasons: expansion, development of new services or products, or entering new domestic or international markets, distribution channels, specialized staff, technical capabilities or access to capital and lines of credit. Businesses of any size can team to strengthen long-term relationships or collaborate on short-term projects.

Depending on the goals of the project, there are several ways to structure your agreement. Once I'm ready to commit, I often use a Memorandum of Understanding (MOU) to specify co-operation with a business or a person in a limited and clear way. On other occasions, a separate joint venture entity was more appropriate to the circumstances. Other more traditional options include formal partnerships, and mergers or acquisitions. Key considerations for me have been the level of involvement of management, and the risk/exposure should things not go according to plan. Professional legal and tax advice is suggested since the structure affects operations, profits and taxation.

One attractive element is the flexibility. A project can have a limited life span and only cover part of what you do. This limits the commitment for both parties and the exposure. The objectives must be clear and the plan well communicated to everyone involved. Goals of the parties must be aligned. Cultures and styles must work well together, and there must be leadership and support from the earliest stages. Each party must value the assets invested by the other. You may want to look at other organizations operating in similar markets. Consider a SWOT analysis (of your Strengths, Weaknesses, Opportunities, and Threats) to evaluate if the two businesses are a good fit.

Here are some partnering examples to illustrate how diverse and flexible they can be. John Snedden started barbequing whole pigs for fraternities and local farms in 1977 when he was in college at Washington & Lee, and has been serving wood-only barbeque in the DC area since 1990. Unhappy with store-bought sauces, John experiments with his original Rockland's BBQ sauce and it's an instant success. John moves to the DC area in 1983, where he caters his first event and wins first place for best ribs at the International BBQ competition. By 1987, John is flooded with requests and is catering full time out of his home. Then in December 1990, John opens Rocklands BBQ and Grilling Company and serves over 20,000 pounds of pork by the end of his first year in Business in 1991.

By 1993, John's ideas are used at the White House at Bill and Hillary Clinton's first state dinner. John's staff increases from 7 people to 20 as he's overwhelmed by catering demands in 1994. By 1995, John open a location in Ballston, VA, expands his staff to 45 people and serves over 66,000 pounds of pork. In 1997, John bottles Rocklands original sauce and starts distribution nationwide. Within a year by 1998 with 2 locations and full-service catering and party planning, John's staff at Rocklands has reached 75 employees serving over 100,000 pounds of pork annually. Rocklands celebrates its 10th year anniversary in 2000 and is awarded the "Good Neighbor Award" by the Restaurant Association of Metropolitan Washington in 2003. The next year in 2004, John opens a new Rocklands location in Alexandria, VA with a restaurant and catering kitchen.

In 2005, Ballston closes as the management agreement expires, and the Rockville MD location opens in 2006 at Wintergreen Plaza. Then in December 2007, Rocklands Arlington opens their doors. In 2009, marking the inauguration of the nation's 44th president, Rocklands introduced limited edition Barack Obama hot sauce. John marks his 20th year anniversary in 2010. In 2011, John's first twitter campaign launches "the blue plate special" from each location. Two more new homemade products launch in 2012 – Malt Salt and Blackening Rub available at retailing partners like Whole Foods and Wegmans. Rocklands is voted Best BBQ in DC City Paper for the 5th consecutive year.

In 2014, John caters for 3,900 people, their largest party so far. Rockland's celebrated 25 years in 2015. This growth and sustainability is clearly a testament to John's vision and to his ability to deliver great food. Our partnering is focused behind the scenes. John also really understands the need for great marketing, controlling his costs, pricing competitively, maximizing the productivity of his team, and getting a return on capital. Our partnering is focused on these elements of his success story. Since 2014, we have developed a real estate-based asset management system. In short, when most business start, the approach to profitability is in residual (meaning the money comes in, expenses are paid, and what's left is the profit). With guidance, companies operate differently as they mature and engineer profits via asset management. John turns a nice profit providing great food at Rocklands. Additionally, we've set up a system to profit based upon real estate.

At the time of this writing in April 2016, Yahoo Finance ranks the return on investment in flipping properties in the Pittsburgh, PA market (where I'm from and where we operate), at 129%; that's 30% above the next closest market. So, money comes in, gets applied to the asset management system (completely turn-key) and every dollar produced in real estate flips or from rentals (John also owns over a dozen rental properties) that is applied to expenses at Rockland's, increases the bottom line net profit. It's a win, win, win!!!! John has recently expanded again with the opening of Earl's Sandwich shops with no end in sight.

Richard Tyler is also proudly celebrating the 26th anniversary of one of the world's most innovative, effective and influential sales training and management consulting firms – reaching upwards of one million people per year through various popular business books, syndicated TV appearances, keynote speeches and conducting workshops and programs. Teaching success philosophies and time-tested techniques in Sales,

Leadership, Management, Customer Service and Quality Improvement, the company has received countless accolades in its industry, including Top US sales training and management consulting firm and Best for corporate growth strategy as well as the Top award for excellence in sales, Management Consultancy of the Year and the Best of Business Award Management Consultancy.

Tyler's philosophies, which have directly helped everything from mom and pop upstart businesses to Global 1000 companies, have been chronicled everywhere from *Entrepreneur Magazine* to *The Business Journals*, *Sales and Marketing* magazine, *Wealth & Finance International* magazine, *Acquisition International* magazine and *The Houston Chronicle* in his adopted hometown. He has appeared on affiliates of FOX, CBS, NBC and ABC.

Renowned as a top business author as well as an influential, in demand speaker, Tyler's numerous books include *Smart Business Strategies™*, *Real World Customer Service Strategies That Work, Leadership Defined*, *Mission Possible* and *Marketing Magic*. His two forthcoming books with Celebrity Press are: *BOOM!* co-authored with Mark Victor Hansen (co-creator of the best-selling *Chicken Soup For The Soul* series) and *Success Today – Leading Entrepreneurs and Professionals Share Their Secrets to Health, Wealth and Happiness*, co-authored with Brian Tracy. Tyler will also soon be publishing *Sales Excellence – Seven Steps to Achieving Extraordinary SUCCESS in Sales*. Tyler recently won an EXPY® award for his interview on the TV show "Success Today."

The variety and scope of the platforms Tyler engages may be expansive, but the philosophies Tyler imparts – whether he's teaching revenue generation, increasing profits or high customer satisfaction – all flow from the same essential principles that transcend race, creed or nationality.

Teaching what he calls "not simply business skills but life skills," Tyler bases his timeless concepts on his nearly 40 years as a Sales Professional and his innate understanding of not only the process of buying and selling but also an instinctive understanding of our nature. His philosophies work across the board because they are based on human behavior. "Most companies develop their concepts and techniques in different arenas separate from each other. They teach sales, then management, leadership and customer service but with completely distinct, incongruent philosophies. Our ideas are congruent across each of these areas and flow seamlessly into each other, with leadership and management training flowing directly from sales, which in turn creates the need for ongoing customer service. Everything we teach – including revenue generation, increasing profits and having high customer satisfaction – flows from the same sales principles. Sales is all about effectively communicating an idea to people so that they can evaluate your position and decide what's right for them. In essence, we're teaching everyone how to be master communicators."

His wild success as a door-to-door salesman in Charlotte – an endeavor he got into originally to make tuition and board money to supplement his scholarship – led him to change his mind and realize he could accomplish just as much good in a different way that drew on the incredible sales skills he discovered and kept developing. Richard was dealing with giant manufacturers, meeting nice local business owners. It was an exciting time." Other wholesale reps he met heard about Tyler's stellar reputation as a salesman, and wondered what his secret was. Why were they only making $20 in the same time frame that he was generating $100 to $150? He didn't know how to explain and quantify the nuts and bolts of his process – his expertise in that would come years later – but he offered to ride along and work with them to see if he could identify any flaws.

He often noted that while he started his day very early, many of his fellow salesmen and saleswomen would wait till late morning and give themselves only a tiny window where a customer might be open to buy anything. Tyler figured out he had to make 45-50 cold calls a day to find 20 who would talk to him and 5 who would buy something and hopefully clear him $100. He discovered that the key to the sale was finding that sweet spot where he had an item someone wanted and they had the money to buy it. Noting flaws, weaknesses, even laziness in the methodology of others proved to open the door to his eventual success as a sales trainer.

Sales is an integrated process where everything has to flow just right and where commitment to following through on a process is foundational. In our process, we start at the beginning. We teach our clients how people learn, along with what a customer's objections are, their wants and needs, how to resolve concerns and how to satisfy them – and multiple ways to reach agreements with them."

Tyler is always looking to help people grow their business and create a revenue-generating culture. We consult on product launches, marketing, designing new products and mergers and acquisitions. Tyler sums up his success philosophy with his trademarked phrase that he shares with all his clients:

Remember, "Your success tomorrow is in direct proportion to your 'Commitment to Excellence®' today."™

About Elmer

Elmer Davis, Jr., MBA, ALM multiple best-selling author in *Victory, Success-O-Nomics*, and *UnCommon* has over 30 years of experience in marketing and finance, with private and non-profit organizations as well as Fortune 500 corporations. He began his business career in marketing with Bristol-Myers in the early 80's, then moved on to industry giants like Mobil Oil, and Accenture.

He was a partner with Anderson, Phillips, Davis and Hoffmann in Washington DC, New York, and Los Angeles and served as Executive Vice President and Chief Diversity Officer for Financial Dimensions, Inc. in his hometown of Pittsburgh, PA.

A graduate of Florida A&M University School of Business and Industry, Mr. Davis holds a Bachelor of Science in Marketing, as well as a Master's of Business Administration from Howard University. He also earned a Master's degree in Operational Management from Harvard University in Cambridge, MA.

He has conducted leadership and entrepreneurial training forums for various groups and professional development clients in numerous industry segments within the public and private sectors and major universities including Harvard University, MIT and High Point University. Elmer has also written several articles, including Understanding the Communication Environment, the True Costs of Miscommunication, Financial Management for Cash Flow and Profits, and Embracing Workplace Diversity and Eliminating Employment Discrimination.

He was recently profiled and quoted in *The Wall Street Journal* as well as *Forbes, In Touch,* and *Global Impact Quarterly* magazines. Elmer was honored with inclusion in *Who's Who in 2004.* Elmer is a well-regarded facilitator of crucial information and a thought leader, having recent forums at Google and Tesla as well as Singularity University at NASA and the X-Prize Foundation with Dr. Peter Diamandis in California. Elmer is a high demand speaker having been chosen as the US Diversity Champion of the Mortgage Bankers Association in 2005, he delivered keynote remarks at the National conference. He has also spoken at Times Square with Steve Forbes, and at the Global Economic Forum at the United Nations in New York City. Elmer has since led training workshops for entrepreneurs in the Dominican Republic with Esperanza International, and symposiums with the International Children's Heart Foundation. He returns to the UN stage with Jeff Hoffman (Founder of Priceline.com) in summer of 2016.

Elmer is a natural communicator and was a guest on The Brian Tracy TV show which aired on ABC, NBC, CBS and FOX and the Massachusetts IT University Radio WMBR.

He also appeared on The Big Pitch radio show with Kevin Harrington as an expert guest.

www.businessradionetworks.com is one of Elmer's current businesses while his continued work at TBK Ventures, Inc. has helped control costs and increase profits for entrepreneurial businesses across the country creating Global Impact via neighborhood reinvestment.

For more information about how Elmer can help you reach that next pivotal level, visit his site at: www.elmerdavisjr.net, call 855-293-0877 or email him at: edavisjr@post.harvard.edu

CHAPTER 26

ROAD TO SUCCESS WITH THE HEALING PROCESS

BY NICOLA BROWN, PhD

The path to Living an abundant life began with my decision to grow, be persistent in my commitment, and never yield in an unending pursuit of my purpose, which led me to ultimate success.

We are all born with greatness within us. Most often we have to be grated for greatness to appear. We must be willing to go through the growth process to begin, enjoy and ultimately lead and live a better life.

Cars don't usually voluntarily wreck themselves without the aid and assistance of others. No car would truly be totaled or even repaired if it had to do so voluntarily. I say this because I was destined to win. I had always succeeded in all that I did. But for a season, I felt like a wrecked car without the proper mechanic to fix my problems.

I had gone to school, gotten good grades and gotten a great job. But I was not prepared or trained for the greatest challenge of my life. Death! In 2007, my beloved was told he had months if not weeks to live. The thread that had held my children and myself together, began ribbing away. From the shock and trauma of the news, it sent an earthquake through my spiritual, emotional, financial, relational and physical world!

My husband and I were healthy, or so it seemed. As nurses, we opted out of medical coverage to receive pay in lieu of benefits. Our worst nightmare ever! Upon receiving the diagnosis of Stage IV lung cancer, no insurance carrier would pick up the tab. So all things not securely fastened would be blown away in the hurricane. Health, money, business, homes, cars, love and life all disappeared.

Somehow, I had opened the wrong envelope that Napoleon Hill spoke about, namely: *Ill health, fears and worry, indecisions and doubts, frustration and discouragement, poverty and want.*

I felt like I had gone to sleep as *Pretty Woman* and woke in the *Nightmare on Elm Street.*

I had taken many classes in school, but none was in failure. So I was, for the first time, flunking this life class. I didn't remember signing up for this class or ordeal. I sat dazed and amazed that 37 years of winning had come to an abrupt end without my active participation, or was it?

Two months after the death of my beloved, I met and married Wesell. A notorious womanizing scoundrel. This was Robin Hood. He stole from the poor to feed his many kids. He demanded loyalty and obedience or death by the fist. It was not a fist full of dollars, but of pain. Leave your kids and come and serve me and mine. So I did not suffer one loss but the loss of all I had: my mind, my kids, my joy, my peace, my confidence, my identity, my businesses, my cars, my career – EVERYTHING!

I woke up in 2012 in North West hospital in Maryland, beaten, broken and bruised. On that day, the police and nurses informed me that if I went back I would be killed! It was then that I decided, I was that butterfly that had a broken wing, but by God I was going to fly again. I began an enlightened journey by declaring ***"I deserve better!!!"***

You could take my freedom, you could take my dignity, but I would never be willing to give my ***spirit*** (drive, will, determination), ***my soul*** (life), or ***my future*** (destiny). That belonged to me. I choose to exercise my rights. ***I am free! I was born free!***

I elected to live in my car in Maryland for five months so I would not be harmed. It was here that I would look up in the trees and dream of a better day. During this time, I began the rebuilding process by reading books: *Think and Grow Rich, The Attractor Factor, Harmonic Wealth, Toxic Relationships, No Matter What,* just to name a few. I must have read over a hundred books. My trunk was my library. I knew if I was going to make it, a new belief system would be required. I remember working as a consultant, and other consultants expressed wanting to be me. But they had no idea I was the woman who lived in a shoe called my car! I would not share that I ate Chinese white rice with sardines or canned corned beef every day that I was not at an event. Survival was key to me. I had to go home to my babies in Florida.

Two days before Christmas, I came home to Florida without fears or so it seemed, provided no one called the name Wesell. With the name called, I'd experience PTSD (self-diagnosed).

A few months after I came home to Florida, I began a business that could not sustain itself or me. I had too much baggage. I closed within five months. I kept on reading. I went to a conference by Dr. Caroline Leaf that gave me the push I needed. I left that event and went to the beach and while there, I asked God to allow me to make this become my everyday reality. Seven days later my desire was granted. In October, I would sign some of the greatest contracts in my life. My financial life began to rebound and would spring board me into a wave that gave me the financial freedom to launch my current company AIRS Global Inc.

I'm often asked about AIRS, what does it mean? Abundantly Inspired to Renew and Strengthen you. The abundant life was what had been a part of my genetic makeup and blue print. In each of us is an awe inspiring little girl or boy that wants to come out and play and enjoy life with others. Sometime due to our environment and mindset, we forget who we are. Abundance is not measured in what we have, but instead in who we are. This is why we must fight to not have this great abundance taken from us. Abundance now allows me to keep both feet on the ground and reach to new heights.

Inspiration for me came from the love that was inside of me for the man that I had loved and lost. The one that would stretch me to go back to school, earn my higher degrees and do something greater with the energy I had inside. When life raised its head as a bully, I was inspired by my kids who I had given birth to, to never let them see me quit. I got up and began to fight back for my beliefs. I believed I was born an ***eagle*** and for a moment, I forgot who I was. ***Inspiration*** separated me from the pack. I was destined to rise above and take my rightful place not as a victim, but as a daughter, mother, lover and a friend. ***Inspiration*** causes us to triumph in life, love and business.

Renewed determination caused me to reach into myself and be willing to find the courage to create methods, systems, and a message that our bodies do not have to succumb to life's challenges and dis-eases, but through proper hydration, nutrition, supplementation, exercise, stress reduction and rest, we can assist our bodies to repair themselves with minimal assistance.

Strength came when I reconnected my mind, body and spirit to Divine and Universal order. We live in a world that is chaotic in its operation and we are expected to function by an alarm clock and shuttled like cattle into environments that create stress. We send our bodies into a hormonal abyss, never expecting it to malfunction; I see this every day in our offices. Bodies whose systems are so drained, they can no longer sustain life. When tired, broken and exhausted, clients come to our centers to be ***renewed***. We have state-of-the-art equipment to communicate without touch and to restore a sense of vitality and wellbeing. With our internal GPS and check engine lights, we are often not willing to listen, and cut the switch so we will not observe the warning signs. At our offices, clients do not want to leave at the end of their sessions. Our slogan is "When life has knocked the wind out of you, we help you to breathe again."

In our first year, we made five figures and knew this was a reflection of what was internal. We knew we had the right vehicle just not all the operational parts intact. There were no systems in place; therefore we were not fully operational. This I knew was fixable, and so it would require raising our internal BAR (**B**elief, **A**ctions and **R**esults) to produce what we knew we were capable of.

For one, I knew getting the right systems in meant becoming FOCUSED (A willingness to **F**ollow **O**ne **C**ourse **U**ntil **S**uccessful without **E**xcuses or **D**elays). I had to have:

- A keen **Sense** of direction, **Understanding** my needs and my customers' needs
- **Courage** to be willing to implement and apply changes
- **Compassion** had to be given generously

- **Esteem / Self Respect** were core to our growth
- **Self - Acceptance** would set the stage for my life
- **Self Confidence** had to be aligned with my core values in serving.

The mindset training that I would receive surpassed all that I had learned in school and more. I had to be willing to take responsibility for my actions and hold others accountable for theirs. In learning to respond well to our life's challenges, we are given more. Learning to become respon-sible, we begin to be, do and have more. It's all in the response. Are we deliberate creators of our lives or are we only reactors? That which I'm responsible for I can change.

In our second year, we had crested multi-streams of six figure incomes. We then began to give more. Not just looking out for ourselves but the welfare of others. We were able to see the vision process take on a whole new meaning. We began to connect with our audiences and began to fulfill their needs. We no longer believed in the philosophy of surviving but we have consciously adopted a place to thrive. My team and I had also learned to no longer desire to be lone rangers, but to create long-range goals. We also learned not to compete but to complement, after all, we are providing complementary wellness services. My MD partner and I joined forces in enhancing the quality of life for our clients to better improve clinical outcomes. It would require our hiring the right people to get the job done well, and not just done.

For me, falling in the ashes was not a bad part of the lesson, it was the falling backward. One of my mentors said "when you fall you must learn to fall forward, for if you do, you will be able to get back up." For me, falling was the only thing I never wanted, but for me, never to have fallen would have been my greatest mistake. I have learned how to fall and can do it with grace, ease, peace and comfort.

Life is a series of lessons and often it has an open-book test. But we must choose to see it. My perception makes it so. Limited thought comes from a limited source. Limited thought comes from a limited mind. Limited minds lead to limited lives. I took the caps and skates off to be able to run my race with excellence.

When I got home to Florida, I had a 1999 Honda Accord. One day I went out to my car to move it and it made the most awful sound I had ever heard, it sounded as though it was being choked to death. After which, I went to put my car in reverse, it would not go backwards. When we parked the car, we had to make sure it was on an incline. We also had to push the car when we had to move forward, Flintstone style. One day as I was becoming agitated, a thought flittered across my mind, what if my car was telling me it was time to move forward without any regrets of looking or staring backwards? I had to be willing to take the life lessons that I was being taught by my car and apply it to my life.

After learning my lesson, I would move from that car to brand new cars following that season. What if I had not made myself flexible enough to change and make the shift from poverty to prosperity? It might not have taken place for me. Will you make the necessary shifts in your life to move forward?

About Dr. Nicola

Nicola Brown, PhD is a dynamic mother and fabulous grandmother, leading her tribe as RN, Transformational Educational Speaker and Coach, Professor, Business Consultant and Maximization Strategist, Life Optimization and Empowerment Specialist, International Conference Speaker and Author.

Her recent projects include collaborating and Co-Authoring with Jack Canfield. She is a part of the **Global Entrepreneurship Initiative™** and **COUNCIL MEMBER**. She has been invited to be a **United Nations Guest Speaker**.

Dr. Nicola Brown is the Founder and CEO of AIRS Global and Therapeutic Services Inc. AIRS (Abundantly Inspired to Renew & Strengthen you) was created in honor of her beloved husband Lance, who died from Cancer.

Dr. Brown helps her clients through transformational techniques. She can be found in one of her AIRS Centers inspiring and empowering her clients to obtain maximum energy, productivity and performance. AIRS is an intuitive, cutting-edge technological leader in the health and wellness industry. Through bio-energetics therapies, she aids her clients to 'breathe again when life has knocked the wind out of them.' AIRS is a global brand that is bringing traditional and holistic care to a whole new level.

Dr. Brown has developed her programs and philosophy based on five core principles of wellness which are the key foundations to the healing process. The principles are: Hydration, Nutrition, Supplementation, Exercise and Stress reduction.

Dr. Brown's education includes Business Management, Hotel and Restaurant Management, Medical and Health, Wellness, Theology, Psychology, Counseling, and Natural Health Degrees and Certifications.

She has been featured in several magazines, newspapers articles, and television.

Dr. Brown's corporate clientele includes Physicians, Attorneys, Politicians, Business Owners (Large and Small), celebrities, athletes, educators and many more. She has built and established the foundation of her business with hospitals, institutions and facilities where she worked in key management and administrative roles. Her experience is vast and her success is life-transforming.

CHAPTER 27

LIVING A FAITH-FILLED LIFE

BY TONI THOMAS DURDEN

Have you ever imagined yourself living a fairytale life? Of course, we all have. Who doesn't want to have the life of their dreams? We want to be the apple of someone's eye, the hero and save the day. We want to walk through peaceful gardens and embrace our beautiful surroundings, to enjoy the sunrise and sunsets doing what makes us happy. We long for meaning and purpose.

It doesn't always turn out the way we planned. Too many of us are sleepwalking through life, doing the same thing over and over again with negative results. Unfortunately, many of us go through this in our lifetime, burning out before we reach our potential. The good news, there is an ingredient guaranteed to change your life. It's called FAITH! I know, because my life was transformed because of it.

What is FAITH? Well, the Bible tells us "Faith is the substance of things hoped for, the evidence of things not seen." Heb.11.1. For me, Faith is the "Impossible being possible." I was the underdog with everything going against me until I applied my faith. The world opened up and I saw limitless possibilities.

Before I started living the life I always dreamed of, I was a statistic in every sense of the word. I was sexually abused at six years old, lived in a fatherless home with a single mother and two siblings. My mom remarried an abusive, alcoholic man when I was eleven and things progressively got worse. I was bullied in school and no direction or guidance; I turned to drugs and alcohol. My bad decisions led me to unhealthy relationships that nearly cost me my life.

When I was 18, I felt I was headed on a path to destruction and desperately wanted to change. It was at that time I found myself in church during revival. The topic, oddly enough, was "Headed to the Junkyard." The message brought me to my knees. I recognized that I was lost, drowning in sin and in desperate need of a SAVIOR. At that moment, I asked God to guide my life and I immediately felt the power of his presence. The pressures and fears I had dissipated and soon my life began to change. The very next month I was hired as an international flight attendant and suddenly I was off to see the world and start a new beginning.

Was everything perfect after that? Absolutely not, but I was in a much better place to learn and to grow. I had a personal relationship with God and became eager to know what he had planned for me. Years later I began to realize that all the shattered pieces of my past were merely a refining process to help build my strength and character. I still had many problems emerge in my life, but instead of running from them (like I did so many times in the past), my faith helped me to confront them. Faith in God's grace made me understand that all problems were temporary, but the lessons they taught were permanent.

Faith connects us to a power like no other. It's like sitting in a dark room not able to see until the switch is turned on. I look at life as a GIFT! It's because of tragedy and near death experiences that I really learned to LIVE. Your life may not look anything like this, but I can assure you that even the smallest obstacles in our life will keep us from moving forward.

It's a wonder how we have any dreams or ambitions at all. Most of our foundations were built on sand which crumbles when things get tough. We were influenced our entire lives from people who were not qualified in teaching us how to live successful lives. You may not have had good role models for parents, you weren't loved, couldn't speak openly, and heard "no" more often than "yes." We are broken, hurt, and disillusioned when life doesn't go our way. The good news is it's not too late to learn from the mistakes. We can't blame anyone. We have to take responsibility. It's OUR lives; we must take control of them. Look within yourself and what you've been through. Identify the lessons you learned along the way and how they can help you.

What is success? It's the accomplishment of an aim or purpose – a person or thing that achieves desired goals or attains prosperity. Years ago, I thought success was having a big house, a fancy car, and a glamorous wardrobe. In a nutshell, about being "rich and famous." I couldn't have been more wrong.

It took me years and many tears to realize that in order to be truly successful, you have to be successful in all areas of your life. Not perfect, but willing to put the time and work in. I used to think making a lot of money would be the benchmark to success until I met many wealthy people who seemed just miserable. Who wants that? Wealth without happiness is just crazy. I saw more happy poor people than happy rich people. So did that mean that "successful" people were unhappy while "unsuccessful" people were happy? Maybe my idea of success was wrong. I eventually found that the reason behind their pursuit of success made the biggest difference in their happiness levels. The ones who made money to benefit others far exceeded the ones who made money to amass for themselves.

Even in my pursuit of a successful relationship, I was found wanting. I expected others to bring me happiness. I was like a chameleon, so nobody could see that I wasn't the confident, strong woman I portrayed. I became a people pleaser so everyone would love me. I earned awards to make myself feel appreciated and give me a boost of confidence. I didn't know what love was, but learned it was impossible to love someone else until I loved myself. I was selfish and I couldn't seem to get me off my mind. I then met my ideal partner. He was handsome, his parents were still married, from a loving family, great sense of humor, loved adventure, hardworking and he was extremely affectionate. It was easy to believe that HE could be my knight in shining armor.

We soon got married and that's where the fairytale began, so I thought. I expected my husband to make me happy. We were for a while, but then we had children, job changes, moved to another state and began to enter the COMFORT zone. We became miserable at times, treating each other disrespectfully, dishonoring, and being ungrateful. I was not the ideal wife for many years. A marriage will only be as great as the effort you put into it. I had to learn to edify instead of criticize, love instead of manipulate and respect instead of gossip. I learned how to be careful with my words because life and death is in the power of the tongue.

True happiness doesn't come from wealth, beauty, relationships or anything external, it comes from within. We figure as soon as we get that job, lose weight, or have a great relationship, our problems will be solved. Happiness isn't something that just happens; it's something you need to actively pursue.

How do you define success? Where did you get the idea from?

Imagine this! Today you went to the doctor for an annual check-up. It was just a routine physical. Your doctor tells you he found an inoperable brain tumor and you have three months to live. You're looking at the doctor, but unable to speak. You exit the doctor's office wondering, what am I going to do? How do I tell the people I love? You're probably questioning your life, thinking about some broken relationships you wished were repaired. Did you say everything you wanted to say? Did you do what you wanted to do? Did you make a difference? Are you leaving a legacy to be remembered?

How is your life going to look during the next three months? Two things happen when you know death is certain. First, you decide what's important to you and second, if you get well you appreciate every day from that point on. You only begin to truly live when death is inevitable. We all have the same destination; we're not getting out of this world alive. Success is a process of discovery and is measured by the heart, not by what one can see. You woke up today which means you've been granted another day to make a difference.

Are you wondering how living a faith-filled life will make you successful? The Bible says: be faithful with the little things, you will be ruler of much. Matt.25:23. We need to be trusted with what we currently have. How are you handling what you have been trusted with? It's like giving a child a bicycle and he leaves it in the rain to rust. If he is not taking care of what he's been given, as a parent would you get him another one? No, you must appreciate what you have.

If success is your end goal, faith runs the engine to get you there. I wanted to give up so many times when something wasn't going right in every aspect of my life. You have to decide what goals you ultimately want in your marriage, health, finances, businesses, and your emotional state. We are responsible for the outcome. We have to stay committed throughout the good times and the bad. If you don't think you have any faith, remember that we use faith every day without realizing it. Have you flown on a plane without meeting the captain? Have you had surgery without looking at the doctor's credentials? Why? You trusted they knew what they were doing. You can look back on your life and see many instances where FAITH has pulled you through.

We are here to enjoy the journey, not to focus on the destination. Each destination will be a new beginning to explore. We have the opportunity to correct our path and live more meaningful lives.

We settle for mediocre relationships. Why? We didn't start with definitive goals. You weren't in full agreement about what you both wanted to accomplish as a team. You can have the relationship you desire, but you must go back to identify what's important to you both. Learn to communicate in one another's love language and realize you are doing this thing called life together.

You need to set your financial goals. Whatever your goal is, know why it's that amount. When your number is too high and you don't reach that goal, you quit. Quitting is not an option. Apply more faith. Also, what will you sacrifice for it? If you achieve your highest financial goal, "What is it all for?" Money can have a great benefit to build homes for the poor, feed the hungry, and help others in need. It can also be self-serving, buying every luxury you can afford. Money only makes you more of what you already are. Is it charitable or greedy?

Life lessons have a funny way of showing up in the most unusual ways. For instance, imagine a delivery man coming to your home. He sees a sign on your gate that reads BEWARE OF VICIOUS DOG; however he doesn't see a dog. His heart begins to beat rapidly, sweat starts pouring down his face because he knows he has to make the delivery or risk being fired for not completing his task. He ponders his dilemma and decides not to take the chance in getting bit by the vicious dog.

While he waits in his delivery truck, he sees a little girl walk through the gate to knock on the door. The delivery man yells, "Didn't you read the sign?" She said, "No, I can't read." He was fearful of what the sign said although he didn't see the dog. This is how we go through life fearful of what **could** happen without evidence that it **would** happen. It's all a matter of perspective.

We must practice and release our faith to take risks and test our limits. Your breakthrough happens when you defy the odds, have a greater vision, champion people, do what you love, then success follows.

About Toni

Meet Toni Thomas Durden, best-selling author of *Life in the Jetstream*. She has been a world traveler and adventurer for more than 27 years. She is a successful entrepreneur, real estate investor, Certified Dream Coach®, Life Coach, speaker and philanthropist.

Early before starting her career, Toni was from a small town with limited resources. She had won a national pageant that opened many doors and broadened her horizons. She met many celebrities, appeared on the Regis and Kathie Lee Show, and went to see Oprah, Phil Donahue, and Geraldo. She later received a letter from Oprah saying, "Do what you love and success will follow." She also appeared on the Silver Screen with Earnest Borgnine, Norm Crosby, Norm Fell, Pat Priest Hansing and Allen Garfield.

Toni is the Founder of Teen Life 101. It's a 501(c)3 not-for-profit organization helping teens to learn life skills to transition to the real world. This is done via media and events. The idea is to make learning educational and fun.

She has been involved with charity work her entire life. She was a former Little Sister of Big Brother Big Sister of South Sarasota County. She felt blessed later in life and wanted to help others. Her contribution expands from working with many other non-profits like Adam Walsh Children's Fund, Big Brothers Big Sisters, Make-A-Wish, I Have a Dream Foundation. It extended out to orphanages in Peru and Africa, building homes for the extremely poor, children's homes and hospitals, jail ministries, nursing homes, at-risk and working with terminally-ill patients.

Toni's hobbies include traveling around the world, reading anything that she can learn from, roller coasters, kayaking, biking, entertaining, spending time with like-minded individuals, and spending time studying the Word.

She has been married for 22 years to Rob, with two sons Austin, 21 and Kieran, 17. They reside in Southern Virginia.

CHAPTER 28

RETIREMENT IS A MYTH: USE "THE LIFESTYLE SECRET" AND LIVE THE LIFESTYLE YOU DESIRE STARTING NOW

BY TROY WEST

Did you know that 99% of the U.S. population will never be financially free by age 65? (U.S. Census Bureau of Labor Statistics)

It's not your fault. Retirement is nothing more than a "brand" setup by the government, financial institutions and large corporations to ensure you struggle and stay working to create tax dollars for the government, so your money can be used by investment companies, and so you can make your employer money. You get to do this until you are no longer needed or drop dead, whichever comes first. How appealing does that sound?

Whatever the mind can conceive and believe, it can achieve.
~ Napoleon Hill

Life should be a "GET TO" not a "HAVE TO." You don't have to defer time, money, and passion in the hopes of one day taking more vacations, spending more time with family, and buying the things you've always wanted. You can work towards these things now, but you must be smart, methodical, and refuse to listen to what you've been taught your whole life about retirement. Retirement actually tells us to defer our lifestyle now for a better lifestyle tomorrow but has consistently proven to fail us over the last 200 years. This is “The Retirement Myth.” One privilege of being a financial consultant is that I can always live through other people, sharing their success and challenges. Money doesn’t lie, it always has a story. What's interesting is that all stories have patterns to them (good and bad), that are directly related to how people think and feel. Being in business and continually evolving strategies to effectively improve people’s lifestyle is not an easy task.

Fortunately, I’ve always had great mentors, books, and experiences to leverage. There are simply too many to list here. The bottom line is people talked about challenges but nobody was getting to the core root of the problem, the "Retirement Myth"™. Nobody was labeling this a branded idea to serve the few. Nobody was talking about how to turn the system upside down to use the ingredients in our favor.

Being a systems guy, I studied the problem, I studied the system. I concluded if 99% do not live financially free why would I become a pawn and teach them what doesn't work? Instead I modeled bits and pieces of HAPPY people living the lifestyle they desire. Through my journey, I have concluded that you can defer to systems like “The Retirement Myth” and fail, or you can apply “The Lifestyle Secret” to successfully plan and improve what is most important to you.

“THE RETIREMENT MYTH” EXPOSED

Retirement has PROVEN to fail people for 200 years!

Retirement is a cancerous trap. Government and large corporations have taught us since the Industrial Revolution that if you spend money on the best colleges, get into debt, and then work hard enough, save hard enough, and defer your time long enough, you’ll no longer have to work anymore, and can live happily ever after in security and freedom. Yet even having a discussion about retirement will upset most of us, because we know it's a far off reality. What if there is a way to get there faster while at the same time enjoying the life you have now?

If you’re like most of us, you’re living the common problem, influenced to work hard by an employer that pays you just enough, for long enough, until you are no longer needed, and can be replaced by someone younger, cheaper, or better looking. In the process, you pay taxes to the government who subsidizes corporations, who then in turn use the media, and manipulate financial professionals, to reinforce this myth called "retirement." Retirement was designed so that we continue to work to make money, to consume, to go into debt and to defer our happiness longer and longer. Instead of retiring comfortably, we unknowingly give our power to the few, feel powerless, and are compelled to feel dependent, because we don't have answers or get educated about the real root of the problem, "The Retirement Myth." You think there is a reason why we feel dependent on Social Security and health care? Of course there is! It is controlled by the same system!

Listen – we pay approximately 1/3 of our earnings to the IRS in taxes, 1/3 of our money to big banks for interest and are left with 1/3 to feed our families. We are left to save less than 5% for this so-called retirement that may never happen. Plus, where are we taught to save our money? The answer is places where we can't touch it unless we want to be taxed and heavily penalized to use OUR OWN MONEY! Yes, it is large investment companies and banks reinvesting our retirement money while they charge us to use it. This is outrageous! In the process of saving for retirement, we are paying our brokers outrageous upfront commissions for investment products that may not even serve our best interests and are so complicated we don't understand them. It doesn't matter if you make north of $250,000, $25,000 or somewhere in between, following "The Retirement Myth" designed by the government, financial institutions and large corporations will not create your desired results or lifestyle. According to research, most Americans save less than 5%, yet pay 33%-85% in lifetime interest payments. Many of us also pay Uncle Sam before we see our pay check. Wouldn't it be nice to function like you own a bank or investment company instead of being a pawn for big government, financial institutions, and large corporations? Wouldn't it be nice to know you get paid first and could give yourself a raise by more money working for you, rather than against you?

If you are at or near the end of your career, inflation is eating at your dollar like a rat, healthcare feels like a mortgage, and there is a good chance your savings are disappearing slowly like an illness you never see. Have you been taught how to optimize income and mitigate these risks? Likely not to the extent you should, because after all, you've been neglected now that you're no longer needed. Even extremely bright financial advisors are prey to "The Retirement Myth," being taught systems that cater to large investment and insurance companies. These companies pay well but they still don't put the advisor in the forefront to be able to have systems that are congruent to their truly desired lifestyle. They are trained to trade time for money like the rest of us. "Retirement" is forced upon them with so much influence it's hard to think differently. Everybody is manipulated down the path of "retirement" to face the TIME-MONEY DILEMMA – either trading time for money or conserving time, but suffering financially.

It is in this way that we are told what we need. We lose time, money, and our passion in the pursuit of a dream that may never manifest itself, and in some cases may turn into a nightmare. The paradox resides in our choosing to put ourselves in the time and money dilemma. This makes us choose where we suffer. Is it our relationships, our health, our spirit or another important aspect of life? Thus we defer time and money to live in a small future window of time, and then, we hope too much of life hasn't passed us by.

99% of us are in the wrong system, working over eight hours per day with very little savings, dependent upon the government, financial institutions, and large corporations. Yet less than 1 in 3 of us will use a financial consultant because at best, it is a win-lose relationship. You lose money and time simply based on the limitations on the ability to save and also on how some consultants get paid. It's neither parties fault, it's part of how "The Retirement Myth" was constructed. The good news is that it is possible to live a life of your dreams. All you need is to learn "The Lifestyle Secret" formula and how you can apply it for financial stability and constantly improve your lifestyle. Wouldn't it be nice to know you could do what you wanted now? Wouldn't it be nice to know you could do what you love and have flexibility of time and plenty of money?

Money + Time + Passion = "The Lifestyle Secret"

How did I discover "The Lifestyle Secret?" It came by accident, from life lessons, vast research, and unbelievable mentors. Some major events in my life that have shaped my thinking include:

(i) Suddenly being diagnosed with epilepsy, a struggle that, in the past, made me lose my sense of consciousness throughout the day; losing substantial productive time not knowing what went on and trying to figure it out. If you've ever seen the movie, Memento, that will give you an idea of what life used to be like for me. It was pure hell. Eventually, I learned to use my condition as a blessing given to me to learn a new way, eventually finding out how to organize time in a way that gave me opportunity and constant lifestyle improvements.

(ii) Another life lesson I learned was jumping into the financial industry during the worst economic period short of the Great Depression. Whole neighborhoods were being foreclosed on! How did I make money in a time like that? First, I studied the systems and applied learning what the successful lifestyle experts were doing. I quickly found myself living my dreams traveling the world and checking items off my bucket list. I bought a house and rented out the other rooms to cover most of my expenses. I traveled the world through creative means. I used technology to work from abroad so I could travel regularly. I didn't need to become a millionaire overnight.

In fact, I actually saved more money working from overseas over a computer than I would have in the U.S. because the cost of living was less abroad. I simply used money principles in a way that functioned towards my immediate objectives while positioning myself for mid and long-term objectives. I didn't let "The Retirement Myth" of deferring time, money, and passion stop me. I asked myself "How can I do it?" and took action.

Thinking Outside the Box

Everyone wants the lifestyle they dream of. Yet why continue to be the person that wakes up in a box, eats out of a box, follows a box calendar, drives a box to go to another box to sit at a box, so you can listen to your superiors yell at you out of their boxed-shaped heads until you turn 65, so you can finally try to live the way you want outside the restrained box. Am I right? If you're already or near "retired" you don't want to feel trapped in a box, because you are on a fixed income, worried your money won't last, right?

The Box Problem creates horrific challenges, as time and money are limited. If you have no time for family and friends, how will they feel? How will you feel? What happens to your relationships? You are probably constantly stressed or fatigued and pounding the pavement in hopes of making more money or worried about your health. Regardless of a great attitude, if you never feel in a position to live your passion or to become your highest version of you, then what will that do to your spirit? Your self-esteem? Your true happiness?

However, what if you had more time for family and friends, more money for your immediate and future needs, and lived your passions and desires? What if you had a recipe that would constantly improve these areas? How good would it feel to be flowing with excitement, energy, and passion? If you were constantly living better, what would that do to your spirit now? What would it do to your legacy later?

Given a way to constantly improve your lifestyle: doing what you want, when you want, where you want, with whom you want, as often as you want, with fulfillment and happiness, what is that worth to you?

THE THREE PHASES TO THE LIFESTYLE YOU DESIRE

Here are the three phases to obtain a better lifestyle. Each phase has distinct steps to follow:

I. **Financial Foundation –** Position yourself where expenses are met, your risks are mitigated, and you take advantage of opportunities by using principles such as leverage and opportunity cost.

   Here are the steps:

   1) Goals and Objectives - Know what you want to do, have, and become. Identify the amount of money it will entail and the time frame you want to accomplish it in.

   2) Increase Savings - Develop clear strategies to increase income, eliminate debt, minimize taxes, and free-up wasted money in your budget. Direct money towards your goals and objectives.

   3) Emergency fund and short-term goals - Protect against future debt and cover emergencies. Work towards 3-6 months' savings for your personal and 6-12 months' savings for your business. Use lucrative strategies to make your money work for you.

4) Protection Planning - Mitigate against life risks so you can always maintain an income and the assets you have accumulated.

II. **Freedom Baseline –** Build from security of having time, freedom and building wealth. Transition into strategies that take advantage of how money functions, so you'll have your expenses covered each month without the need for your labor or time input. The "money machines" you set up pay your expenses. Start utilizing systems that create time-efficiency so you can use time for what you want. Here are the steps:

1) Identifying your Lifestyle - Expand your objectives into the lifestyle you desire. Dig deeper into the core of what you really want to do, have, and become. What would your perfect year or perfects days look like? Identify options and systems that can begin working towards the lifestyle you really want.

2) Getting in the Game - Use new sources of income that align to your passion. Build towards automated processes so you can increase your income and assets while you sleep.

3) Optimize and create Infrastructure - Get your money machines working for you, get the right experts involved, processes working in ways that make the machines as "well oiled" as can be. Ensure your processes sync together.

4) Income Distribution - Ensure your income covers your lifestyle needs and grows your assets, and that your sources of income can last your lifetime. Optimize growth, opportunity cost, and leverage what you can. Mitigate your risks.

5) Your Legacy - Put a plan in place to ensure your assets last and transfer them where you want them to go effectively.

III. **Lifestyle Level –** Modify your machines in such a way that continually optimize your lifestyle. Your processes should continually mature, working and developing to serve you and your people more effectively.

1) Your Roadmap - Adjust your plan for business or investments to maximize efficiency.

2) Leverage and Opportunities - Execute the best opportunities you see, leveraging what you can.

3) Congruency - Adjust your messaging, actions, your persona, systems, and tools to align to your mission and lifestyle.

4) Execution of revenue/investments - Capitalize on maximizing your targets based on your risk tolerance, philosophy, and opportunities in front of you.

5) Know Your Numbers and Risks - Get feedback on how you can improve your financials and avoid liability.

6) Optimization - Tweak your processes for maximum efficiency. Add in new processes if necessary.

7) Culture - Bring in people that fit the mentality of the lifestyle you want and use experts to ensure you and your client's deepest desires are met. Be attentive in listening and proactive in creating.

I applaud you for refusing to be a victim of "The Retirement Myth" and instead joining me and my friends on the journey to living the lifestyle you desire!

About Troy

As the President of Lifestyle Financial Planning (LFP), Troy West helps people break through traps associated with retirement, a concept created by the government, financial institutions and large corporations to systematically use us for their advantage. Troy's unique skillsets in Social Science, personal development, time management, and financial savvy have combined to help people understand how they are conditioned to follow what he coins "The Retirement Myth" and break through time, money, and passion barriers to improve what they want starting today. Troy is committed to his passion of reshaping ineffective, disempowering, and outdated principles that have proven to fail us over 200 years and founded "The Lifestyle Secret"™, the formula that combines time, money, and passion to constantly improve your lifestyle.

Troy is known by his friends and colleagues as a "Systems Guy." Troy's blend of learning, modeling, and innovating, have led him to take patterns of what works and shape them into strategies that can be followed and executed consistently by his clients. Currently, Troy is in the midst of creating more and more proprietary programs to help professionals, senior citizens, and financial consultants develop from their current financial state, and build the lifestyle they want.

His philosophy as a "Lifestyle Entrepreneur" and financial consultant is that any objective can be achieved if it is clear and planned out with options congruent to one's core values, understanding, and commitment to newly-learned strategies. His goal is to create long-term winning relationships that educate people how to first be financially secure and then consistently improve their desired way of living. Troy went through 12 years of having constant lapses of consciousness (epilepsy) but still managed to do things that would seem impossible given the circumstance. In college, he graduated at the top of his class (in 3 years), was part of developing one of the most improved NCAA basketball programs in the country, and took full semesters "while on vacation." In one of the worst economies in U.S. history and new to the financial industry, Troy was traveling the world and checking-off bucket list activities (while living comfortably and running his business). Troy is a highly sought-out consultant who develops programs and workshops. Clientele of LFP range in financial experience, assets, income, job occupations and age groups. LFP can help nine out of ten people as long as they are motivated, open, and committed.

Troy graduated *magna cum laude* from San Diego State University. In his personal life, Troy enjoys traveling the world, culture, NCAA basketball, NFL football, working out, and spending time with friends and family.

For consultation and help, please visit Troy and LFP at:

- www.lifestylefp.com
- Toll Free: 1-844-342-1735
- admin@lifestylefp.com
- linkedin.com/in/lifestylefp
- facebook.com/lifestylefp

CHAPTER 29

THE HEALTHY WOMAN

– TAKING LIFE'S LESSONS WITH GRACE AND TENDING TO OUR NEEDS

BY STEPHANIE KORKOR

The setbacks and failures we experience in life are really wonderful signs that we need to pay attention to what will make us whole again.

Everyone has experienced at least one setback or failure in an area of their life. When you have unaccomplished dreams and unfulfilled goals, there is always a nagging voice in your spirit reminding you of the goal, a pang of guilt when you look at your untouched project, a wave of panic when you look at how quickly your health is degenerating or how fast your finances are dwindling, and a sinking feeling in the pit of your stomach, when you think about what you haven't done or how different your life could have been if you had done it. When you are unable to meet the reasonable standards and expectations you have set up for your life, are not doing what fulfills you, or are doing something that is totally inconsistent with who you are and what you stand for, you will remain drained, uninspired, restless, empty, unfulfilled, and unhappy. Even when you are engaged in activities or work that gets your basic needs met, you will always feel that something is missing, sense the call of a higher purpose, be more interested in certain causes or ways of life or in pursuing a certain career path.

The journey to how I ended up being a Transformational Coach for women who were struggling to find a balance between health and emotional well-being came about in a most unexpected way. I learned about a solution to common problems that many women suffer from through a story from a friend of a friend. This Russian woman, Tatyana Kozhevnikova, had a program where she could help women address the variety of concerns that are unique to women. Perhaps her wisdom was something that had been around for generations, passed down from wise woman to wise woman to help those who could not afford medical care, but I didn't know or care, because it was fascinating. It did not matter half as much as what I came to realize from hearing about it—we live one life and have one body, but what happens inside of us can often be quite different than what our outward health appears to be.

It's the entire picture – inside and out – that brings us true fulfillment.

Both men and women have a need for all-encompassing health, but the thought of helping women was what really resonated with me. I saw how beneficial it would be to offer them heartfelt and caring guidance that was practical, holistic, confidential, and effective. Some people ask, "Do you replace the doctor?" The answer is no; however, I do offer options that may not exist through traditional western medicine and therapy.

From that moment on, my passion was born and my journey to success through service to other women began, and what an amazing adventure it has been. Ups and downs. Sorrows and moments of genuine joy. Then everything in between; this is life, after all.

LEARNING TO SERVE AND SOLVE

There are endless amounts of wisdom out there for anyone to take advantage of if they truly are passionate about something. As they say, when there's a will there's a way.

Working full-time in the governor's office, I began to spend my free-time pursuing ways that I could learn how to fuel the fire of this new desire to help and serve women. And it didn't take going much further than my circle of friends to realize that so many women were embarrassed and secretive about the problems that bothered them, thinking they had to put up a front that suggested that things were always "fine", when in reality, they often were not. It's not always easy to share what plights us, and I get that. Most everyone has been in that place in life at one time or another: facing great obstacles, going through some trying situations, experiencing some humiliating, tight, tough circumstances. Having empathy for this type of situation compelled me even further.

I took three steps that were so powerful for me that they changed my life rapidly, despite it being a period of a few years. More importantly, my opportunity to help women in need had begun. Because for me, that's the true blessing of life and knowledge—helping others.

First: I reached out to Tatyana, that woman that had captured my attention, and after an initial rejection to even talk to me about it, I didn't feel ready to give up—at least not without giving it a full-out attempt. So, I emailed her and poured my heart and soul into it, offering logic and reasoning and passion, as well as a specific message about the need for this type of information in the US. It was an amazing moment when she did respond and gave me fifteen precious minutes of her time. Those fifteen minutes turned into over two and a half hours of conversation. She was willing to teach me what she knew!

Second: I had to find a way to actually learn to be an effective Transformational Coach and mentor to the women that I had begun working with. Having passion and determination isn't enough; you need the right mentors and strategies to help you really connect and guide them toward results. It's not just the actions at this point; it's also the approach.

Third: I came across a course, *A New Dawn with Yaye Fatou Diop*, and it was there that I learned to understand, master, and implement effectively the Laws of Attraction, Deliberate Creation, and Allowing, all of which help one to get into vibrational alignment with the universe. I began powerfully manifesting my dreams into reality and my setbacks into successes. I finally saw how I could align my mindset and business with those who needed it, as well as ways to help the women who I was working with do the same, down to the smallest details. This was the missing piece, and now I was better able to reach out and connect with women in a more effective, deep, profound way. When we're connected to our world, wonderful transformations can begin.

Because of these three steps to help me help others, I am now a

Transformational Coach who has the ability to have compassionate outreach to women who are struggling and help them get their lives back.

THE KEYS TO INTERNAL HARMONY

The keys that help us unlock the mysteries that would otherwise go unsolved is what my clients and I focus on—together.

There are many coaches that go by many names: business coaches, success coaches, wellness coaches, etc. I'm a Transformational Coach—all of those things wrapped up into one. By working with women to address fitness, exercise, nutrition, and holistic solutions to better physical health, I can guide and lead them toward greater emotional balance and wellbeing, as well. The key to starting this process is the same, regardless of what specific solutions are needed.

Cleansing our bodies to remove the toxins that impede them from operating at their best is the first step in breaking our body back down to the basics so we can build it back up in a healthier, more functional way.

Having innovative, powerful, and effective solutions was necessary for my work, along with helping women to understand what it was that I offered, exactly, and how it could benefit them positively—removing the barriers that stopped them from experiencing the full joy that comes from being a woman—a mother, a friend, a daughter, a provider, a vessel for life, and a contributor.

Since my success and rewards in life are so closely linked to helping others, I want to share with you a few of the areas that my coaching taps into. These areas are gateways to better physical and emotional health, which is a beautiful thing to experience and to watch others experience, too.

1. Helping to bring awareness to the level of vibrational energy that the client is exerting out into the universe. Our positive and negative thoughts have an impact on our physical, mental, psychological, spiritual, financial, and emotional well-being. By recognizing the importance of the alignment of mind, body, and spirit, we shatter our artificial barriers.
2. Developing a fully effective, progressive training program to spur on better health and internal strength in all core areas.

3. Mindfulness as to the movement in the body, taking note of how muscles respond and tighten in response to mental imagery of those muscles in motion.
4. Talking and exploring the concerns that exist for the client, thereby finding ways to address the emotional as well as physical hindrances.
5. Actions that lead to enhanced self-esteem, self-confidence, and self-awareness of the messages that the body does share with us, which impact how we respond and navigate through our lives. We are meant to be out there living, loving, and smiling, not secluding ourselves out of fear or concerns!
6. Information and education regarding how the female body functions—which is imperative for all women to fully understand. It's amazing how few women do fully understand this—another motivator in my quest to help others.
7. Holistic solutions that help to avoid the frustration, heartache, and other negative emotional energies that come from unsolved medical problems or continuous solutions that involve invasive surgeries.

These seven steps are vague in nature, but the foundation of everything it takes to help bring back the thriving, strong, and assured woman that may have gotten lost along the way. In many cases, women recognize the power of being that type of woman for the first time in their lives. As their coach, I can tell you that nothing feels so wonderful to me as when I hear, "Stephanie, I've learned more from you in a few months than I've been able to learn anywhere else." Statements like that are the jackpot that increase my emotional wealth. They represent success, both for those that I've helped and for me. It's so inspiring, and their smiles, they generate a level of happiness and appreciation that far too few people have the privilege of seeing firsthand in their lives.

TO BE LOVED AND FEEL COMPLETE...THIS IS SOMETHING WE ALL WANT

We all have a story, and through others' stories, we can all learn valuable things.

One client whose story truly impacted me in an incredible way was someone that I worked with a few years back. Her name was Kathleen and at the time she was sixty-two years old. She had no children and had never been married; in fact, she didn't even date, as she had roadblocks and barriers that made that a frightening thought. One day, she happened to come in contact with her ex-fiancé Mark after thirty-eight years of being out of touch. They got together and realized that the spark was still there, but with all the concerns that Kathleen had, she was so scared to enter into this place she hadn't been for so long. Fear and uncertainty… two powerful motivators to avoid life instead of living it.

Kathleen sought out help from doctors, who only offered medication and surgery, nothing to address her problems as a whole. Through a friend she'd heard about my coaching program and decided to give it a try. She did want to have a relationship and love, but it was just so agonizing for her to even think about. Over the next four weeks, we worked together diligently, addressing her problem as a whole (factoring in internal and external health). Then, much to my horror, she just disappeared. I didn't hear from her for four days, which was quite uncommon. Finally, I'd had enough and I called. Then I texted. Then I emailed. Still nothing. Finally… on the fifth day she contacted me with the best update I could have heard: she was fantastic and had been on an adventure with Mark. She was happy, and he was grateful to see the vibrant woman he'd known once upon a time had returned.

Two wonderful lessons were reiterated to me that day. First, I am so glad that I personally worked to conquer the concerns I once had about becoming a coach. It took some work to brush off the nay-sayers and rise above the waves of doubt that I'd created within myself and that others hurled my way. Second, and most importantly, I realized that by helping "one", it carried over into helping others. In this case, Kathleen's rekindled romance, but for most women, feeling and being healthier can lead to better relationships with their spouses, friends, children—everyone. We all do better when our friendships and connections are in a good place, don't we?

EXPLORING, SEEKING, AND FINDING OUR BEST SELVES

Be inspired and empowered to research and find what you know will bring a sense of wholeness to your life; and to complete you in one way so you can begin to explore everything else.

My greatest wish for you is that you feel encouraged and empowered to seek out the solutions that just may give you a reprieve from whatever it is that is holding you back. We have so many options that are within our control and that means that there is no one—other than us—who can begin the process. Are you ready to begin?

Today is the day to begin claiming what you deserve.

Today is the day to acknowledge that you deserve to feel amazing—inside and out!

Today is an opportunity to accept what is, and then accept what does not have to be.

For me, *every* today brings about this newfound success that has me so excited. It's all consuming to me. The thirst for knowledge to better understand women, our bodies, and every way that I can help connect the pieces and break down the barriers that prevent us from reaching the fulfillment that we deserve and desire drives me.

To many, success is defined by a certain set of tangible goals. For me, it's so much more than that, because success is directly linked to the actions that we are willing to take to make ourselves the best we can possibly be in all areas of our lives. It's a sense of well-roundedness that comes from being whole and knowing that holistic solutions are those that come from within us and the universe around us, helping us to have this vibrational energy that heals and promotes complete health. And this is my wish to you—that you may do what you must to find your success. You'll know when you've arrived, because it actually becomes possible to look at the world around you through those proverbial rose-colored glasses. It's a pretty sight, too!

About Stephanie

Dr. Stephanie Korkor, Founder and President of The Velvet Grip Inc., is the premier holistic women's mentor. She has a unique set of skills and training that gives her the ability to revive, rejuvenate, accelerate and motivate women in their physical, mental and emotional life. She is a highly sought-after expert in women's health, well-being and empowerment. Her extensive knowledge and deep passion for helping women live the life they have always wanted has been the driving force behind her success. Her holistic and naturopathic approach to healing and well-being is just the beginning. She believes that to be truly empowered, one has the power to tap into her deepest self – physically, mentally and emotionally.

Stephanie is a Board Certified Naturopathic Doctor specializing in women's health. She is also a Certified Personal Trainer with National Academy of Sports Medicine and a Certified Fitness for Fertility Specialist and a Certified Pre/Post Natal Fitness Consultant. Stephanie is a highly respected Intimate Gymnastics Master Coach and Trainer as well as a Pompoir Trainer and Coach.

Stephanie has done all that she can to make sure that she can offer the most success to her clients. Understanding that in order to have a holistic approach, she had to know more that just the science and fitness behind everything. She knew that in order to help women truly take control of their health and see them transformed into passionate, alive, youthful and vibrant women, they must also work on the emotional and mental aspects of their health. As a Jack Canfield Certified Trainer in the Success Principles, Stephanie is a master at helping her clients overcome their limiting beliefs and to take action toward creating the life that they want.

Because of her unique knowledge and unrivaled experience, Stephanie is also a member of America's Premier Experts and has been quoted in *Newsweek*, *The Wall Street Journal*, *USA Today* and *Inc. Magazine*.

To connect with Dr. Stephanie:

- Email: DrStephanie@thevelvetgrip.com
- Website: www.thevelvetgrip.com

CHAPTER 30

THE SEVEN SECRETS OF SPIRITUAL SUCCESS

BY WILLIAM A. GASPAR, MD

What is the essence of spiritual success? Is it being recognized in the media as someone famous, making a lot of money, or knowing that you did something outstanding for humanity? Everybody defines spiritual success differently. For the great scientific and spiritual minds of the last few millennia who established world-changing religions, who saved their people from exterminations, who discovered scientific miracles and lifesaving medical treatments, huge financial reward was not necessarily the first thing on their mind.

I was an American-born citizen, living in communist Hungary from the age of 5 years old with an US identification card. Not being indoctrinated into the communist ideology mostly blacklisted me from any advance. This adversity taught me early on to stand up for what I believe in, even if it was not convenient. I knew as a child that I'd rather die trying to escape from communism than to live in submission. Being an American citizen in beautiful Hungary made me feel very special and almost superhuman. I felt convinced that the Creator Force favored me to achieve great deeds. This bloated self-confidence humbly propelled me toward my great successes later on in life.

Finally, at 23, with my wife Eva and daughter Rubina Xenia, we bravely escaped communism. It happened through hair-raising adventures filled with a number of life-threatening situations. On one level it was insanity to plan this escape, but deep inside our heart, we already felt joy about our future successes. My philosophy is that if I have to run against much faster Olympians, I still see myself succeeding by imagining how one of my opponents fell, another one quit because of dehydration, and so on. . . and I won. No question about my success. I never doubted that we should succeed in escaping communism and then we will establish a great life in the USA. From not speaking English in my mid-twenties to earning a Bachelor degree, then to become a medical doctor and be able to write books and be interviewed on great programs, proved to me that America is still a great country and success is in the attitude.

Looking back on our journey of successes, my wife and I concluded that the FIRST spiritual principle was our belief that we could not fail, because we are part of an everlasting, omnipotent, SPIRAL SPIRIT. The science that is emerging from my studies show that we have originated from an eternal Spiritual Source who endowed us with unlimited potential. My early studies made me realize that this cosmic spiral breaks into five parts.

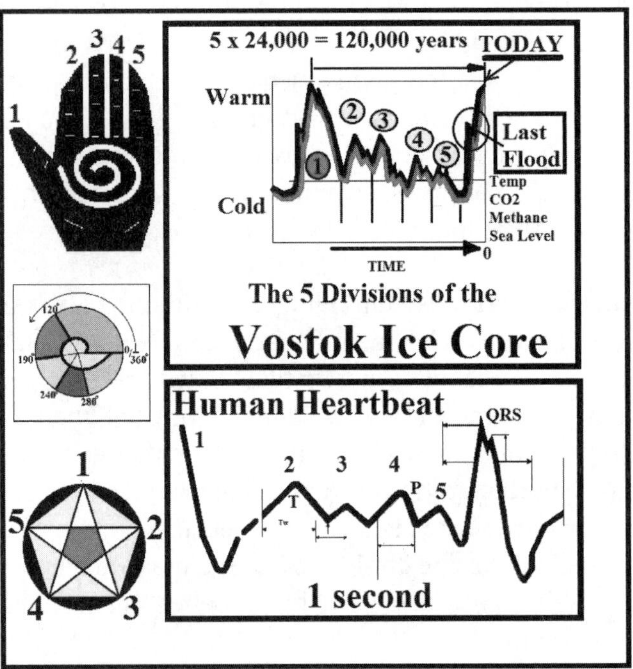

Diagram 1.

The Creator formulated us in His Spiral Spirit image and in the divine division of five. Four extremities and our head. This Spiral Fractal force keeps displaying itself as a 4 + 1 division, as one can also observe on the fingers and thumb of our hands. Therefore, the Hand of God is involved in every aspect of Creation. We can observe that in the diagram of the Ice Age cycle that is almost identical in appearance to the five divisions of the human heartbeat. Take a look at our first diagram where we illustrate our star dust origin. There is a point in our Black Hole of the Milky Way where the Two Big Spirals meet, this region I call the Heartbeat of the Galaxy.

This cosmic Goose or Northern Cross, known in astronomy as Cygnus is now identified by NASA as one of the most powerful electro-magnetic sources from the Black Hole in an area around Cygnus X-3.

Just as the rainbow breaks into various colors, our spiritual hues and talents are different from each other, but individually perfect. The SECOND spiritual success principle is to find out what SPECIAL talent this Nature Source equipped us with. We owe it to the Grand Architect of the Universe who constructed us, to discover our specialty and share our nature with the rest of the world. As one cell in the Cosmic Human body, we all have a function to carry out for the health of society.

In the THIRD principle, we must become active SEEKERS of our truth. Meditation and prayer is just one of the multitude of ways we can search for answers. There is certainly a Theta wave of the Shamans and Angels that bring us celestial clues. How many times we wake up at 4 o'clock in the morning, half asleep still, but downloading great knowledge from above? Our gut feeling in the Solar Plexus is one of the best guides for discernment of any information received. How many times we drive by a portion of a road to work, observe a large rock or a grove of trees that almost magnetically draws our attention each time we see it, and we never have ten minutes to stop to wonder? How can we find the truth if we do not listen to our gut feeling about an intended message that the Great Spirit planted all around us? If a fellow human is propelled to talk to us, we should intently listen. There is a chance that occasionally another person's information is spirit-derived and was heavenly directed toward our spiritual growth.

Once we receive a new impetus that tickles our spiritual interest, we need to intensely STUDY it as our FOURTH principle of spiritual success would recommend. Numerous connections to the subject we study will open up a limitless highway of knowledge. Just as a good detective, we aim at understanding concepts in their totality. All clues must add up to a new Eureka moment.

In our journey, my wife and I tried to learn from a variety of cultures and types of religions to understand the yearning humans have for the Divine. Initially, we spoke no English, we had no money or substantial help. We learned fluent English in two years as we worked extremely hard, and bought investment houses. I completed a Bachelor's degree in the next four years and by our sixth year in America, I started medical school. Besides becoming a medical doctor, I also discovered a number of important cosmological and sacred geometry concepts. Our daughter Rubina Xenia, who is gifted with the talent of awesome communication skills, helped us develop a more refined set of vocabulary and artistic design to our thought processes early on. The few books I wrote, I financed myself and made it onto the famed Art Bell Show, the Laura Lee Show, Global Radio and became a speaker in Sedona for the 1st International Sacred Geometry conference. I was even interviewed on TLC and on the Ancient Aliens of the History Channel, even though the programs have not aired yet.

It was our spiritually-gifted son, Austin Keane, who showed me through the power of the imagination and applying the Law of Attraction, how to get an interview initiated with Giorgio A. Tsoukalos. The process began within a couple of days without lifting the phone. So little time and so much more to learn. Our powerful minds can visualize and manifest awesome deeds. By far my greatest achievement was that I could keep my family happily together with the outstanding participation of my wife Eva, who herself earned certifications, college credits and a Diploma of Master of Herbology and Iridology. Big deal? Yes, at the age of 27, she did not speak a word of English. Her curiosity lead us into the Native American Spirituality that became an important step for spiritual learning.

The Lakota Sioux Indians pray toward the West first with their Peace Pipe, saying that the 'Power comes from that direction'. That wisdom made me wonder if maybe I should be searching in the West for the power that turns our Earth from the West to the East. This is where the Black Hole of the Milky Way Galaxy is located, the elusive source of the Galactic Heartbeat. The Mayan, Egyptian and the Christian Cross, the

Blackstone, along with the Wild Turkey of the Navajo Creation legend, all pointed me toward Cygnus in the Black Hole as the main source of Power.

One day a Lakota friend of ours whose flute music plays at DIA in Denver, Calvin Standing Bear, came over to our house in Denver and enthusiastically pointed out the star constellation Pleiades. I looked it up and found out that it was the shoulder blade of the Taurus Bull in the sky. It brought my attention toward the Golden Calf, the Bull fight of the Spanish culture and the Buffalo of ancient Creation legends. It started me on a journey of exploration into a lifelong study and search for the meanings of star constellations, Egyptian hieroglyphs, and the origin of letters. My main focus of study was to understand the timing and the event that causes a switch in Nature. I needed to understand how the island of Atlantis sank and why the Egyptian Winged Disk destroyed humanity thousands of years ago.

The Sumerians depicted the Winged Disc as the Lord itself, and most cultures honored it as the Eagle or the Hawk of mythology. The symbol of Icarus, the medical emblem of the caduceus and even the Winged Serpent's concept of the Mayans and the Aztecs derived from this mystery. Most interestingly, a number of secret societies and car manufacturers also picked this curious emblem as their logo. The study of these phenomena and their meanings helped me understand how we spiritually honed in on obtaining information from the ether. Even more important was the fact that I could join prestigious organizations, such as the Freemasons and others where more avenues of learning opened up. One only needs to 'ask one to be one'.

This brings the FIFTH spiritual principle into focus. One must SOCIALIZE within churches, synagogues, trade organizations, seminars, join clubs or groups of ancient knowledge to be able to learn about spiritual practices, good communication skills and a way of applying them. There has to be an exalted platform where people of experience will recognize your talent and root for you to express them. A mentor and apprentice model is one that has worked well throughout the ages. You need to meet people such as Jack Canfield, Brian Tracy and others who started where you are now and made it up to the top, so they can instruct you how to accomplish the same. Whether it is a business venture or a spiritual journey, gaining the trust of successful mentors is essential to learn the skills to grow. Going the extra mile in any of these relations without expecting an immediate return is also essential in this path.

The SIXTH spiritual principle is to recognize that you have something to SAY, SELL or to offer up a talent as a SERVICE. As the world changes, we always need new scientists, bold entrepreneurs who can keep up with a new way of being. One only needs to look at the smallest organisms around us, such as the viruses and bacteria who are relentlessly searching for new ways to exist and be virulent. They don't seem to have excuses why they wouldn't succeed. There are no blocks in their thinking of why they could not flourish. They keep manifesting new resistant ways to be thriving in any hostile environment. The Force of Nature naturally is plentiful. From a small seed grows a tree and soon there is a forest that provides life to a myriad of species. We possess the electromagnetic basis of that force to propel us toward a successful spiritual and financial existence. It is easier to help people when we have the abundance to create, teach, share and gift others.

The SEVENTH spiritual principle is to find a definite way to SUCCEED. It is important to recognize and copy the attitudes of successful people. Who do we listen to for advice? Our teachers have to be people who themselves succeeded against all odds. Every time we fail, or have a temporary setback we need to learn from that and get stronger from it. Gloom has to change to happiness and feeling great right now about how we will succeed in the near future. Have a great plan about your colorful success that will enrich humanity at least for seven generations ahead.

About Dr. William

William A. Gaspar, MD was born in Pittsburgh, Pennsylvania in 1957 from newly-arrived immigrants. By 1961, his parents moved back to beautiful Hungary. Then in their twenties his wife and he escaped from communism in a dangerous adventure. In 1981, they arrived back to 'the land of the free' with his wife Eva and daughter Rubina Xenia. Their son Austin Keane joined them later. They did not speak English, they had no money, but they were highly motivated to fulfill the American dream. They worked extremely hard, learnt English with excitement and entered into college as soon as they could. Within short six years in the United States, they flipped a few houses, William received his bachelor's degree at Kean University, and he started medical school. After 10 years in the USA, he received his MD degree in 1991, and Eva progressed toward a degree of Master of Herbology and Iridology.

They were extremely satisfied that they had achieved everything they ever wanted. That is, until the spiritual research bug hit him. Seemingly out of pure ether, silly questions in his own mind swarmed at him like angry bees: 'Why there are exactly 24 hours in a day?', 'Why do we have four fingers and a thumb?', 'Why an ice age cycle looks exactly like a human heart beat?', 'Where do letters and symbols originate from?' and so on. He developed an obsession with Cosmology, Sacred Geometry and Comparative Mythology. The answers arrived magically. They had great times sun dancing with the Native Americans and chasing cattle with the Cowboys. During this process, they had the great fortune to meet with a number of authors and great spiritual minds.

William's first book, *The Celestial Clock*, came out around the year 2,000 – about the Mayan Calendar ending. The great Mayan scholar John Major Jenkins, edited the book. Although, it was self-published, he had the honor to be on the Art Bell Show in 2001. Several other interviews and documentaries followed and he wrote a couple more books, including the *Sacred Cosmic Marriage* and co-authored *The World Tree*. At least seven authors quoted from his discoveries in their books. These scientific discoveries did not make him famous, but they opened up new frontiers and memberships in organizations. In his research, he discovered 'the ancient secret design of the Phoenicians that provide our Roman letters and the Egyptian symbols based on the knowledge of the Galaxy.' The emerging science is proving his theory that the 'sacred heart of our Milky Way Galaxy is around the star constellation Cygnus, the Northern Cross, that is also the likely originator of our own human electromagnetic heartbeat.' Many more discoveries followed. Initially subconsciously – later by design – his wife and himself employed a number of techniques that helped them become spiritually successful in what they do. They call it the Seven Secrets of Spiritual Success. It is their honor to share this with those seekers who are interested.

To contact and for more information, visit:

- www.thecelestialclock.com
- E-mail: gasparvili@gmail.com
- William 'Vilmos' Gaspar on Facebook and Gaspar & Jaramillo The World Tree on Facebook
- William A. Gaspar MD@gasparvili on Twitter
- William A. Gaspar MD@worldtreegaspar on Twitter

CHAPTER 31

THE OWN IT. WIN IT. CRUSH IT. SUCCESS FORMULA

– HOW TO PUT YOUR INCOME & REVENUE ON AUTOPILOT

BY ASH SEDDEEK

[Are you feeling stuck in your job or business? Are you looking for a breakthrough to make your job or business enjoyable and successful but don't know how? In this chapter you'll find the answer you're looking for. The essence of the breakthrough is in how much control you get when you follow the success formula presented here. In this formula, you'll see the thread of the need to have a passionate and relentless commitment to (1) your mindset mastery, (2) your expertise or business and (3) your client outcomes. ~ Ash Seddeek]

When Michelle went into her real estate office, she found several messages from her assistant. They were not so much different to what she found on her desk the day before. These messages were from former clients asking for her services; even though it'd been a long time since they were her clients for a home purchase or sale. There were also a number of messages from people she had never met, referrals from former clients or those that found her through her website. Michelle is a 'top producer' in the real estate industry. To become a top producer, you have to earn more in real estate commissions than anyone else in the same office you're working in.

The "book of business"

As in Michelle's business, customers are the lifeblood of all businesses. It doesn't matter what job, service or product you sell, customers are at the heart of keeping your business alive.

Have you ever been in a situation similar to Michelle's? Your answer will be an accurate indication of what stands between you and your ability to put your success on autopilot. Let's explore this more. Michelle's customers constitute what is called her "book of business." Another real estate agent can come to Michelle and offer her thousands of dollars for her client list. I want you to have your own book of business. Even if you're a corporate employee: your book of business is 'your LinkedIn' and internal network of sponsors and recommenders that you can tap into for your next opportunity. Remember: You're always running your own business, wherever you are.

Have you ever had several job offers and didn't know which one to accept, or had too many customer referrals and didn't have enough time or resources to dedicate to them. Both of these situations are good problems to have.

Customer referrals are a clear indicator of a healthy and thriving business. They indicate:

- Whether you're doing well financially, and not struggling to get repeat and new business.
- Or whether you're having to start from scratch every day in your business.

Michelle's example gives you a concrete picture of what life is like for some people. You too can start achieving the success you desire through the Own it. Win it. Crush it. Success Formula. Let's get started.

IT'S TIME FOR YOU TO SOAR

The solution is a simple yet powerfully profitable 3-step formula. This formula is the result of working as a peak performance expert at Deloitte Consulting, Oracle Corporation and Cisco Systems. At each company, I created award-winning professional development programs for thousands of global leaders, managers and the top 1% sales, services and engineering professionals. I also apply it in my own businesses as well. When these three steps are applied, they become your modus operandi for achieving repeatable, sustainable and ongoing success. The steps represent three mastery areas critical for success. These are:

- Self-mastery: We will call this 'Own it.'
- Value Creation Mastery: We call this 'Win it.'
- Customer Outcomes Mastery. We call this 'Crush it.'

We will use "Own it. Win it. Crush it." to refer to these three masteries in the rest of this chapter.

I will share with you some of the key elements in each of the steps.

THE OWN IT. WIN IT. CRUSH IT. SUCCESS FORMULA

Each step has three key components designed to help you create mindset and behaviors shifts critical for your success.

Step	Components
1. Own it **Self-Mastery**	1. Responsible Mindset 2. Abundance Mindset 3. Consultative Mindset
2. Win it **Value Creation Mastery**	1. Brand Standard 2. Differentiated Service Offer 3. Memorable Experience
3. Crush it **Customer Outcomes Mastery**	1. Customer Wow Factor 2. Repeat Business 3. New Business

STEP ONE: OWN IT: SELF-MASTERY:

You are responsible for your present and future. We will focus on three mindsets that shape this step. Owning this is fundamental to the life philosophy you need to embrace so you can start to achieve the financial independence, personal and family quality life you desire.

(i). **Responsible Mindset: Your mantra here is: If it's to be it's up to me.** When you adopt a responsible mindset, your motto is: "I accept responsibility regarding anything that needs to happen in my life: work, play, exercise, love, success, financial independence, happiness."

On the flipside, when you give that up, you live with a victim mindset and you concede to being powerless.

But with a responsible mindset, you're the master of your own universe. Your powers, dreams, motivations and passions are all yours. You feel extremely strong and empowered. The more you protect, nurture and apply these "powers," the more in control you are of your destiny, and what you are able to achieve. You'll also create more positive energy around you, and you'll start attracting people to you, your cause, business or initiatives.

Here are a few examples of how these two mindsets manifest themselves in our daily language:

Victim Mindset	Responsible Mindset
I don't exercise because I have so much work to do; there is no time for me to exercise.	I will exercise today!
This job is not working out for me. My manager doesn't support me, let me get the training I need to get the job done.	This job is not working out because I haven't yet given it my 100%. From now on, I will ask my manager lots of questions only after I have done my own extensive research and contacted everyone I need to contact in this company to get my work done. I will also look for training opportunities on the internet and learn fast to get really good at this job.

(ii). Abundance Mindset: Your mantra here is: I am an abundant being living in an abundant universe.

This mindset is about seeing opportunities and abundance where others may see scarcity. You hear the scarcity mindset when someone says:

- I can't find a job. The economy sucks. Everyone else I know is out of a job as well.

Whereas someone with an abundance mindset will be saying:

- Even though the economy may be slow right now and many people are out of work, I am going to see what companies are hiring and see if I can re-work my resume to address these needs.

An abundant mindset business owner may say: "Just because we are not able to find customers in this town for our business doesn't mean there aren't any customers out there. I am going to contact owners of similar businesses and find out what solutions worked for them and see which make sense for my business and customers.

Like a coin, an abundance mindset has two sides:

An Abundant You

On one side, it's the belief that there is a lot in each one of us in terms of potential, terrific ideas, dreams and aspirations. As Les Brown, a well-known motivational speaker, says: "There is greatness in you." You are whole. There is more in you that you can bring out in the form of 'personal productivity' by not settling for the status quo and always creating opportunities for yourself and others.

An Abundant Universe

The other side of the abundance mindset is when you strongly believe that there are abundant opportunities around you. When we shift our thinking from "I have to go get a job" to "I want to create jobs for myself and others," you start letting your creativity flow and you may say: "I can do this by partnering with others, and start a business or start a business by myself." If you are in a full-time position now, you may say: "I could look for an initiative or a project that I can kick-start."

(iii). A Consultative Mindset: Your mantra here is: Everyone around me is my client.

When I joined Deloitte Consulting my eyes were opened to the consultative mindset and I:

1. Discovered what it means to be a consultant.
2. Learned how management consultants manage their own professional development.
3. Learned how they manage the client relationship and adopt a long-term relationship view.

I knew that the best take-away for me from Deloitte has been the consultative mindset. When you adopt this mindset, you:

1. Represent your own brand and, at times, business brand with you as its ambassador.
2. Everyone you work with is your client.
3. The long term view trumps the short term view.
4. No one is going to remember your name before they remember the quality of your work. Always do your highest-quality work.
5. Satisfied customers lead to more customers: you can ask your client to be a professional reference and to share the experience they had working with you with new clients. If you walk away from a client project without making sure your work is going to be referenceable, then you know how much harder it is going to be get your next client, because you don't have a recent client testimonial or reference you can point them to.

STEP TWO: WIN IT. VALUE CREATION MASTERY; ACHIEVING THE CUSTOMER WOW FACTOR

Always do amazing work. Consistently deliver excellent work and exceed your customers' expectations. Have your own 'personal brand' and demonstrate your 'differentiated service' to others.

Brand Standard:

A good exercise here is to write or create a personal brand statement. This will help you define yourself and tell people what you stand for and how they will experience you when they work with you.

An example of a brand standard (statement):

"I will be the best social media consultant for small businesses in my community. By understanding their markets and the customers they serve, these businesses will find my marketing services focused on their success. I will do everything I can to ensure I deliver high quality services. When business owners in my community think of the best social media consultant, they will remember my name, call me and tell others about me."

Your Differentiated Service Offer

This applies to you whether you are a full-time employee, part time consultant or a full-fledged business owner. Sit down and think about what your business 'brochure' will say in terms of the service you offer. What makes you different from others? Why should others use your service rather than that of your competitors? For example, if you're a financial analyst, how good are you going to be vs. others?
Here is a brief exercise, take a moment to answer the following questions:

- You should hire me because ______________________________

  ____
- The results you and your business will receive when you work with me include ______________________________________

Memorable Experience:

Why do people go back for more to Starbucks, Apple, Disney, Amazon, Zappos, Ritz-Carlton, or ASOS? The common factor is an excellent, consistent customer experience. How about you? Why would people come back to you with more work?

In order to understand this concept, answer this question:

When people work with me, they will feel:

- I have their best interest in mind.
- They will get excellent value for their invested time, money and effort.
- What else? _______________________________________

STEP THREE: CRUSH IT. CUSTOMER OUTCOMES MASTERY: BUSINESS MULTIPLIER EFFECT

When you wow your customers with your service or product quality, they become your best marketing tool: generate buzz and referrals for you. These happy customers do more business with you and bring more business, money and abundance your way. That's the natural progression from satisfied customers to repeat business to new business.

The Crush It step is about what you 'leave behind' every time you interact with your customer. The 'leave behind' can be a solution to a problem or a new productivity tool you implement. Now let's look at these points in more detail by exploring some results of these behaviors:

Result 1: Customer does indeed use your product or service.

When you have done a great job at serving your customer and having their best interest in mind, they are more likely to use the product or service you provide, and get the highest possible return on their investment. You've seen examples of companies that go the extra mile in serving their customers. You can also assess how well you're doing here based on the quality service you have with your customer. At the lowest end of the spectrum, your business is providing a nameless transaction and at the other end you are a trusted advisor. Where do you stand on this spectrum?

Result 2: Repeat Business: Empower your customer with the knowledge and skills they need to move forward.

A lot of consultants try to create a co-dependency with the customer. This is to create a cycle in which the customer must return and give them more work. This is not, however, the right approach. You should show the customer how to get things done on their own after you have left. Consequently, you become someone they endear, trust and willingly bring you back in to do more work.

Result 3: New Business: Referenceability.

When your customers are more than satisfied with your excellent service, your customers will become one of your professional references for life.

The customer may also agree to give you a testimonial that you can use in your marketing efforts.

Referenceability results in repeat business from current customers and new business through new customer referrals via the power of word of mouth and the testimonials you have gathered along the way.

Your active role here is about scaling your business and having one customer win lead to another. This is when you reap the rewards of the three masteries above and see their results in your business.

SUMMARY: OWN IT. WIN IT. CRUSH IT.

Finally apply speed and timeliness in all of the above in your career, business or organization. Clients and managers always welcome people who deliver excellent and timely results. When you apply all of the above, work becomes enjoyable and highly rewarding.

About Ash

Ash Seddeek is dedicated to empowering people to honor their abundant potential, create profitable businesses and prosperous communities.

Ash is the creator of the Own it. Win it. Crush it.™ Success Formula to accelerate mindset shifts, add business value and create multiplier effect revenues and profits. He is an international business success and leadership speaker and author. He delivers a message of unlimited opportunity and potential.

Ash inspires his audiences in highly interactive keynotes and workshops and challenges them to think differently and adopt a responsible mindset to accelerate results. He helps companies create an organizational culture that empowers employees and inspires initiative and massive action. He believes that a responsible mindset is the highest form of personal accountability.

Ash Seddeek is also an expert on the top 1% sales and leadership success strategies and behaviors. He worked for Fortune 500 companies such as Deloitte Consulting, Oracle, BroadVision, and Cisco.

Ash has one 7-figure revenue business and is the founder of the Top 1% Sellers Factory, a boutique high-performance sales training and consulting firm. He studied at Harvard, Stanford and Santa Clara University Business Schools and is a Fulbright Scholar. Ash is the author of the forthcoming book: *Funnel Vision Strategies: How Top Sellers Deliver Exponential Client Value and Grow Wallet Share.*

His other books on sales and leadership are:

- *MEANING: How Leaders Create Meaning and Clarity during Times of Crisis and Opportunity*
- *Start with a Vision: How Leaders Envision a Better Future and Show Others How to Get there*

Ash, a national speaker, has been featured on CBS News, Fox, NBC, and ABC covering sales and leadership topics. He spoke recently at the prestigious Harvard Faculty Club on how to create massive business revenues and shared the stage with some of the top speakers in the world including Jonathan Goldsmith, the *Most Interesting Man in the World.*

You can connect with Ash at

- ash@connectwithash.com
- www.connectwithash.com
- twitter.com/ashseddeek
- Linkedin.com/in/toponepercentsellers

CHAPTER 32

WOMEN EMPOWERMENT: REACH YOUR FULL POTENTIAL AND FULFILL YOUR DREAMS

– THE SECRET TO HOW WOMEN CAN REACH THEIR FULL POTENTIAL BY BECOMING AWARE OF THEIR INNER SELF AND USING THE RESOURCES AROUND THEM

BY CATHERINE (ECATERINA) CANTER

As we become more enlightened, as we know ourselves more, truly anything is possible. When you connect to your true self, then life is limitless and anything you can possibly imagine can be your reality.
~ Yut

Laura had always been a cheerful young woman who inspired those around her with her positive nature. She had been known for her determination to follow her dreams. However, as time passed, Laura seemed to change. She felt stuck in her life; empty on the inside, and without a sense of direction. Daily routine and rushing absorbed her to the extent that she felt lost in daily tasks and she started to actually define herself by those tasks. "I have a crystal clear feeling that I live on a surface of myself," Laura confessed to her mother. She also felt that the fear and anxiety of performing and fitting in gradually expanded to fear to try new things, and worse, fear to live. "I live with constant pain in my chest caused by this feeling of smallness," Laura admitted.

One day the pain was so excruciating that Laura felt an urge to stop and totally allow herself to live the sensation. "I literally feel I've shrunk; my energy level has contracted to the maximum and is vanishing. Can I just disappear?" she asked herself in total stillness and helplessness laying alone on the floor in her room. Tears started to roll down her cheeks when a feeling of peace and surrender overwhelmed her. Yes, it is this sensation when you hit rock bottom that it can only get better. She laid there in solitude for a while. Finally, she fell asleep…and had a dream.

In this dream, Laura was following a woman but her silhouette kept disappearing in the mist before entering a mysterious white door. Finally, Laura managed to reach her; she was about to say hi but remained speechless. The woman stunningly resembled her. "Who are you?" asked Laura. "Are you my twin sister?" "I am you, yourself," replied the woman. "What do you mean?" asked Laura. "I am your inner self, the core being about whom you forgot because of your daily routine. Look, you have many roles that you perform in life, such as being a mother, daughter, employee, wife, friend and so on. But imagine you are taken away from all your roles? Who is left then? I am your inner self that is left when there are no roles; the part of you that is full of wisdom and wants to express itself – this is the part of you that gives you courage to live fearlessly and act, love, and be happy." Before Laura realized, the woman hugged her. Suddenly Laura felt enveloped by a feeling of connection, peace, confidence, and simplicity. She was yearning for such a feeling for so long.

"What is this door for?" asked Laura. "When you reconnect with yourself you become inspired to follow your dreams," the woman replied. "But you need to have courage to take the first step. When you want to pursue a dream, just step through that door and take the first step towards your dream. When you step through that door, you enter a space of uncertainty and unknowing, but also a space where you get support and answers. Do you want to enter that door now?" Laura looked at the door and took

a deep breath. The door was standing tall, wide, and still. A familiar feeling of fear to step over the line overwhelmed Laura. "Everything you want is on the other side of fear," whispered the woman. Laura needed the relief from fear. She closed the eyes and stepped through that door. Then an overwhelming feeling of curiosity, playfulness, and creative energy surrounded her.
Tears started to roll down her face. When she turned around, the woman was no longer there, but she left a note: "I am the real you, you can access me any time. Remember, you are more than anything that comes against you. It takes courage to step into dreams, but if you do you will get help."

Know yourself and you will win all battles.
~ Sun Tzu

How many of us can at least partially identify with Laura? Many of us long for a transformational change. In such situations we need to:

(i) reconnect with our inner self - a core being that is yearning to fulfill our dreams.
(ii) take actions to follow our dreams. Below are few steps to reconnect to our inner self and reach our fullest expression of ourselves in life.

I. RECONNECT WITH YOUR INNER SELF

1. Spend time in solitude. Have quiet moments apart from life clutter, people, and events. Take a walk in a park or forest, contemplate while watching the ocean's waves. Try not to watch news or TV. This will help free your mind and you will get into a habit of reconnecting to the silence within you.

2. Think about your life and connect the dots. Allotting time to think about your dreams, purpose, and possibilities makes wonders. The phenomenon of synapse tells us that if we give an issue enough time and attention to reflect on it, the numbers of neuron circuits increase which leads to more ideas and breakthroughs about the issue at stake. Train your brain to connect the dots and generate new ideas. One of my most rewarding activities has been to make connections between my career paths, talents, and events in my life. I was asking

myself: how can I bring together all these parts of my life? What is the universe leading me to, where is the synergy that I can interpret as my purpose?

3. Get yourself deliberately in a state of inspiration every day. Visualize and write down ideas that come in this state. This is key to our journey to know ourselves and be able to reach our potential. The Latin translation of the word inspiration means being in spirit. When we are inspired we connect to our inner self, the core being that is yearning to express, to expand, and realize our dreams. It is a higher dimension of our conscience, and for me it is the sweetest space to be, because in those moments I have an enveloping feeling that everything is possible and that I will get support when needed. When the state of highest inspiration passes, I look at those ideas and think they are a bit scary. But I know for sure that the inspired state is the real state, not the one obstructed by our conditioned mind. There are many ways to reach that space. We can intentionally listen to music, walk or exercise in nature, watch an inspirational movie, listen to inspirational messages, meditate or pray, write, or dance.

4. Become aware of, and eliminate, self-sabotage mechanisms that hinder your self-confidence. These are destructive self-limiting beliefs that operate like default mechanisms which have been attached to us as a result of our parents' attitude towards us, our cultural heritage, and social norms. We are often not aware of them but they prevent us from "seeing" opportunities and cause us to think small.

5. Dream big! Always seek to move to the next level. Our human path is to evolve. We find excitement and fulfillment when we expand our boundaries and embrace higher realms. It says that small vision leads to small life. Maureen Dowd asserted that, "the minute you settle for less than you deserve, you get even less than you settled for." This is incredibly true. Life gave me so many insights that we shall think big because the lower we aim the lower the prospect of success or failure, but often the level of effort, mental energy, and time is the same. And we should not know exactly how our dreams will be realized. Paulo Coelho said that, "When you want

something, all the universe conspires in helping you to achieve it." It is said that if you can see the invisible, God can do the impossible.

II. TAKE ACTION TOWARDS YOUR DREAMS

Take the first step in faith. You do not have to see the whole staircase, just take the first step.
~ Martin Luther King, Jr.

1. Step through the 'door' that Laura had to step through; have courage to take action towards your dreams in spite of fear and uncertainty. Often what separates us from knowing what we can do is just one step, one action, a phone call, or a question. I have learnt that if we overcome the fear and act, we are amazed by what we are capable of. You will discover that your potential is really much bigger than you thought. Quantum physicists affirm that the Universe is yearning for anything new and will render support.

2. Stretch your comfort zone to grow. It is known that 'when you stop growing, you stop.' Eleanor Roosevelt said, *"You gain strength, courage, and confidence by every experience in which you really stop to look fear in the face. You are able to say to yourself: I have lived through this horror. I can take the next thing that comes along."*

3. Develop new routine habits that bring you to your goals and dismantle habits that hold you back. Indeed, as Einstein said, *"Insanity is doing the same thing and expecting different results."*

Being exposed to opportunities of personal development is still a privilege that many women lack. For example, women and girls in many developing countries are deprived of this privilege. Therefore, they could be supported to develop their potential. The international development community can play a major role in bringing such a vision to the women empowerment field and, thus, contribute to poverty eradication and transformational social change.

I believe there is a shift towards an increasing human beings' quest for fulfilment and meaning. Philip Kotler, in his book *Marketing 3.0*, states that, "one of the key characteristics of an advanced and creative society is that people believe in self-actualization beyond their primal need for survival." (Kotler, 19) Aaron Hurst in his book *The Purpose Economy* argues about the emergence of a new economy's paradigm and shows how, "people's desire for impact, personal growth and community is changing the world." It talks about changes in business models of the private sector, non-profit organizations and charities which tap into our deepest cravings for meaning in our lives and work through creating new products, relations, and conditions that help people develop themselves and make a contribution. "Purpose is a universal need, not a luxury for those with financial wealth; even those in challenging situations still make it a priority." (Hurst, p.102)

Being aware of the need to develop our potential, we become increasingly cognizant of the need for us to scrutinize our mental models, analyze our beliefs, and thinking patterns. Yet, exposure to these concepts of personal development may be mostly the privilege of people who have been blessed with visionary parents, an unordinary inspiring education system, or mentors. But what about women and girls in developing countries, who have been born into poor families and social environments that often have imposed the "narrative" of their self-identity related to their social status.

The neuroscience and behavioral economics have already brought to our attention that human perception of reality is strongly influenced by past experience and external environment. Recent studies indicate that psychological barriers perpetuate poverty and obstruct people from discovering their potential, opportunities, and capabilities to contribute to society. The 2015 World Bank Development Report brings evidence that we think through mental filters conditioned by our background.

Neurocognitive science sustains that we can perceive only things that we can conceive, that is, we can experience only those things that we allowed ourselves. The UNDP study *Barriers and Opportunities at the Base of the Pyramid* highlights that detrimental belief systems heavily affect the life of people with low social status, including women. This is very relevant for women and girls in developing countries, many of whom live in a setting influenced by poverty and social prejudices regarding their capabilities, roles, and aspirations.

We are losing enormously in the cause of sharing prosperity and social justice by not supporting women and girls to become aware of their human spirit and potential thus tapping into women's ability to live their purpose and passions. Hillary Clinton reminds us that, 'women are the largest untapped reservoir of talent in the world.' I believe it is time for the development community to focus on individual transformation which would complement the conventional approaches that focus on sectors. I believe human connection to issues brings social change. Instead of developing a mindset of receivers for specific needs, we could inspire women to be the core of their inner change.

Kofi Annan stated that, "to educate girls is to reduce poverty." Yet, educating girls in the 21st century involves more than learning to read or write. Albert Einstein was affirming that, "education is not the learning the facts but the training of the mind to think." There is now an increasing recognition of the importance of non-cognitive skills and emotional intelligence (EQ) as opposed to intellectual coefficient (IQ) for people's success in life. Results reveal that such interventions' impact is more significant on women than on men since women carry more of the societal "bondage."

I think true women empowerment occurs when women think of things they never thought about; act in a way they never dreamed about; and connect the dots of what they are all about.

The development community could embrace the vision of women empowerment through the paradigm of human potential: providing women with tools on self-discovery, "growth mindset," grit, and removing their limiting self-beliefs induced by social status, poverty, and cultural prejudices. Such an approach would be in alignment with the current thinking supported by neurocognitive science, behavioral economics, and psychology experts. These innovative approaches could be attached to the new Sustainable Development Goals (SDGs), which aim at women's economic and social empowerment, and be part of the gender transformative approach aiming to change mindsets and social norms related to women. It could also be realized in partnerships with other "purpose economy" players and leverage their need to contribute.

Amartya Sen expanded the field of development with his work, *Development as Freedom,* where he highlights the human deprivations and the need for freedoms and opportunities to ensure human progress. Women's contributions are indispensable in this process. Amartya Sen believes that "women are increasingly seen, by both women and men, as active agents of change, the dynamic promoters of social transformations that can alter lives of both women and men." (Sen 1999:189).

Therefore, I believe we need to educate women and girls not only to struggle for equality but also to aspire to transform lives, to educate women not only to engage in their communities but also be visionaries for their communities. I believe we owe it to ourselves that women discover themselves and fulfill their aspirations. There is unimaginable leap frogging power in uncovering women's spirit and realizing women's dreams for the progress of our societies.

About Catherine (Ecaterina)

Catherine (Ecaterina) Canter is an international expert on innovative approaches aiming to improve international development impact, boost democratic governance, and enhance women empowerment. She has worked at the World Bank focusing on policies to make the development more inclusive, such as tools for citizen engagement and interventions on women empowerment. Catherine earned a mid-career Master in Public Administration from Harvard Kennedy School of Government and is a Fellow of the Mason Program for Public Policy and Management in Developing Countries from the same school. Catherine has also been awarded the Harvard Kokkalis Scholarship on Southeastern and East-Central Europe which promotes leadership, public service, and innovation in policy making. In addition, she holds an MA in Politics and Mass Media from the University of Liverpool, and a BA in Journalism and Communications from the State University of Moldova.

Catherine has a deep understanding of women empowerment and inclusive social development. She conducted World Bank's project screenings to identify opportunities for citizen engagement and women empowerment interventions as well as provided policy advisory and recommendations aiming to increase women's voice and agency, advance their economic empowerment, and enhance their participation in Bank's projects. She contributed to the World Bank's understanding of key success factors, political economy, challenges and opportunities for citizen engagement and women empowerment in various countries, through extensively researching and publishing eight papers on social accountability approaches, including gender responsive interventions. Her work considerably contributed to the World Bank policy documents aiming for more inclusive and accountable processes.

Catherine has a personal commitment for women empowerment. Her vision is to empower women in developing countries through providing them with tools, and equipping them with knowledge, about their untapped potential that would help reach their aspirations. Catherine believes in the opportunity to tap into an increasing people's search for meaning in their lives to contribute to social good. She has been raising awareness among the development community that self-limiting beliefs influenced by social status, poverty levels, gender, cultural prejudices, and social environment constitute behavioral and psychological barriers that perpetuate poverty and obstruct individuals, in particular women, from "seeing" and embracing opportunities – as well as harnessing their abilities to contribute to their societies. Her efforts have been directed towards creating synergy of recent findings in this area and connecting the dots on what international development field could contribute in this regard, including through Sustainable Development Goals.

Prior to the World Bank, Catherine also served as a spokesperson for the Council of Europe in Kosovo and Strasbourg, worked as a Political Specialist in the American Embassy, and as a TV News Special Correspondent at Moldovan Public Broadcasting. She is an alumnus of Harvard Women and Public Policy Program, a member of the Harvard Adaptive Leadership Network, and a fellow of Kokkalis program on Southeastern and East-Central Europe. Her publications focus on governance issues and social accountability, including women empowerment. She has received awards for her meritorious performance by the U.S. State Department and also for dedicated community service as well as commitment and professionalism in journalism.

CHAPTER 33

FIVE (5) KEYS TO UNLOCKING SUCCESS

BY DAWN BURNETT

As a Wellness Strategist, when I hear the term "success" I think of health, total wellness, but many people think of a destination either in wealth or in status of materialistic measure. When we study the definition of success, it means the accomplishment of an aim or purpose. Sounds simple but there are many layers to the word success, so it's not just as simple as setting a goal and achieving it more so than it is about the awareness of how to arrive at the place of success.

To arrive at success, it is a journey, a road or path that we travel down – the journey of life; to arrive at a destination, which ultimately should be purpose, the reason we are here on earth. Some of us arrive quicker than others so let's examine why.

I. **The journey to success first starts with a thought**
   Thoughts start in the mind and our minds control our outer world. Those thoughts cause feelings, which determine our actions, which supply us with results. But thoughts are tied to our beliefs, belief of personal worth and ability. So there are many factors that affect our thoughts: past parental programming, cultural influence, and past experiences. What we believe is what we achieve!

   But, to arrive at a place of understanding, in our thoughts we must first have awareness, the recognition and observance from a higher place of consciousness and the examination of where we are at in the now, at this present time. It is then that we become connected, aware of our thought process, surroundings, dreams and beliefs. Now this may seem too deep for some people, but if you are thinking that, perhaps this is a mental road that has been lacking and preventing you from arriving at your place of success.

The minds of the greats have all arrived at this place to create a shift from trying to succeeding.

Many of us overlook this foundational step. Instead, we are busy with the chase of success, the appearance of an outer result from efforts until one day a major road block happens in life. Then suddenly, there is a shaking so strong it jolts us to a halt, and forces us to examine what it is we are searching for and why.

This shift in awareness is what leads us to a more awakened place of self because it's within that all environments begin to change. Now don't get me wrong, there is lots of effort and action involved with success, but to arrive at a faster pace we must first master our foundation. Don't believe me? Remember our step to success is mind first then action. **The number one element that stops us from taking the necessary action is fear** – again the place of thoughts and our minds.

As soon as we shift our thinking from fear to faith–belief that we have success before it happens – staying with a steadfast mind and intense focus so strong that instead of the thought of quitting, we fight and persevere, not giving up. But the only thing that will bring us to this place is first determining our 'why.'

II. Determining our 'why'

Our 'why' of what we are aiming for should come from a place of heart and passion, not a position of money. Money is the by-product, the result of our 'why.' Let me give you an example, I decided to become a Wellness Strategist after the birth of my miracle boy who, at the age of two, had a compromised immune system – due to vaccinations that pushed him into five rounds of antibiotics that lead us to a children's hospital that wanted to remove body parts, and he was pronounced with severe celiac disease by our Natural Doctor. Nobody could supply me with concrete solutions.

I became so frustrated that my mind shifted with despair and it's then that I found an article for a university. The words leaped off the page, "Get your degree in Alternative medicine." Without hesitation I had my college transcripts sent, I was in my seat and after many obstacles and intense perseverance, I graduated *summa cum laude* and within six months *I restored my son's health.*

From there, I kept noticing how many people were getting sick and diagnosed with diseases; I know I, before my education, was one of those people. My 'why' is to help put an end to this disease care crisis, a position of passion and heart, finding a problem and supplying a solution.

My success came from being my true self and flowing in my purpose and so will yours.

In healing my son, I did not take time to think, which is great, I just moved towards my aim—getting my son well—and there was nothing in my mind that was going to stop me. A near-death car crash, a major move to a new state (not knowing what was on the other side), a divorce and freedom from a 15-year toxic relationship; all of these things happened, but I experienced success because my mind had a locked- in focus of getting my son well, and I saw him well before I started the journey.

I had waited so many years for my miracle boy to show up after fertility specialists told me it was impossible to have another child and that they couldn't help me. You see, I had no self-doubt for the first time in my life. When that happens, we remove the blocks stopping us from success and we are catapulted towards our dreams, in this case the dream of keeping my son and watching him grow up whole and well.

Wellness to me is passion, and when we don't flow in passion we are missing the key component to success. Put simply, when you do what you love you just flow. Nothing stopped me from finishing up my degree and I learned with passion, the desire for my son to be well. When we flow that's when abundance comes in, it's not a place of forced position. I was flowing in my education and consuming every word to make my son well, and my self-abundance was graduating *summa cum laude* after my ex told me I would never achieve my degree, but my ultimate abundance is my son's wellness.

So abundance doesn't always mean a place of money. I first had a dream and belief that my son would be well, a locked-in mindset that he would be healed and I saw the end result as wellness. This was my 'why' which lead me to take action and go back to college at the age of 38. My passion for him to be healed was so strong it kept me learning with intense focus, despite all the adversities that came in, and as a result, my son is 12 and is well!

This is my abundance, because without good health we have nothing and can do nothing. My focus was not on me, it was on my son. *For there to be abundance and success we must take our focus off ourselves and put it on the desire to help others and solve their problems.* When we do this properly, abundance flows in. So, we are the only one standing in the way of our own success.

Arriving at this place of understanding has taken me many years, my life's journey, so if I can help in shortening those years for your journey, then my place and position on this earth has been served. *If I ignite your passion, cause you to think at a deeper level or provide you with a relatable moment where you no longer feel alone in your journey, then my purpose in joining the greats in this book has been served.* Seeing you catapulted towards your dreams from reading this book is my abundance.

Please don't think I have arrived, I, like many of the greats, am continuously working on mastering my mind. We know that if we don't tame our minds then our minds will tame us and all success will be lost – that's why we call success life's journey. Since our thoughts and experiences are stored at a cellular level and if negative, they can affect our health and create disease we have to heal and transform our thoughts. We the greats know, that although we have advanced on our road to success, speed bumps, triggers that spark thoughts of the past we thought had been healed, pop up like a weed that was never removed at a root level in the back yard. Apparently, we never got to the true root so when that happens we have to revert back to taming our minds.

People arrive at this place differently. For me, it's vision boards, prayer, meditation, laughter, mirror work, positive affirmations, mindful living, healthy eating and yoga that bring me to the place of restoration and taming my mind. The realization that what goes in must come out and the knowing that if I hang around negative people I won't live a positive life. Having survived that last car crash by a hit-and-run drunk driver, and having my lights knocked out and my son nearly taken from me, I already feel as if I am on borrowed time. I have a message to supply and I know I won't be leaving this earth until the message has been released and lives have been transformed to greatness. This is my purpose that became clear when the lights after that crash were turned back on.

So let's zoom in on our target of success. What other components are we missing for success?

III. Gratitude

Despite what is happening around us, during our launch to success we must learn to operate from a place of gratitude – a knowing that all things appear for a far greater reason and show up to teach us a lesson that will advance us on our journey to success. Successful people constantly learn and grow and they learn from other successful people. Who you surround yourself with is who you become, and if you look at truly successful people, not just the wealthy, but also the true whole success of people, they operate from a place of gratitude. After all, if there is no gratitude then we are cutting off the source of supply for abundance, so put simply, gratitude will transform our lives.

IV. Giving

Another component to success is giving, what we put out is what we receive. It's important to operate from a place of love, love for people and what we are doing, and then giving will become easy. Giving can't come from a place of calculation, it has to come from a place of heart with no measurement to the end result, but rather a knowing of the principal law that what we put out comes back to us in multiple forms. When we love what we do then we never have to wonder what we will receive. As we continue to remember our key components to success and flow in them, then everything else will fall into place, come into perfect alignment with what we are working to achieve with passion, . . . our life's purpose.

V. Determining the "How"

The final key component to success is the surrender and understanding that you don't need to know the hows of making it from point A to point B of success; they will turn up if you have put everything else we spoke about into place. We just first start with the belief and surrendering, knowing that all will be well as we take one step at a time down the road to success while staying focused on our "why," so we don't quit while we continuously work on our thoughts and tame our minds, dodging sink holes along the way that will cause the wheels to pop off and derailment to happen. Will you fail? Do you fear that? We have all had these thoughts; greats have all thought this at one time or another. The reality is 90% of life is our perception to the actual 10% of events that are truly happening. After all, we are the only ones who really remember what we perceive to be as our failures. We can learn from them and move forward, creating something new or we can allow them to cripple us, keeping us from success, planting us on the road mostly traveled.

So we hold the power of choice. Stop and ask yourself,

- Am I really doing what I'm meant to do with my life?
- Am I letting fear stand in the way of my dreams?
- Am I looking for security in things outside of myself?
- Do I believe in myself?
- Am I afraid of success?
- Do I feel worthy of success?
- What is preventing me from achieving and flowing in life's purpose?

It's time to remove your conditioned-thinking glasses, free yourself from your blockages and release from the pitfalls of past behavior. Success and happiness await you, the choice is all yours.

Life is not a dress rehearsal, so GO FOR IT. What have you really got to lose? You just may actually find yourself

About Dawn

Dawn Burnett, CSA is founder of A New Dawn Natural Solutions, Inc. A *summa cum laude* graduate of Alternative Medicine from Everglades University at Boca Raton, Florida, Dawn provides Wellness Strategies to those who are frustrated with their current health situations and are ready to embrace alternative healing solutions.

A regular fixture on the high-profile airways of national television, Dawn believes we can all access a healthier, more balanced life by using natural approaches for boosting our energy, purifying our eating regimes, and recalibrating the connection between mind and body. As a wellness strategist, her advice and insight have helped her satisfied clients achieve that in their personal lives, while, as the curator of a line of products on her website: www.anewdawnnaturalsolutions.com, she also makes these solutions accessible to fans and devotees across America.

Dawn's impressive roster of television and speaking appearances include FOX and TBN. A writer as well, her work can be found in the pages of publications such as *Confident Woman Magazine.* As a contributing Writer for *The Huffington Post,* she engages readers in the powerful world of connection.

A published author of *True Confessions of the Heart* (Carpenter's Son Publishing; Ingram Distribution), Dawn's premiere book is an inspirational autobiography, demonstrating how, through the use of natural medicine, readers can heal their lives from the inside out — just as she has done herself. Her forthcoming book, *Connect, How To Know If He's Really Your Man,* published by Health Communications, Inc., shifts the focus to dating and personal relationships, putting Dawn's insightful voice at the forefront.

Dawn is working on her forthcoming book *Behind The Scenes On The Journey To Success* shifting the focus towards what High Profile People have had to endure to make it big.

Ms. Burnett is an advocate for children's health, and is an ardent believer in "paying it forward." As such, Dawn has collaborated with a noteworthy recording artist and co-wrote a song titled: *Right Now.* At the request of HTV, Dawn produced a video that she donated for use in children's hospitals in an effort to raise awareness for childhood obesity prevention. Dawn's forthcoming song, *I AM A Trainwreck*, shifts the focus to inner connection, and for this song, she collaborated with a noteworthy recording artist and music producers.

Dawn is also expanding her focus towards radio where she will be co-hosting *Wake Up And Listen*, putting her wellness expertise at the forefront. *Wake Up And Listen* talk show radio will inspire and empower listeners to achieve the fulfilled life they have been dreaming of.

Are you ready to connect to your well-being? Dawn has the strategies to help you achieve ultimate wellness so connect with her on:

- Twitter: @anewdawnnatural
- Facebook: anewdawnnaturalsolutions
- LinkedIn: andnaturals
- Website: https://anewdawnnaturalsolutions.com/

CHAPTER 34

SHUT THE FRIDGE! OPEN YOUR MIND

BY AMANDA J. STENTON-DOZEY

At some point in your life, you have tried to change a habit, and really struggled. The struggle with any habit is not the behaviour, it's with your thinking (subconscious response). If you don't change the thinking, the behaviour will always go back to what the subconscious mind is most familiar with.

17 years ago, I embarked on my first real weight loss journey. I was really serious about getting rid of the excess weight I'd gained after having my first child. In the 11 years of dieting that followed, I had spent in excess of $14,000, I was 30 kilos heavier than when I started trying to lose weight, and I hated myself enough to question my existence.

I reached the conclusion I was going to be obese for the rest of my life, and told myself there was no point in fighting my genes. I was **FAT**, and there was nothing I could do to change it. I was going to have to accept that I would hate myself forever. What a depressing concept!! I tried everything on the market and even if it **did** work, it was only ever temporary. I would run out of money, stop the product or the program and back on the weight came (plus a few bonus kilos!).

I did everything I was told. I weighed foods, bought exotic ingredients (that then sat in my cupboard for the next 4-5 years), I counted calories, fat, carbs, it was **INSANE** what I was doing to myself. I did more than the required exercise (and I wasn't a fan of exercise). Yet the results were always the same.

I was even accused of lying to my program 'support' person about what I was eating – not how I imagined being supported?

But all the same, all these processes did was give me more evidence as to why I was such a loser, and a fat one at that! **So I gave up.** I ate what I wanted, when I wanted and as much as I wanted. Being above average height, people would say to me "oh you can't tell you're THAT size because you're tall" and that pissed me off no end! Who cares how tall you are - fat was fat in my mind! I got sick and tired of wasting SO much money, time and energy on things that wore me out to the point I couldn't maintain them, emotionally or financially. I'll bet there's a few of you out there nodding your heads right now - you've had this experience yourself, haven't you?!

So have I actually overcome the cause of my weight problem by consuming pills and potions or using someone else's food plan? Have I really changed my habits for good?

Have I learnt **WHY** I eat the way I do? What would happen if I never dealt with the cause of my eating habits?

Honestly, if you don't ever deal with the **core** triggers that turn you to food, your weight problems will continue to yo-yo for the **rest** of your life. Whilst you feed those negative voices in your head that are telling you, "You're not good enough, you don't deserve to be happy. You're lazy, you're stupid, you're just fat." You're just a self-fulfilling prophecy of your internal talk. You've given up control of your life, your choices. All the while, you just continue feeding the **Fat Cats** of this multi-billion dollar industry who are just waiting, preying on good people just like you.

"How do I get off this merry-go-round?" I hear you ask. I'm going to give you a couple of ideas here, and I want you to base your decisions on what you can sustain, at least for the next 6 months. If you won't commit to it for 6 months, don't start it. The reality is, you're not doing yourself any favours other than giving yourself a kick in the guts, and that's not going to achieve anything positive.

Firstly - **stop going on diets!** We're all on a diet - it's either healthy or unhealthy. You DO have a choice and, because you're a grown up now, take responsibility for your thinking and your behaviour.

If you **eat** crap, you'll **feel** crap - **deal** with it or **don't do it** - it's a choice. If your body is telling you "don't eat carbs after 3pm or I'll give you heartburn for the rest of the night!" Don't eat carbs after 3pm! Listen to your body, it's job is to get you through this life in peace. But remember, whatever you do to your body, it will do back to you ten times bigger, so choose wisely, it's much better at this game than you!

Swap and reduce. Don't take on too much change all at once. It's a brain drain and chances are you'll give up. Start by reducing how much you eat. Maybe take off 1 dessert spoon of food from your plate every night for a week, then more the next week. You can also swap foods. Instead of eating dairy chocolate, swap it for dark chocolate - and if you don't 'like' dark chocolate, it's a good sign that you don't really want anything to eat anyway!! Think about trying to coerce children to eat veggies. They say 'I'm full' until you offer dessert! Truth is, if they were really hungry, they would've eaten whatever was put in front of them!

Very Important - Don't deny yourself! If you want to eat a piece of cake, eat a piece of cake. BUT... add these two rules:

1) **Give yourself permission to really enjoy it.** If you're going to eat that cake and then beat yourself up for the next 2 hours - **STOP**. **DO NOT**, under any circumstances, eat that cake, until you're at peace with it. If you feel like you can't find peace, walk away from the cake, for now, and come back when you're ready to make an effective and calm decision.
2) **Stop when you've had enough.** The waste doesn't matter. It's still wasted in your body anyway, it just comes with an additional cost to your health and your hip pocket for the extra medications later on! Much better to just 'waste money' than the quality of your life as well!

I want you to refocus on **where** you're seeking information about what's best for you. I want you to learn to **trust** yourself again. Your subconscious mind has been keeping you alive and protected since you came into this world, so it knows what's best for you and how to protect you, better than anyone else.

All of this "Health" information is given with a generic approach, comparing your situation to that which is similar to yours. What it doesn't take into account, is your self-talk, self-image, values and beliefs.

You're forgetting that you were born with an intuition designed to keep you safe and alive at all costs. **Listen** to it! For every article or research that tells you fat is good for you, you'll find another that disagrees. Trust in **yourself**.

Okay, here are some simple ideas on how to change your behaviours, without it feeling like you're pulling teeth without an anaesthetic!

- **Turn off** the TV/Internet/tablet, etc.
- **Avoid** online and magazine quizzes and questionnaires that tell you how bad your situation is.
- **Remove yourself** from the negative influence of others. It's merely their opinion, it doesn't have to be yours.
- If it doesn't make you feel good about yourself, it's not for you!
- **Move your mind and body**, and then build on that. Remember the KISS principle – Keep It Simple Sweetie!

Purely focussing on what we eat and how much we exercise is **not** the answer. We have become a culture **obsessed** by food – Cooking Shows, weight-loss shows, 12-week challenges, healthy choice ranges, frantic media releases about obesity epidemics, etc. "It's basic math," they say, ". . . put in less than you burn off!"

We can logically figure this stuff out. Those experts are right, it is basic maths. But the issue lies in the **subconscious** part of our being. The **'feeling'** part of us. The part of us that stands in front of the fridge, for the third time, hoping that something ***yummy*** has magically appeared since our last look. Hoping that this food will take away the boredom, loneliness, anger, or whatever that problem is that lies within.

But if the **problem** lies within, then the **answer** must lie within too. And I'm not talking about inside your fridge either! You already **know** what you need to eat, you already **know** what you need to **do** with your body, to be healthy. You **have** the knowledge already. It's the DOING that escapes us. But why?

As a Behaviour Coach and Hypnotherapist, I speak to people everyday, who really want to change the way they look. Hell, I was one of them!

I went to a hypnotherapist 16 years ago because I hated my body. I hated how I looked, how I felt. It didn't seem to matter what I did, I just hated it. I went through the process knowing there was a money-back guarantee, so I had an *'out'* if it didn't work. And you know what? I walked out of that session, and this was my internal talk:
"Well that was enjoyable, but I'm **sure** it didn't work. That was way too **easy**. I'm sure I'm going to be one of her *'failure'* clients, because I have no will-power. I couldn't even walk past the takeaway next door without giving in! Which reminds me, it's lunch time, and I feel hungry. I'll just have a look at the takeaway shop. I won't buy anything, I'll just see if there's anything that appeals to me."

Well guess what? I walked out of there with a hamburger with the lot and a chocolate milk! As long as I was having negative self-talk, there's **NO WAY** I was going to have success.

It wasn't until many years later, and over $14,000 in pills, potions and plans, that I finally realised: ***It's my INSIDE that needs an overhaul.*** As long as I'm beating myself up internally, I'm going to keep treating my body like the rubbish dump in my mind. Mind and body have to agree, it's the way we're designed.

Have you ever met, or even **BEEN** one of those people who loses a fantastic amount of weight? Looking great, feeling great, shopping for clothes is easy, everyone's complimenting your look. Only to put it all back on again?

If it's such a great experience, why do we go back? Because the compliments lessen, the joy of buying smaller sizes wears off, the thrill has gone. Then the mind starts thinking 'fat' thoughts and creating all the reasons **WHY** you aren't feeling good about yourself anymore.

"It's because you're worthless, nobody likes you, you think you're SO good now that you're thin. People are jealous of how you look."

We all need to feel safe and secure. We want to fit in, we want to feel wanted, accepted, loved. So we return to old eating habits, gradually at first, and we think – "it's only a couple of kilos, I can get rid of that next week." And so the cycle kicks back in, and the heavy thoughts return, bringing the heavy body with them.

The missing link is changing the way we **think** about ourselves. Only when you are truly **kind** and **gentle** to your being, using your thoughts and internal talk, will you permanently change how you **treat** your body. The **body** is the bi-product of your thinking. Being healthy is merely 5% what we put **into** our body, 5% what we **do** with our body and 90% what we **tell** ourselves.

If you're feeding your mind crap, the other 10% won't make a scrap of difference, because you'll get tired or bored or angry or frustrated, and your 10% will come undone. Your outside is just a reflection of your inside.

So how do we make changes that support what we're putting into our bodies and what we do with our bodies? **Stop obsessing over food!**

- Give yourself **permission** to indulge, really engage in the activity and BE in the moment.
- Be **kind** to yourself, no self-loathing allowed EVER!
- Be **aware** of negative self-talk & change it - swap and reduce your negative thoughts.
- **Disconnect the food from the emotion.** Food is a source of fuel, not a feeling suppressant.

I want to leave you with this thought: Weight loss companies are very clever. They spend billions of dollars each year on 'buying psychologists' to make sure their marketing is making you feel **SO** awful about yourself that you just **HAVE** to buy their products and services until you feel better about yourself. AND THEN, you're back to square one! This merry-go-round epidemic is what makes them money.

Stop participating. Give up this mouse-wheel existence. THE MOUSE IS DEAD PEOPLE! I know, first hand, how disempowering and soul-destroying that lifestyle is.

For over five years now, I've maintained my weight of 80kg with ease. I'm more fit than when I was a teen, and I still LOVE food! After having success changing my thinking, I realised the key difference in my results was purely my desire to change how I treated myself, and how I related to food. Yes, I emotionally eat on occasion, but you know what? I'm in control of the food, instead of it controlling me. I'm at peace with myself, because I know I **will** get back on track tomorrow. I only exercise in ways that I enjoy, and my body craves healthy foods far more than anything else!

About Amanda J.

Amanda J. Stenton-Dozey is no stranger to the School of Hard Knocks. Exposed to bullying by her peers throughout her schooling, domestic violence, bankruptcy, failed relationships, addictions, obesity, and an array of other life challenges, Amanda J. has used these experiences to help thousands learn to see their personal value and to grow their potential.

Amanda J. developed her philosophy, "you are what you think you are," from a very young age. Her passion for human growth and development has guided her through multiple career paths, accruing a diverse knowledge and understanding of thought-based behaviours. Amanda J. has a unique and intuitive understanding of what makes people tick and has successfully nurtured thousands of her clients to reframe their thinking and 'behave their way' into new results.

Whilst her work has been primarily conducted one-to-one, she has now made it her personal mission to spread her message and offer her teachings on a larger scale, to those who know they deserve more from life.

An enthusiast of Human Behavioural Science and research, Amanda J. holds qualifications and extensive experience in Hypnotherapy, Life/Self-Esteem Coaching, Master Practitioner and Trainer of NLP (Neuro-Linguistic Programming), Early Childhood Development and Business, and possesses over 20 years of experience developing and growing people to their potential.

You can connect with Amanda at:

- www.AmandaJ.ThinkingIntoResults.com
- www.AmandaJ.com.au
- www.facebook.com/AmandaJdownunder

CHAPTER 35

GOING THROUGH FAILURE IS HOW YOU ACHIEVE SUCCESS

BY RONDEA WINE

Rejection and Correction equals Education and Acceleration... Rejection is the start of education...Most people are not successful because they have not been rejected enough.
~ Robert Kiyosaki

As a child, we have unending wonderment, amazement, and curiosity. We have an overwhelming ability to focus on what we want with unrelenting persistence. As a child, we have crystal clear dreams and a belief that all is well with oneself and the world. We have no limits and no fear.

When we become a young adult, we develop the characteristics of commitment, dedication, drive, loyalty, and responsibility. However, we also allow the negative thoughts and negative words to stifle our dreams, hopes and wishes. We hear more "no's" than "yesses". We have to decide if we are going to do what we are told or not. We have to weigh the consequences of our actions. We still keep striving, however, it has become a little more difficult and not as much fun. It does not have to be this way if you know how to think and what to do.

"...Too many people give up too early. If they are disappointed, lose a few dollars, or have their feelings hurt, most people retreat back to the world of their lower mind. I believe this is one of the primary reasons why so few people attain great wealth, even in the richest country in the world. I also believe it is the reason why so many people choose security over freedom. The fear of not having enough money to put food on the table has replaced freedom as a priority in our society. The more security you see, the less freedom you have."

When we become an older adult, we are tested in our abilities to keep up with the other folks whether that be with our intelligences, our finances, and/or our skills and talents. There is another way and that is to beat to our own drum. However, that way is full of obstacles and other peoples' lack of understanding and put downs. It does not have to be this way if you know how to think and what to do.

When we become an elder, we may become lost. Hopefully, we are with loved ones who want to have us around, watch over us, and remain a part of our life. If not, then we may have to deal with despair, loneliness and /or death. The opportunities at this end of life could be much less than preferred. The folks of the world may show little tolerance or patience with us. It does not have to be this way if you know how to think and what to do.

"Within you, whoever you may be, regardless of how big a failure you may think yourself to be, is the ability and the power to do whatever you need to do to be happy and successful. Within you right now is the power to do things you never dreamed possible. This power becomes available to you just as soon as you can change your beliefs."

So, what is success and what is failure? Success is having the right thoughts about life such that you are, do and have everything that you want. This could mean being poor and perfectly happy. This could mean being wealthy and supporting charities. This could mean spending lots of quality time with your family, children, and/or friends. This could mean having good health. This could mean doing what makes you feel good (of course without hurting yourself or others). So, what is failure? Is it the negative of success? Interestingly, failure is having thoughts in the wrong direction. In other words, you are, do and have nothing that you want. Failure is only limiting if you allow it to be. Failure is only disgraceful and/or shameful if you think it is. Failure is only discouraging, depressing, heart wrenching, lonely, pitiful, spiteful, and non-forgiving if you allow it and believe that it is so.

"All frustration is due to unfulfilled desires. If you dwell on obstacles, delays, and difficulties, your subconscious mind responds accordingly, and you are lacking your own good. Success means successful living. When you are peaceful, happy, joyous, and doing what you love to do, you are successful."

You did not get all of this junk in your life overnight. You may think that you have no way out. There is always a way out! There have been many people who have been to the brink or edge of disaster, and have lived to tell their story. You can do it too – you can be a survivor! Just take one step at a time towards your new and better goal. Think of only positive and good thoughts. Do not listen to the negativism. Be persistent. Keep going. Never give up on reaching your dreams!

So, how is it that the title of this chapter is all about going through failure in order to achieve success? May I enlighten you with my own personal stories: The first two are about love and relationships and the third one is about financial illiteracy:

As a child, my family was the epitome of what a loving family should look and act like. Everyone expressed love to each other with lots of hugs, kisses, and wonderful adorations of praise – how beautiful you are, how smart you are, how funny you are, etc. This idealism continued until the age of eleven years old. After my biological father divorced my mother, it felt like the world as I knew it had been shattered to pieces, and the pieces would either need to change or by the grace of God, be put back together again. Needless to say, the pieces changed. My family changed, a step father (a good man) came into the picture, a new living environment was established, and I changed.

Then during my early 40's, I finally got my act together and finally realized just who I am, and what I believe in. I now know exactly what I want in a man who will become my husband. Now, if I had quit in high school and gave in to the thoughts of others about who I am, or gave into the negative consequences of my actions later in life, I would not be where I am today. Today, I am happy and finally at peace with myself. Please do not think I am perfect; far from it. I have weaknesses and strengths just like everyone else. However, knowing who you are and what your purpose is in life gives you all the hope that you need, to have an amazing life.

After four years of college, I decided to change careers and went back to school to learn a trade. Upon completion of that schooling, I became an employee for six years. The other side of the fence looked more exciting and glamorous. So, I left that company and went to work for a different company. After a little over one year, and after the 9/11 event in the U.S.A., that company laid off 1,500 people, including me.

Due to a lack of financial education and indiscriminate spending, I filed bankruptcy. Finally, another job came long. I went back to school thinking that a different career would make things right again. Two years later, after obtaining a Master's degree in Primary Education, I worked as an elementary teacher for one year and realized that that was not for me. I then went back to being an employee with my first employer. Still not sure I had enough education and another two years later, a Master's degree in Business was obtained.

After six years with my first employer for the second time around, I gave notice again and started my own business working from home. It was a successful year, however, the client was the employer I had just left. That employer again approached me and asked me to come back, which I did. Now, I still have a business entity, but am back to being an employee. So, has all of this jumping around been good? I believe everything happens for a reason. You have to get your financial education somehow, even if that is through the school of hard knocks. Finally, I am learning to network with people who have what I want. I am learning how they think to change how I think. Luckily, every decision I have made has made me a better, stronger, more courageous, more independent, more initiative-taking, more humble, more empathetic, and more knowledgeable type of person.

Remember that you learn more in your valleys than you do on your hilltops. Now, you can look upon this fact as disturbing. Or you can look upon this fact as a challenge. A challenge that will inspire you to keep going.

"Apart from the benevolence of God, we cannot amass wealth. While our labor, diligence, planning, and wisdom are vital, God remains the sole source of blessing. He is the fountainhead of life, health, food, sun, and all other elements necessary for prosperity. As Creator, all of life is His gift. He is the Prime Giver.... Since all wealth flows from the provision of God, our role is to act as sensible, faithful stewards. God gives it all and God owns it all. He designates us as caretakers of His assets." So, you may ask, how is it that the people who do harm to others and to this world have wealth? There are certain universal laws that may be followed by everyone. It is up to you whether or not you follow them and it has nothing to do with whether or not you are a good or bad person. Below are five of the laws:

The first law is: The Law of Gratitude. If you are ungrateful for all that you are, do and have in this world, then do not be surprised if what you have, be and do, is taken from you and given to someone else who does have gratitude.

The second law is: The Law of Like Causes Produce Like Effects. "Getting rich is not a matter of environment…[and] is not due solely to the possession of talent, for many people who have great talent remain poor…Getting rich is not the result of saving, or thrift; many very penurious people are poor…Nor is getting rich due to doing things which others fail to do…Getting rich is the result of doing things in a Certain Way. Every act is, in itself, either a success or a failure. Every act is, in itself, either effective or inefficient. Guard your speech. Never speak of yourself, your affairs, or of anything else in a discouraged or discouraging way…Never speak of the times as being hard, or of business conditions as being doubtful…Train yourself to think of and to look upon the world as a something which is Becoming, which is growing; and to regard seeming evil as being only that which is undeveloped. Always speak in terms of advancement…"

The third law is: The Law of Habit. How you repetitively talk to yourself and others, how/when/where and what you do every day, and how you think on a repetitive basis establishes your beliefs, then your feelings and finally your actions.

The fourth law is: The Law of Economics. This law is all about giving and receiving. If you go through life only trying to get, you will ultimately thwart any chance of receiving. You may have also heard of this as 'the Law of Reaping and Sowing.'

The fifth law is: The Golden Rule. This law is all about treating others as you would treat yourself. Give more than you receive and give it more often than expected.

My hope is that you will use the five laws above to change your life around for the better, or at a minimum, keep making your life the best ever. May you always have hope. May you always serve others. May you always be/do/have your best.

About Rondea

Rondea Wine has a passion for helping people with their overall well-being, whether that be with health (involving the mind, body and spirit), wealth or overall happiness. She grew up in a family plagued with health ailments; lost both of her fathers to diseases; and has noticed the impact that a lack of financial education has done with her own mother's retirement fund. Rondea naturally gravitated toward finding ways of improving health, wealth and overall happiness for everyone.

She continues to take responsibility for her good and bad choices, and continues to move forward learning from her mistakes. One of the things that has helped her overcome her weaknesses is experiencing a variety of cultures. Rondea has traveled to all 50 states of the United States of America, overseas to Western Europe and Asia, and she continues to explore the world and discover and experience how other people live.

Rondea Wine's Bachelor of Science degree helps her understand the science behind things. Her Master's in Teaching degree helps her better relate to others and pass on the knowledge gained. Finally, her Master's in Business degree helps her discover cost-effective solutions. In addition, Rondea has had two successful businesses. She continues to educate and immerse herself with financial knowledge. Rondea is a lifetime member of CEO Space America, a level 3 affiliate with Global Information Network, and a member of BestLife Coaching. Rondea holds a personal life coaching certificate. She is an affiliate with Karatbars International and a believer in economic insurance. She is a published author as of 2014 with her book entitled, *Stop the Junk.* She has two cats and loves God and her family.

You can connect with Rondea at:

- rleoandlenny@gmail.com

CHAPTER 36

FAITH, PERSEVERANCE AND LOVE

BY YESENIA MIRANDA GIPSON

Whether one is spiritual or not, most all things are done through faith. A mentor once said to me, "Faith is the belief in something which has not yet been proven, in one's life." There is so much truth in this statement. And when faith is proven, the subconscious receives it as being as natural as breathing, knowing that the air will never be depleted. Most people get in their cars believing that it will take them where they want to go. They do not doubt in the car's ability to function how it is intended to. That is having faith in your car. Those that work get up every day and get ready for it because they believe they have a job. They have faith in their employment. Every night, one goes to sleep without fear or doubt of waking up in the morning. Many make plans for the future, be it near or far, under the principle of faith; that belief, which has yet to be proven, that tomorrow will always come.

Part of faith is to believe in something until it is proven. In all of the examples above, the one thing they have in common is that they get proven in our lives. Every time the car takes you to your destination, your faith in your car's ability has been proven. Every time you arrive at work and your office or desk is still there waiting for you, you prove you are still employed. Every morning you wake up, you prove that it is safe to go to sleep at night. Because your faith has been proven over and over again, doing these things become as natural as walking, knowing you are stepping on solid ground.

I have always known that I wanted to work for myself but I never thought it possible. Neither my husband Deshon nor I had college degrees, or ever made an attempt at starting a business of our own. So when we decided to start our company, we were overwhelmed with trepidation, plenty of doubt and treading on unsettled waters. We were well versed in the technical and manual part of the installation business. My husband had been a technician for quite some years. However, we knew absolutely nothing about the business aspect or where to begin. We did not even have the money or the credit to get a business loan. Nonetheless, we had determination, desire, each other, and the strong belief that 'we could if only we would.' We needed to take that first step, that leap of faith, and we did.

This is when our journey of many leaps of faith began. When one believes strongly in something, one works hard to achieve it, or better yet, to prove it. The first leap we took was getting a business license without any guarantee of having a functioning business. Once we acquired the business license, we had to invest money, of which we had none, to obtain the required insurances to even be considered as a sub-contractor. With still no guarantee of being selected, and when money we did not have, was being poured into our company, our stress level increased, to say the least, and our faith began to waiver. It was not easy and fear almost paralyzed us several times. But we pushed through, we believed harder, and we kept working on proving our faith.

Deshon's work was impeccable as a technician and was recognized among the peers within his market. He took pride in his work and genuinely cared about his customers' satisfaction. This afforded him the opportunity to speak directly with the regional director in his market about putting a bid in for the sub-contract. We landed the contract and the largest company in the satellite industry became our first client! We were humbled and grateful that they would give us the opportunity. There was no turning back and failure was definitely not an option. My husband kept working as a technician and I kept my corporate job. This was a small home business that was to remain that way. Our regular jobs were the "bread and butter" that kept us afloat. We hired four independent contractors, as our client required a minimum of five technicians to activate the contract. As I mentioned before, we had no money. The savings we had, we had used the year prior to purchase our home and pay for the move. We paid the technicians out of our job salaries until the company made enough money to cover payroll.

Then began the real work. We had to ensure that our client was satisfied with our service and our technicians were happy with our company. We wanted to grow but in order to do so, our company had to be better than the rest. We were competitive in pay and we provided our client with the highest level of service out of all sub-contractors. All of a sudden, technicians began to call us wanting to come work for us. Unbeknownst to us, our technicians were spreading the word of how much they enjoyed working for us. They were saying that not only were we fair, but we treated them with respect and like family. Who knew that just doing what God asks of us to treat our brethren, as we would like to be treated, was going to be key in our growth and become a business tool for others. It is not a tool for us because it is part of who we are, be it in business or in life.

In staying aligned with our values, all technicians that reached out to us for work were advised of our protocol to contact their current employer and inform them of the technicians' desire and to give the employer the choice of allowing the transfer or not. Scouting or taking technicians from other companies is not how we wish to operate. Again, "do unto others as you would have them do unto you."

Curious as to what exactly we were doing right, we polled our technicians. What they said was surprising to us because again, we were just being us. They mentioned how appreciative they were of the "lay-a-way" program we offered. Deshon and I implemented this program because we know how costly getting into this line of work can be. This program allows technicians to get started with minimal out-of-pocket money. They purchase the tools they need to succeed from us and pay us back in small incremental payments. We do not mark up the price of the tools nor do we charge any interest or fees for the program. Our company cannot be successful if our technicians are unable to do their jobs because they lack the proper tools.

Several of them reminded us of how we paid for their vehicle repairs upfront and allowed them to pay us back in small incremental payments. Again, no additional fees or interests charged. While, it is not our company's responsibility to pay for repairs or replacement of vehicles, as the technicians are all independent contractors, it is our responsibility to ensure they all have work to feed their families. And in order to work they need their vehicles. Remember that a team is only as strong as the weakest member. So, if one of our members is down, we are all down.

Another technician reminded us of how we purchased a van for him, after he totaled his truck, and allowed him to pay us back in small payments over an 18-month period. He was so grateful to us because he was able to keep working and taking care of his family without any lapse or getting into more debt because he did not have to take out a loan that will charge fees and interests.

Hearing these stories was humbling because we had no idea of the magnitude our love for our brothers had on them. We were just doing what we knew to be right, and what we knew we would want done for our family and us.

The greatest compliment we could ever get is still having our four initial technicians after 10 plus years and to have grown from just five technicians in one market to over 70 technicians in more than five markets. In today's world where human life has no value, people act more like savages, and corporations are more interested in fattening up their pockets than properly compensating those that work hard for them, Deshon and I are proud to say that we stand above the rest because we put abundant love for our brothers and sisters above any dollar we could make.

We are often asked what is our business and the practical answer is that we are a company that provides technical installations for entertainment. However, in a more in-depth evaluation of the question, the technicians provide the technical installations and we provide an avenue for our technicians to make an honest and dignified living with an unparalleled support system.

Over the past years, we have learned that there are far more important things to being successful in business than what is taught in school. The following are the key elements that have worked for us in life and in our business:

The first key to our success is having faith.
Remember my friend's definition of faith? Faith is the belief in something that has yet to prove itself. I'll add that when your belief proves itself, it now becomes as natural as walking, knowing you are stepping on solid ground. You must believe, first and foremost, in yourself, in your capabilities and potential. Without a shadow of doubt, you should know within your soul that you are capable of creating whatever it is you want.

You should have faith in your product or service. No one should be able to believe in your creation, product or service, more than you do. This faith in your product or service can be considered passion. When you believe in something so strongly, you become passionate about it and no one can describe it, depict it, or defend it better than a person with passion for it. When Alexander Graham Bell had the idea for a machine to transmit sound via electricity, the telephone, many opposed it, ridiculed it, and even thought it impossible. Yet, here we are today using the most advanced technology in our cell phones. He had a belief and he did not waiver; he defended it until he created it.

Faith is your conviction. It should never waiver, be questionable, or be easily changed. Many wars have been fought because beliefs conflict and neither party is willing to give up on their beliefs. Your beliefs should be that strong.

The second key to our success is perseverance.
We never gave up. The times when things were tough and we barely could make ends meet or when we didn't know how we would make our payroll, or even when we initially began with no money and no guarantee of securing a contract, we pushed through.

Giving up is really easy to do. We could have done so many times. But not only would we be giving up on ourselves, we would be giving up on our work family. We would be taking the food off their table, the clothes off their backs, the opportunity to provide for their families and give them a chance at a decent life. Thomas Edison once said, "Many of life's failures are people who did not realize how close they were to success when they gave up." Do not allow yourself to give up because your success can be just one more step, phone call, or door knock away.

The third and final key to our success is what we consider to be the most important of all. It is to love everyone, especially those you employ or do business with.
Treat them, as you would like to be treated, like family or close friends. Whether you have a large corporation or a small business, your employees, business partners, or clients should always know that they are loved and appreciated, valued, and well compensated for all that they bring to your company. Not everyone is motivated by money, but most love to know that they matter and that their production has value.

Treat employees like they make a difference and they will.
~ Jim Goodnight.

This quote applies to everyone, not just employees. When you treat people less than, you get a less than response from them. But when you elevate people to their greatness by acknowledging their worth, appreciating their efforts, and loving who they are, you receive more than just their best. You receive their loyalty, respect, and eternal gratefulness.

That is how we choose to treat our technicians because they do matter, they do make a difference, they are appreciated, and they are worthy of being part of our family. In return, we receive loyalty that has spanned over ten years, we receive the very best they have to offer, and we receive family members for life.

About Yesenia

Yesenia Miranda Gipson was born and raised in New York City. Raised in a single-parent home by her mother, an immigrant from the Dominican Republic, she understood at a very young age the value of family and hard work. Her mother is one of the hardest working women she has ever known, and soon, she followed suit.

At the age of 12, she began baby-sitting the neighbor's daughters to earn extra cash to help alleviate some of the household burden; and has not stopped working since. She has held several positions in corporate America ranging from mutual funds trading to corporate training and development, and mortgage lending.

Yesenia met her husband in 1996 and they were married in 2000. In 2005, together they started a small, independent contracting business, landing a pretty big client. Juggling being a wife, mother, student, and business owner, Yesenia put to use the lessons learned during her younger years; family values, hard work, and failure were not optional. Today, she has a Bachelor's of Science in Business degree with a concentration in Sustainable Enterprise Management from the University of Phoenix.

The small business has grown beyond their expectations. The company has grown from five technicians to over 60 and has expanded across six markets. With the success of the business, a great understanding of sustainability, and the massive need to increase sustainable practices in both business and life, Yesenia and her husband have embarked on a new business venture. In this new endeavor, they will educate and promote sustainable practices and offer alternative solutions through renewable sources, to include solar systems for homes and businesses.

In early 2016, another business opportunity presented itself that Yesenia and her husband could not pass up. While their current businesses are centered on independent contracting, this new venture is completely different. However, they will still provide a service, except it will be in a lifestyle transformation. They will be opening up a transformation center in Tempe, AZ mid-summer 2016. This center will provide nutritional and physical guidance for healthier lifestyles with a support system unlike any other.

Not everything is business with Yesenia. She still finds time to remain very active in her son's life through sports and educational activities. As a family, they make time to visit with their immediate and extended family, in addition to plenty of leisurely travels. She is also very engaged with her closest friends, almost never missing out on the important moments of their lives. She cherishes everyone that is a part of her life and demonstrates, every chance she gets, their importance to her and her love for them.